SEEK … IN
T…

The Story of Conflict and Christianity in the Central Solomon Islands

Brian Macdonald-Milne

Brian Macdonald-Milne

Christians Aware and The Melanesian Mission

Published 2020 by
Christians Aware, 2 Saxby Street, Leicester LE2 OND
(Registered Charity No. 328322)
and
The Melanesian Mission, 21 The Burlands, Feniton, Honiton EX14 3UN
(Registered Charity No. 1104551)

Printed and bound by Creeds, Bridport, Dorset DT6 3UX

ISBN 978-0-9955428-9-1

In memory of Norman Kitchener Palmer and Ellison Pogo, Archbishops of Melanesia, valued friends and colleagues, and also as a tribute to my fellow Christians in the central Solomons and throughout Melanesia, especially my "one-talks" on the beautiful and important islands of Gela, the Florida of the Pacific, and others with whom I have lived and worked.

May the Lord God bless all the people of the Solomon Islands.

Na Maghutu God ke vautora na lei vure soko iga.

"This book is full of valuable information about the history of life in Melanesia. It truly links the past, the present and the future, filling in the gaps of our history that no one else has ever done before. As I was reading the book I was amazed at the fine details that Father Brian has researched and included as background knowledge to inform the future generations in Melanesia, and those elsewhere who want to know and learn about Melanesia. The Melanesian Mission (UK) has over the last 171 years sent mighty men and women of God who have given so much for the proclamation of the Gospel in Melanesia, and Father Brian was one of them. We are the product of that faith and love. I was one of the few lucky and privileged disciples taught by him at theological college.

"This book is a treasure, as it has resurrected and breathed new and fresh life into our Melanesian history. I commend it to those who want to study Pacific Church history and who have a desire to be a missionary."

Right Revd. Willie Alaha Pwa'isiho
Assistant Bishop of Chester
Former Bishop of Malaita, Solomon Islands

"There are many books that are born out of a lifetime of intimate relationships and experiences with a particular context and people. This is one of them! The Anglican Church of Melanesia is grateful and indebted to Fr. Brian Macdonald-Milne for his many years of service to the Church and people of the Solomon Islands, and for his contributions through this work to the limited annals of recorded history written about the Church and this archipelago. We commend this historical work to any and all who wish to capture a holistic but condensed background to the growth of Christianity and the Church in this archipelago and the political development of this young nation from someone who has harboured a lifetime of passion for its people, islands, languages, cultures and history from the very beginning of his vocation."

Father Nigel Kelaepa
Secretary of the Melanesian Board of Mission

CONTENTS

ILLUSTRATIONS

Key to credits:

MM	Melanesian Mission
BMM	Beattie of Tasmania, commissioned by MM
ACoM	Anglican Church of Melanesia
MAA	Museum of Archaeology and Anthropology, University of Cambridge
NLA	National Library of Australia
ANU	Australian National University Press
ATL	Alexander Turnbull Library, Wellington, NZ

FOREWORD

By the Right Reverend Nigel Stock, former Chairman of the Melanesian Mission (UK)

It is just over 500 years since Ferdinand Magellan discovered a route from the Atlantic Ocean through the straits which today bear his name. His fleet emerged from the straits into a vast ocean the size of which was vastly undercalculated by this first expedition to circumnavigate the globe. Nevertheless, after the terrifying conditions of the Magellan Straits, the calm of the Ocean led Magellan to call it the Peaceful ocean or the Pacific.

Peace is a state that humanity longs for, but is very adept at avoiding. We learn to our cost that peace is a prize that must be worked for constantly. Brian Macdonald-Milne records here the story of one part of the vast Pacific, the central Solomon Islands, and the particular endeavours of the Christian Church to bring peace.

It is a remarkable story. With the growth of trade and exploration from the Western world, the encounters with the peoples of the Pacific were often anything but peaceful. Too often the records are very one-sided views from a Western perspective. But the people of the islands had their own long-established way of life. The shock of encounter often led to mutual incomprehension, and sometimes to tragic conflict. There were too easy opportunities for exploitation.

It would be very easy to paint a picture of cultural domination, paying little attention to the views of today's islanders. Brian Macdonald-Milne comments in his opening about the lack of books on the long history of the central Solomon Islands. Yet the stories, as you will read, are remarkable. There are some that are better known than others, perhaps most of all the pioneering role of Bishop John Coleridge Patteson. But there are many other people whose life's work deserves to be better known. Not least those Islanders, so often overlooked, who were the backbone of the early efforts at education and the teaching of the faith.

This is a book about the effect of the Christian faith in bringing peace to these islands. Christian Peace is the peace that comes from the reconciling love of God in Jesus Christ. The love that reconciles human beings to the Creator, and human beings to one another. It is a message that needs hearing in all parts of our world, but this book is the record of how people sought to be faithful to the message of reconciliation in the Solomon Islands. It is told by a person who knows and loves the islands, and who has exercised a much respected Christian ministry there.

This book is very timely. So many of the stories and facts of the coming of the Christian faith to the Islands are scattered in the archives of different organisations. In bringing together so much of the history in an accessible way, the author deserves to achieve his hope that others will be encouraged in the future to explore different facets of this story.

May it also encourage today's bearers and hearers of the great message of Christian reconciliation.

Nigel Stock

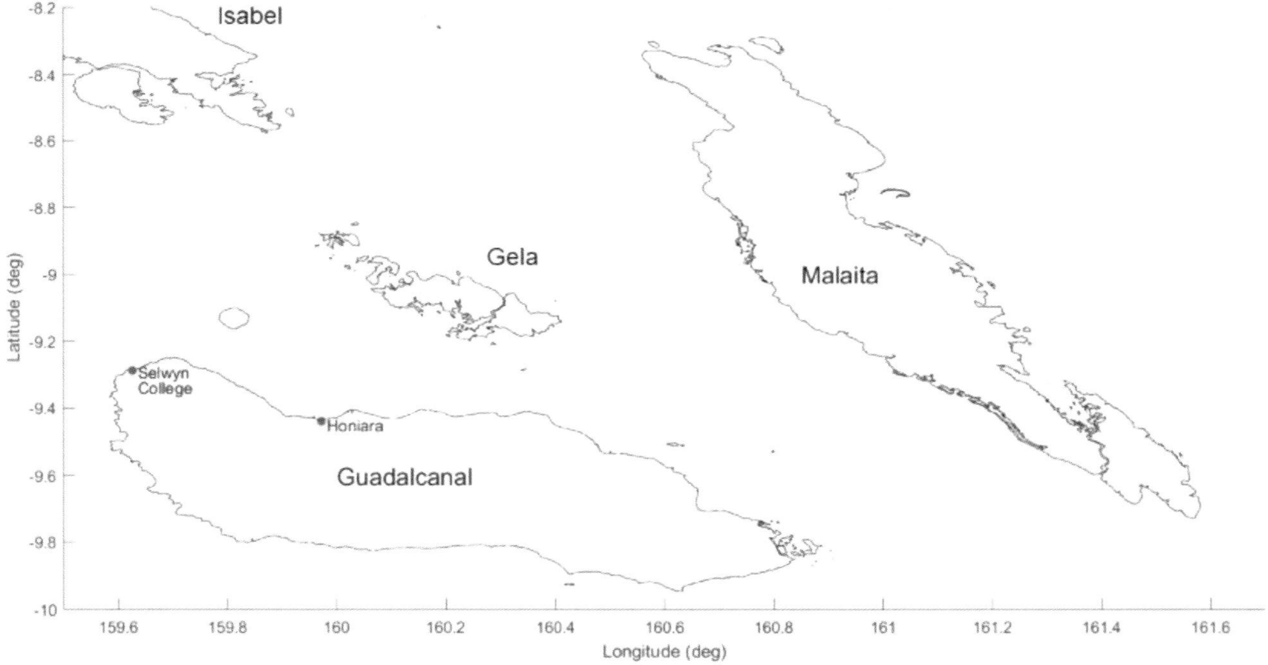

Figure 1 : Map of the central Solomon Islands. [Credit : Sayre, R., S. Noble, S. Hamann, R. Smith, D. Wright, S. Breyer, K. Butler, K. Van Graafeiland, C. Frye, D. Karagulle, D. Hopkins, D. Stephens, K. Kelly, Z. Basher, D. Burton, J. Cress, K. Atkins, D. van Sistine, B. Friesen, B. Allee, T. Allen, P. Aniello, I Asaad, M. Costello, K. Goodin, P. Harris, M. Kavanaugh, H. Lillis, E. Manca, F. Muller-Karger, B. Nyberg, R. Parsons, J. Saarinen, J. Steiner, and A. Reed. 2018. A new 30 meter resolution global shoreline vector and associated global islands database for the development of standardized global ecological coastal units. Journal of Operational Oceanography – A Special Blue Planet Edition. DOI:10.1080/1755876X.2018.1529714. https://doi.org/10.1080/1755876X.2018.1529714]

PREFACE

I arrived in the Solomon Islands in 1964, sailing on the "Canberra" from Southampton, England, to Sydney, Australia, probably one of the last overseas missionaries from England to travel by sea to the islands of Melanesia. After waiting three weeks in Sydney, staying at the House of the Epiphany in Stanmore run by the Australian Board of Missions, I and my baggage (some of it in a large wooden box), travelled on to the Solomon Islands on the trading ship, the 'Tulagi'. It was named after the former capital of that country, situated on a small island in the Gela or Florida group in the central Solomons. We called in at Norfolk Island, where I visited the Bishop Patteson Memorial Chapel, and then at Port Vila and Luganville, the two main ports of the New Hebrides (now Vanuatu), on the islands of Efate and Espiritu Santo respectively.

On arrival at Honiara, the present capital of the Solomon Islands, I expected to be able to take up my new appointment as Sub-Warden of St Peter's Theological College at Siota on the island of Small Gela. However, arriving at the college, I was asked by the then Archdeacon of the Solomon Islands, Harry Reynolds, if I would go to teach at Alangaula Senior Primary School for a while. This was on the small island of Ugi (Uki-ni-masi) in the Eastern Solomons. The rest of my service in the Solomons, till 1978, when the country gained its Independence, was spent mostly in the central Solomons, five of those years being on Gela. From 1978 to 1980 I served in the New Hebrides, setting up the Pacific Churches Research Centre in the capital, Port Vila, on behalf of the Pacific Conference of Churches. I returned to Great Britain in 1980 soon after Independence, when the Anglo-French Condominium of the New Hebrides became the Republic of Vanuatu. While there, I heard about the German Pacific Society, as its founder, Dr Friedrich (Fred) Steinbauer, a former Lutheran missionary pastor in Papua New Guinea, was doing a tour of the Pacific. On my return to Britain in 1980, I suggested to others that we should have a similar Society, and the Pacific Islands Society of the United Kingdom and Ireland (PISUKI) was founded in December 1981,with myself as the Founding Secretary, and Fred as an enthusiastic advisor and friend. I toured the

Pacific myself when I later became Chairman of PISUKI, my first return visit to the Pacific.

After the 'ethnic tension' or civil war in the Solomon Islands from 1978 to 2003, as a result of which seven peace-making members of the Melanesian Brotherhood were killed, I returned to Melanesia on periodic visits during the period in which I was the Advisor of the Brotherhood, between 2005 and 2013. This was at the invitation of the Archbishop of Melanesia the Most Reverend Ellison Pogo -- who, as Archbishop, was also Father (Visitor) of the Brotherhood -- and of the Brotherhood Council.

I was deeply conscious, while teaching Pacific history at the theological college and the Brotherhood, of the lack of books about that part of the country. Early missionaries and administrators had written about their experiences, but there was no overall history of the region, and those books were not readily available.[1] There had been some anthropological, historical and linguistic studies by expatriates, but much of it had been of a technical nature and not available to the general population. This situation has spurred me on to undertake more research and also to draw on my own knowledge, as a result of working for nearly fourteen years on Gela and Guadalcanal, as well as visiting other parts of the country. I was also adopted by Melanesian custom into a family from the Reef Islands in the Outer Eastern Solomons, now known as the Temotu Province.

My hope is that this history will be of interest to Solomon Islanders and other peoples of the Pacific, and will encourage them to do research and publish histories of their own islands, before oral traditions and some written and other sources of information are lost. I hope it will also be of interest to people in other parts of the world who have a concern for the peace and welfare of the peoples of the Pacific region, especially in a time

[1] A popular overall history of the country was Dr C E Fox's "The Story of the Solomons" but it was much less detailed.

of climate change, and for good relationships between Pacific Islanders and people from other parts of the world.

I wish to thank Professor Andrew Pawley of the Australian National University, Canberra, for valued assistance and advice in the matters concerning linguistics, and Professor Jean-Michel Massing, Fellow of King's College and former Professor of the History of Art in the University of Cambridge, for sharing with me his interest in the art of the Pacific Islands and his library. I am grateful, as well, for the assistance of staff at the Cambridge University Museum of Archaeology and Anthropology in sourcing some of the illustrations. I have also had encouragement and assistance over the years from colleagues working at Selwyn College, Cambridge, founded in memory of George Augustus Selwyn, first Bishop of New Zealand, the initiator of the work of the Melanesian Mission in 1849. The Melanesian Mission is now the name of the body in England which supports the Anglican Church of Melanesia in the Western Pacific Islands, and of which I was formerly a Trustee and have been, since 2013, the Honorary Archivist. I acknowledge financial help from the Trustees which has covered part of the cost of the publication of this book, and the support of the Executive Officer, Katie Drew, and the invaluable assistance of her husband Ian Drew, a former Trustee, in matters of printing and lay-out.

The comments of Bishop Nigel Stock have also been much appreciated, as well as those of Associate Professor Dr. Thorgeir Kolshus of Oslo Metropolitan University in Norway, who did anthropological research on the island of Mota in the Banks Islands in the northern part of Vanuatu, and of the Reverend Richard Carter, Associate Vicar at the Church of St Martin-in-the-Fields in London, a former Chaplain of the Melanesian Brotherhood, and, for some years, a Brother himself during the period of the 'ethnic tension' in the Solomon Islands. I am indebted to Frank Jastrzemski in the U.S.A. for information about Captain (later Admiral) Albert Markham, R.N.

I am grateful to Carol Sourbutts and Felicity Luckman, who generously undertook the task of typing the manuscript of this work, and to Barbara Butler and the staff of Christians Aware, without whose support as joint publisher I would have found the whole task much more difficult.

I acknowledge with gratitude the encouragement of the Trustees of The Melanesian Mission (UK), the other joint publisher, for this project. Bishop Nigel Stock, the former Chairman, who as Bishop at Lambeth assisted the Archbishop of Canterbury at his headquarters in London, Lambeth Palace, has written the Foreword to this book. At one time he was a missionary priest from England working in the Anglican Church of Papua New Guinea, and he has visited the Anglican Church of Melanesia, so he knows from personal experience about life and work in the Western Pacific.

As I am part of the story at some stages, I have written about my involvement in the third person (except in the Afterword), as I did in my previous book about Melanesia, also published by Christians Aware, which was entitled "The True Way of Service: The Story of the Melanesian Brotherhood 1925 – 2000". The manuscript of that book was typed by Bishop Derek Rawcliffe, first Bishop of the New Hebrides, in his eighties. He died a few years after the book's publication in 2003, and his contribution to that project was of great value, and a tribute to his lifelong commitment to Melanesia. He was well acquainted with all parts of Melanesia, and also with the Brotherhood, over many years.

Some years ago I discovered that I was not the only member of my extended family to have served in the Solomon Islands. In the nineteenth century, two of my grand-father's cousins emigrated from north-east Scotland to the United States of America. A grandson of one of them, Lieutenant Frank James Smith, was a paymaster in the U.S. Navy in the Second World War, so I think he possibly spent time at or near Tulagi on Gela, as he would probably have paid the naval personnel when they were in harbour there - although relatives have suggested he was on Guadalcanal and 'paid the sailors on the ships docked near the island'.

I paid a final visit to the Solomon Islands in 2010 with my brother Alexander, who had trained professionally as an actor. We had gone there mainly to run courses in drama for the four Anglican Religious Orders. I was then Advisor of the Melanesian Brotherhood, and I also held a workshop for leading Brothers and Chaplains of the Brotherhood at the Motherhouse at the invitation of Fr. Leonard Dawea, who was then Senior Tutor. He was later elected Bishop of Temotu, and in 2019 became

Archbishop of Melanesia, and so Father of the Brotherhood. We were also invited guests at the installation of Bishop James Mason as Paramount Chief of Isabel at the village of Sepi on that island.

The Diocese of Central Melanesia was established in 1975 as one of the four Dioceses of the new Anglican Province of Melanesia and I was asked by Archbishop Norman Palmer to be its first Vicar-General and Diocesan Secretary. Over the years it gradually divided into the new dioceses of Temotu, Hanuato'o, Central Solomons and Guadalcanal. Before leaving the Solomons my brother and I paid a visit to the headquarters of the Diocese of the Central Solomons at Tulagi on Gela. The first diocesan bishop had been Charles Koete, who had also been made Paramount Chief of Gela. He knew about me when he was a schoolboy at Boromole on the other side of the Boli Passage from Siota, when I was teaching at the theological college there. In his time as bishop, a small and beautiful Cathedral had been established at Tulagi in which I preached my final sermon on Gela, and afterwards answered questions about my work in Melanesia since 1964. My brother and I were given a farewell dinner there before we returned to Honiara and had another farewell meal at the Deanery given by the then Dean of the Provincial Cathedral of St Barnabas, Fr. Davidson Nwaeramo.

The Solomon Islands are, for me and others who know them well, a special archipelago which has been through a number of traumatic periods in its history when there was no peace. In the pre-Christian period violent conflict between or within families, clans, and islands was endemic, for various reasons. During the period of contact with people from other countries, it was spasmodic, and later was largely suppressed by the colonial powers, or gradually rejected as people embraced Christianity. During the Second World War the Solomon Islands became involved in a critical international conflict, while the later civil war ('ethnic tension') in the Solomons sadly re-invigorated conflict between people from different islands, in spite of their common Christian faith. The country and its peoples still need the interest, support and understanding of the wider world, as they continue to seek for deeper unity and lasting peace.

Brian Macdonald-Milne - Honorary Canon of St Barnabas's Cathedral, Honiara, Solomon Islands

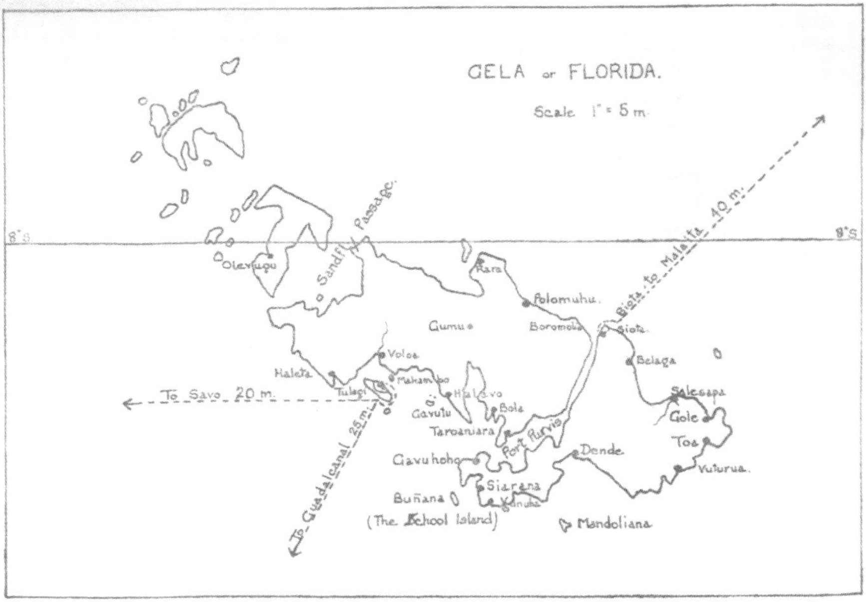

Figure 2 : Gela or Florida. [Credit : From the book 'The School Island']

Figure 3 : A Florida Canoe. [Credit : Beattie of Hobart, Tasmania for The Melanesian Mission, and MAA, Cambridge University]

INTRODUCTION

THE ISLANDS OF GELA, THE FLORIDA OF THE PACIFIC ISLANDS

Looking out to sea from Honiara, the capital of the Solomon Islands on the north coast of the island of Guadalcanal, one can often see on the horizon, about 25 miles (37 kilometres) away, what appears to be a long, low island with no mountains. It is, in fact, a group of over 50 islands of which the largest are Big and Small Gela. Because of this, the group is usually called "Gela", pronounced "Nggela", which is how the word is sometimes shown on maps. The other main islands are Olevuga, often called Sandfly, and Buena Vista or Vatilau, where the people speak Bugotu (Bughotu) language, which is closely related to Gela, the language spoken by the other indigenous people of the group. The whole group is about 36 kilometres long and 391 square kilometres in area, and the Spanish explorers in the 16th century called it (or part of it) 'Florida'.

Gela is significant for a number of reasons. Geographically, it is situated midway between the two chief islands of the central Solomons, Guadalcanal and Malaita. Between the two main islands of Big Gela (Gela Sule) and Small Gela (Gela Pile) is an important waterway called the Boli (or Utuha) Passage, 16 miles (24 kilometres) long, which can be navigated by ships up to a certain size, and is an easy way to travel by canoe or small boat from one side of the island group to the other. From 1897 the capital of the British Solomon Islands Protectorate was situated on the small island of Tulagi (Tulaghi) with its splendid harbour, not very far from the south end of the Passage, while, at the north end, on Small Gela, the Anglican Diocese of Melanesia had its headquarters and Cathedral at Siota, on Boli Harbour. The capital and the cathedral were both largely destroyed by the Japanese during the Second World War, when Gela, like Guadalcanal, became an important centre of operations for both the Japanese and for the Americans and their allies who opposed them. They eventually won the battles on Guadalcanal and on the water between that island and Gela. Because of the number of sunken vessels, this area of sea was renamed Ironbottom Sound after the war. So, Gela's history is central to the story of both 'Church and State' in the Solomon Islands, and closely related to that of Guadalcanal and Isabel (Ysabel).

The term 'Gela' will be used to signify the whole of the Florida group, except when individual islands of the group are being referred to.

The term 'Solomon Islands' in this book sometimes refers to the whole archipelago including Bougainville and Buka and neighbouring small islands in the west (which were formerly the German Solomon islands and are now part of Papua New Guinea), unless only the British Solomon Islands Protectorate or the independent country of Solomon Islands are indicated.

The name 'Santa Ysabel' was used originally for the island north of Gela, but more recently, it has been spelt 'Isabel'. However, the local Anglican Diocese with its base there has retained the spelling 'Ysabel'. Until 1911 Guadalcanal was spelt 'Guadalcanar' on the British Admiralty charts. Many places had names which were spelt in different ways until spelling became more standardized. In this book, alternative names or alternative spellings are sometimes indicated by words in brackets.

The word 'tindalo' can also be spelt 'tidalo', the preferred spelling today. It is the word used for spirits formerly worshipped on Gela. In the Gela language, the letters 'b' and 'd' are pronounced 'mb' and 'nd', and, in the spelling currently preferred by the islanders doing translation, 'g' is pronounced as 'ngg', 'ng' as 'ng', and 'gh' as a gutteral 'g', sometimes known as the Melanesian 'g'. Other Solomon Islands languages, of which there are nearly eighty, as well as Solomon Islands Pijin (the local pidgin), are sometimes spelt slightly differently.

The coming of Christianity to the Solomon Islands is closely associated with the islands of Gela and Isabel, and its influence has affected the whole archipelago, where most people are Christians of one denomination or another today. However, before the coming of Christianity there was much violence and conflict. The early chapters of this book tell of the settlement of the islands through two great migrations into the area, and describe the prevailing culture and languages of the immigrants. There was much fear of the spirits of the dead (ghosts) and other spirits, and the traditional religion is therefore usually described as animism, but it varied in some respects from island to island. The arrival of European explorers from the sixteenth century onwards often added to the conflict and tension, and the activities of traders and labour recruiting ships in the 19th century led to more violence and killings of both Melanesians and white men. With the gradual acceptance of Christianity throughout the Solomon Islands in the twentieth century, and the establishment of colonial Government, there was an emphasis on seeking and establishing peace.

The arrival of Japanese and Allied forces in the Second World War led to greater conflict than the islanders had ever experienced before, and it seemed as if peace had been restored when the Japanese invasion was rebuffed. Political Independence gave hope of closer co-operation between people from different islands in building up new nation states, but in the Solomons disputes over land on Guadalcanal because of migration there of people from other islands, especially to the capital Honiara, led eventually to a violent reaction by the Guadalcanal people and a form of civil war, usually called the 'ethnic tension', ensued. The efforts of peace-makers, especially among local leaders, the Churches, women and traditional chiefs, working together with the Regional Assistance Mission to the Solomon Islands drawn from other countries in the Pacific region, eventually led to the restoration of peace. The challenge in the Solomon Islands and other Melanesian countries now is the maintenance of internal peace and the establishment of more trusting and fairer relationships among all their peoples, with their many varieties of customs, cultures and languages.

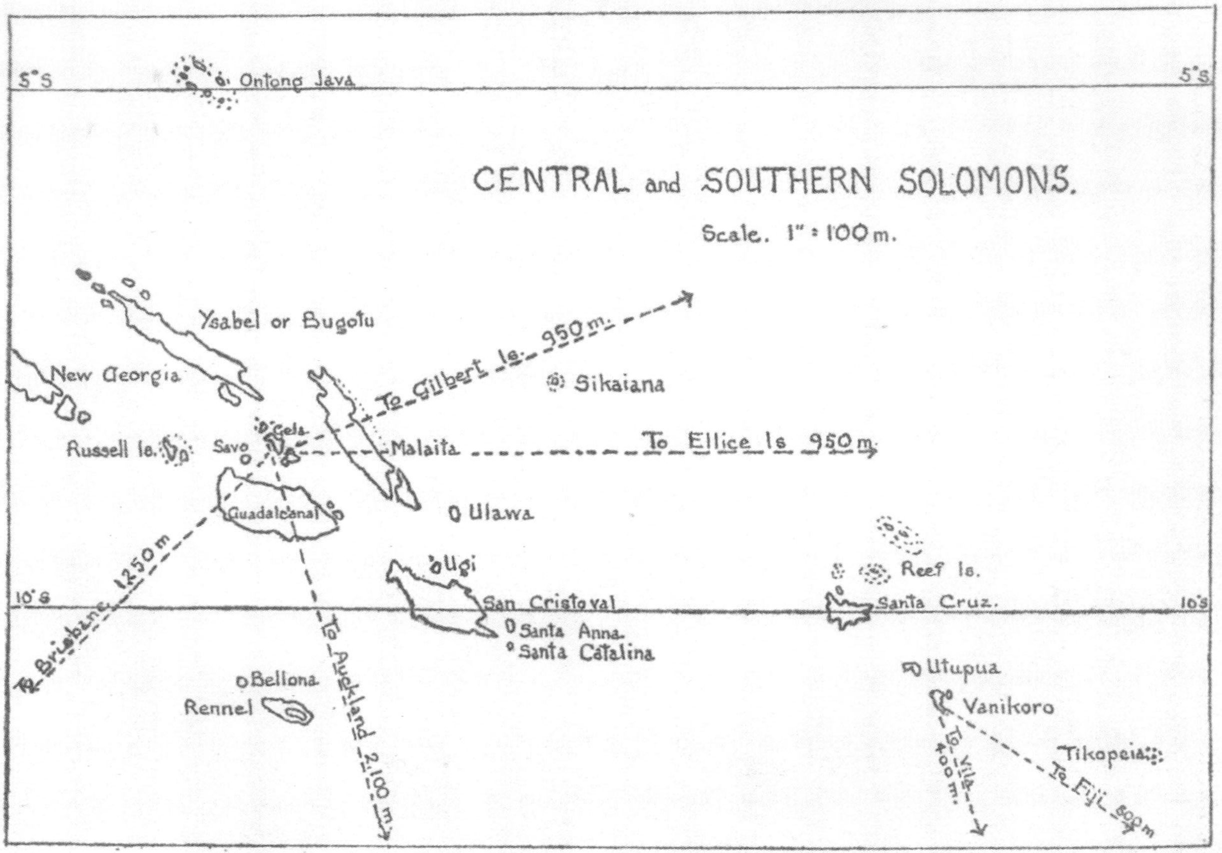

Figure 4 : Central and Southern Solomons. [Credit : From the book 'The School Island']

CHAPTER 1

SOLOMON ISLANDS

A great arc of volcanic islands covers the Western Pacific from New Zealand to Japan. Other islands, some mountainous, some low-lying coral atolls situated on the top of submerged volcanoes, are scattered over the Pacific Ocean from Hawai'i in the far north to Easter Island in the far east. These islands were gradually 'discovered' by European explorers from the sixteenth century onwards, and many were given European names, although most had native names already. In some places, large groups of islands had no collective name, or the islands were so big that each part had a local name without there being a name for the island as a whole, or one for a whole group of islands. European explorers also discovered, in the seventeenth century, that there was a passage north of Australia, dividing it from the land to the north, which they then realised was a large and very mountainous island. They called it New Guinea, as its dark-skinned people reminded them of the people of West Africa, which had been called by Europeans 'Guinea', a word which indicated any remote unknown land. However, southeast of New Guinea, Europeans gradually discovered a chain of islands over 1,000 miles long, which the Spanish explorers called Solomon Islands, perhaps because they hoped they would find gold there, a precious metal associated with King Solomon in the Old Testament of the Bible. The western islands of this chain include the largest of the group, which the Europeans called Bougainville, after a French explorer who sailed by in 1768. In the remainder of the group most islands have a Spanish name, as these islands were 'discovered' in the 16th century by Spaniards. One small group of islands in the centre of this part of the Solomons the Spaniards called 'Florida' – meaning 'flowery' - but the two main islands of this small group have the local names 'Gela Sule' and 'Gela Pile' - Big Gela and Small Gela. The Admiralty chart of 1893 showed that Gela Sule was not fully mapped. By 1911 it was, and showed Mt. Pata having a height of 398 metres.

The country now known as Solomon Islands is only part of the Solomons archipelago. It is 1,667 kilometres in length, and includes 1.35 million square kilometres of sea. There are 27,540 square kilometres of land. Of the 992 islands,347 are inhabited. Guadalcanal is the largest island, and has the greatest population, the majority of them in the capital, Honiara. It also has the highest mountain, Mount Makarakombu ,which has a height of 2447 metres. The other main islands, in order of size, are Malaita, Isabel, Choiseul, Makira (San Cristoval), and New Georgia. The Gela group of islands has an area of about 1,000 square kilometres. Of the indigenous population, 94% are Melanesians and 4% are Polynesians who have traditionally inhabited the outer islands, some of which are low-lying atolls. There is also a small Gilbertese community. The majority of the islanders are Christians, probably about 94 %, with the main Churches being the Anglican Church of Melanesia (35%),the Roman Catholic Church (20%), followed in numbers by the South Sea Evangelical Church, the United Church (formerly Methodist),and the Seventh Day Adventist Church. There are some smaller denominations like the Christian Fellowship Church, founded in the Western Solomons, as well as the Assemblies of God and other charismatic, Pentecostal and Evangelical denominations, which have mostly arrived or been started since the Second World War. Some of the small Chinese community are Solomon island citizens, and there are a small number of residents from other countries in the Pacific and beyond.

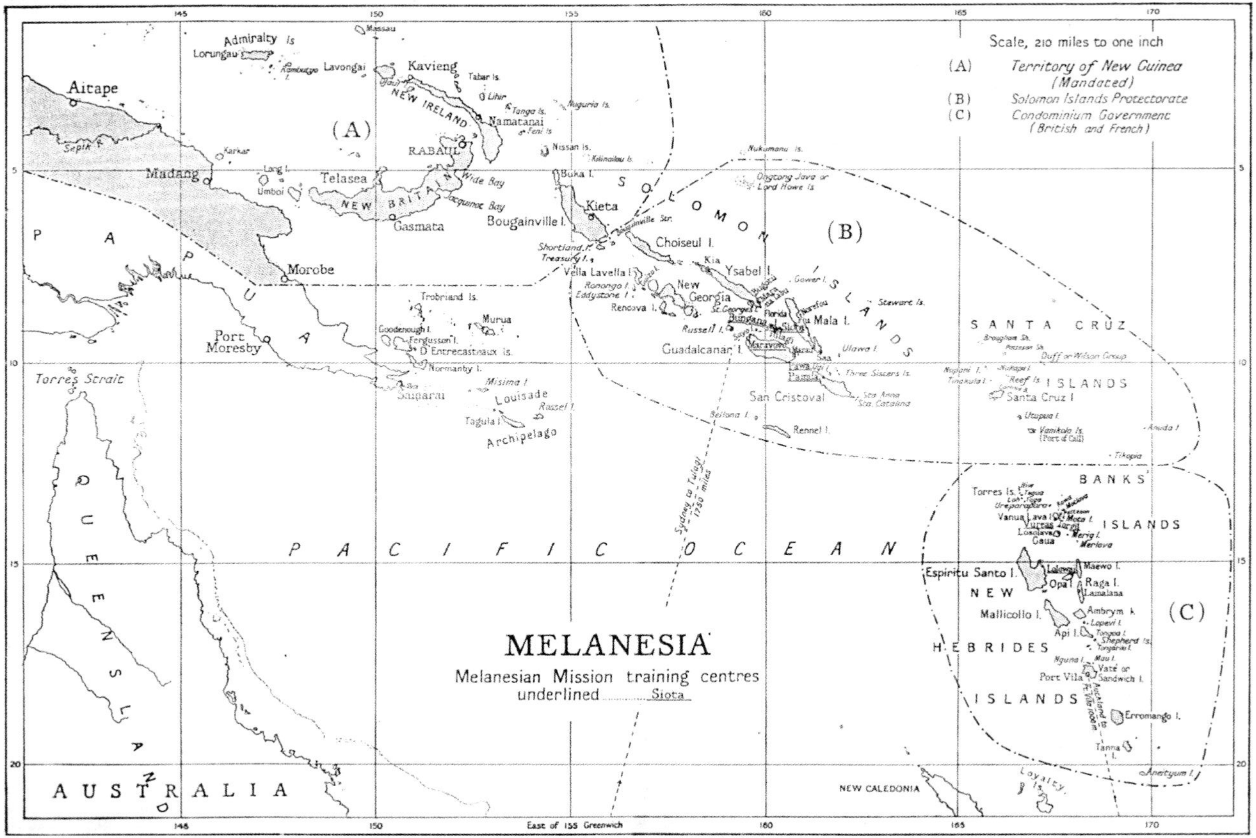

FROM "MELANESIA TODAY" S.P.C.K. LONDON FOR THE MELANESIAN MISSION, ENGLAND 1927

Figure 5 : Melanesia. [Credit : Map from 'The True Way of Service' page 25]

CHAPTER 2

MIGRATIONS AND LANGUAGES

All the islands of Melanesia had been discovered and inhabited by dark-skinned people long before Europeans 'discovered' them. For centuries, people have wondered how Australia and the islands of the Pacific came to be inhabited, and where the people had come from. The story of two great migrations into Australasia (Australia and the islands) has gradually emerged because of the advances in science. The branches of science which have produced this picture are archaeology, anthropology, linguistics and genetics. At one time, it was thought that, in tropical lands, very little from the past could survive, as people there usually have lived in dwellings made of perishable materials, or else they were nomads, moving from place to place in search of food. But when archaeologists began to look more closely, and to search in caves or dig in the ground, they began to find bones of humans and animals, stones and shells and other objects and, in some places, paintings on rock surfaces. Modern science has developed ways of dating such objects through the amount of carbon they contain, known as radiocarbon dating, or by other means.

Some of the earliest remains of our species of human beings have been found in East and South Africa, dating back probably over 200,000 years. Research done in other parts of the world has shown that some people moved out of Africa and across India and South East Asia, about 60,000 years ago, until they reached the island of Timor, from which they crossed into Australia. That was over 50,000 years ago. It is estimated that Australian aborigines probably reached parts of the east coast 23,000 years ago. The type of human beings who emigrated out of Africa appear to have met another type of human being, remains of whom were found in Denisova cave in the Altai mountains in Siberia in Russia. These Denisova people must have made their way originally to the far north, while those who met them somewhere in Asia continued on to Australia and Melanesia. The people of Denisova were related to the type of human beings known as Neanderthals, who passed their DNA in small quantities to those who have become modern humans in parts of Europe and Asia.[2] Many of these people became nomads, spending their time hunting animals for food, and also eating wild plants. At that time, parts of the earth were covered by large sheets of ice and the oceans were at a lower level. There was for a time a large land bridge between Australia and New Guinea, and people from Australia gradually passed over that bridge or through the scattered islands of the strait which later developed, and became the first inhabitants there from about 48,000 years ago. They gradually spread further east, inhabiting the off-shore islands, the largest of which were eventually called "New Britain" and "New Ireland" by the British. These people probably only went from one island to another if the next island could be seen and the distances between them were not too great. By about 30,000 years ago people had reached the westernmost islands of the Solomons chain. With lower sea levels then, Bougainville was joined to Choiseul, Santa Isabel and the Florida Islands. New Guinea, when joined to Australia, had shared many of the same plants and animals with that landmass. After its separation, with the rise of sea levels about 8,000 years ago when the ice gradually melted, the island's animals and plants began to evolve in different ways. In the Highlands temperatures were lower than on the very hot coast (where people could hunt for fish and other animals) and agriculture was developed. Some people inhabited the upland valleys, each of which tended to develop its own distinctive language. One of the tribes there, the Asmat people, have probably been in their area about 30,000 years, There was no malaria in the Highlands and people thrived. As some people migrated further east, they took with them some of the agricultural methods developed in New Guinea, and also some of the animals and plants, especially the pigs and coconuts. As the islands east of New Guinea had been thrust up from the bottom of the ocean at various periods and had probably not been connected with New Guinea at

---

[2] From "A wall of skulls shows why the story of mankind has to be rewritten" by Robin McKie, Science Editor in "The Observer", 13.12.15. See also article in the journal "New Historia" March 19 2016, entitled "Neanderthal and Denisova DNA in Modern Humans", quoting a study in the journal "Science" on "Excavating Neanderthal and Denisova DNA from the genomes of Melanesian individuals".

any time, they only had a quarter of the plants and animals found in New Guinea itself. Saltwater crocodiles gradually swam as far as the Solomon Islands, and fruit bats arrived with the seeds of fruit trees, and eighteen species of bats developed there. However, coral reefs, some of great size, began to develop around most of the big islands, creating off-shore lagoons and sometimes sheltered anchorages. There are more species of life on these coral reefs than in the islands of the West Indies and the whole Caribbean area. As one moves further east from the Solomon Islands across the Pacific, there are less plants and birds and fewer languages. In Fiji, for example, 1,300 miles to the south-east, there are half the number of plant species than there are in the Solomon Islands. Cyclones form in the Pacific, sometimes thirty a year, and they can have a devastating effect on people, animals, coast-lines and reefs, but the strong winds can also carry insects, birds, bats and lizards (such as geckos) from one island to another. The jet stream in the upper atmosphere can carry spoors and insects, which is how some have reached even the isolated islands of Hawai'i in the north Pacific.

The first area of the Pacific Islands to be peopled was New Guinea with its neighbouring islands and then the Solomon Islands archipelago or chain of islands. Some scientists have decided to call this area "Near Oceania". The rest of the Pacific Islands they have designated "Remote Oceania" as archaeology has shown that these islands were inhabited thousands of years later than those of Near Oceania. Near Oceania has some special features which distinguish it from most of Remote Oceania: the people have been there for many thousands of years; they were among the earliest people to develop agriculture; and some of them are darker in colour than all other Pacific Islanders. Near Oceania has more languages than any other part of the world – about 1,100. The island of New Guinea has about nine hundred languages, while the whole of the Solomons archipelago has about one hundred, twelve of them "Papuan", although those mutually unintelligible number about 60. The whole world has about 6,000 languages! In Remote Oceania, only Vanuatu (formerly the New Hebrides), south of the Solomons, has anything comparable – about one hundred and twelve languages, all 'Austronesian'. What makes <u>Near</u> Oceania special, however, is that it has these two families of languages, which are known as 'Papuan' and 'Austronesian'. Anthropologists and linguists have become very interested in the links between migrations, culture, physique, skin colour and languages. In the Solomon Islands archipelago the Papuan languages are often spoken by the people who are darkest in colour. Speakers of 'Austronesian' languages tend to be lighter in skin colours, especially those who have come to be known as Polynesians. About 74 indigenous languages are currently spoken in the country called Solomon Islands.

Some speakers of Papuan languages may have reached the central and eastern Solomons by 25,000 years ago. There is evidence on Guadalcanal of people living there before the arrival of those of the second (Lapita) migration. At Vatuluma on Guadalcanal,inland from Lungga, the Tavura rock shelter has evidence of people using the previously undisturbed forest, and collecting shellfish from waters inland or near the coast. There is evidence of rats and the tree skink and 'canarium' nuts. The sago palm was important, not least because its edible starch could be stored. The development of fishing was indicated by the use of one-piece fish-hooks made of trochus shell.[3] At Posovi rockshelter, also at Vatuluma, a small number of shell artifacts has been found including adzes made of clam shell, arm rings made of trochus shell , and simple beads. Some adzes were made of stones, with their edges ground. Vatuluma in Kaoke language means "stone house". The remains dated from about 2000 BC. The people appear to have been living on the shores and in the bush, and not on off-shore islands, which were later occupied by people who probably used the Lapita-style pottery, and who came in the second migration.[4] 'Posovi' means 'hunting in the water' (for fish and prawns), while 'Tavura' means 'hunting for anything, by land or sea'.

In the eighteenth century, some French scientists, largely on the basis of skin colour and other physical characteristics, invented three words based on Greek to describe the people of the Pacific -- Melanesia for those in the

---

[3] "The Lapita Peoples" p40

[4] The Lapita Peoples", p.41

west, Polynesia for those in the centre (including Hawaii and New Zealand) and Micronesia for those in the north-west.[5] Melanesia was said to include New Guinea, the Solomon Islands, the New Hebrides (now Vanuatu), New Caledonia and Fiji (although eastern Fiji is more Polynesian than Melanesian). But why do they vary so much in culture, skin colour and language? A discovery in a place called Lapita in New Caledonia provided a clue. During the twentieth century pottery of a similar kind had been found at different times in various places – at Waton Island, off the coast of New Britain, at Tongatapu, the main island of Tonga, and on the Isle of Pines, off the southern tip of New Caledonia. The discovery of it at Lapita beach, however, proved that there was a link between the type of people who had settled there and those who had originally come from New Britain and had eventually reached Tonga. The pottery from Lapita was dated by the radiocarbon method to about 1000 BC. The people who used this style of pottery have come to be known by some scientists as "Lapita peoples", and they include some 'Melanesians' and some 'Polynesians'. These discoveries pointed to a second migration into the Pacific, probably originating in Taiwan, where the aboriginal people still speak Austronesian languages. From about 4,000 BC onwards 'Austronesian' speakers moved into some of the islands of tropical south-east Asia and reached the borders of what is now called Melanesia by about 1,500 BC. One group reached the north west area of the island of New Guinea, and expanded eastwards along the New Guinea coast into the islands to the east of the mainland, which are now known as the Bismark Archipelago, including New Britain and New Ireland.

When people of the Lapita culture first arrived in the area of the Solomons, they appear to have established themselves most strongly at first in the Reef and Santa Cruz groups, to the east of the main Solomon Islands archipelago. People there traded with Ulawa in the eastern Solomons for chert flake tools quarried there, and with Gela and Guadalcanal for other items. However, pottery of the Lapita type is almost absent from the main Solomon Islands, and was not found in the rock shelters on Guadalcanal.

---

[5] p.40 Meaning the "black islands", "the many islands" and "the small islands".

There was trade between the Reef Islands and the D'Entrecasteaux islands off the east coast of Papua, and with islands of the Bismark Archipelago, showing that the people of the second migration could undertake long voyages, taking them 2,000 kilometres to the east in search of obsidian, which was highly valued. It could be used, with its sharp cutting edge, for many purposes, and its dark glossy volcanic structure made it very distinctive and a rather rare kind of stone.[6]

Archaeology in the Reef Islands and Santa Cruz have shown that people had arrived there by about 1,000 BC and had developed already some decorated pottery, which gradually became simplified over time, then eventually ceased.[7] A feature of the people using the distinctive pottery was that they settled in rectangular houses, often on stilts, in villages occupying coastal situations and often opposite reef passages, or on small off-shore islands but near arable land, freshwater springs or streams. They combined fishing and shell-fish gathering, using a range of fishing gear, with horticulture and the care of pigs and fowls. They also traded widely,not only obtaining obsidian from the Bismark Archipelago and chert from Ulawa for axes and adzes, but also pottery and oven-stones from far away, if they were not obtainable locally. They fashioned tools, weapons, money, personal and household objects from many materials, and did weaving as well. Their life was closely related to the sea and the marine environment in which they preferred to live, and they had outrigger canoes of various sizes. As they moved through Near Oceania, they appear to have displaced the Papuan-speaking people in some places, or intermarried with them in others, leading to great diversity in skin-colour, culture and language, especially in the Solomon Islands. Alongside the Gela (Florida) group of islands in the central Solomons is the volcanic island of Savo, where the most eastern of the Papuan languages is spoken, and where some of the people are darker in colour than their Gela neighbours, although there must have been contact between them over

---

[6] "The Lapita Peoples" pp.53-56

[7] "The Lapita Peoples" pp.155-156 (continuing to be made in N. Vanuatu).

many hundreds of years. The "Lapita peoples" moved on from the outer islands to populate the eastern and central Solomons and later the rest of the Pacific islands. For a period, there was probably a band of islands stretching across the western and central Solomons where the people were speakers of 'Papuan' languages, thus dividing the speakers of Austronesian languages in parts of the north-west from speakers of those in the south-eastern islands.

LANGUAGES

The study of languages has been very helpful in working out the probable pre-history of the Solomon Islands. On their arrival in the Solomons about 30,000 years ago in Buka and West Bougainville, speakers of 'Papuan' languages probably spread rapidly to all of the central Solomons, including Malaita and Makira, as well as Gela. Remains of human habitation on Guadalcanal dating from about 6,000 years ago have been found in Poha cave. However, the 'Papuan' people in this area seem to have been few in number because the Austronesian languages now spoken there have been little affected by 'Papuan' influences. This is very different from the Western Solomons including most of Santa Isabel, where the languages appear to have been much influenced by Papuan ones. However, only two Papuan languages have survived in the area of the Western Solomons south of Bougainville. Although two others are still spoken in the Central Solomons, in the Russell Islands and on Savo, namely Lavukalele and Savosavo, they appear to have had little influence on nearby languages, except for some on Santa Isabel. Only on the islands of Bougainville and Buka are the 'Papuan' languages dominant. In the rest of the Solomons archipelago nearly all the languages are Austronesian, either Melanesian or Polynesian, and this is true also in the islands of the Santa Cruz and Reef Islands groups to the east. The speakers of Austronesian languages may have arrived at different periods in the northern/western Solomons and the central/eastern Solomons – possibly arriving in the central/eastern area from the eastern Outer Islands when Austronesian speakers arrived over 3,000 years ago.

Gela is one of a sub-group of 7 Austronesian languages in the Central Solomons, being closely related to certain languages on Guadalcanal and to the language of Bugotu, spoken at the eastern end of Santa Isabel and on Buena Vista island. These languages were probably mutually intelligible until about 1,000 years ago. The other subgroup of languages in this part of the Solomons includes the languages of Malaita and Makira and nearby small islands, together with two languages of eastern Guadalcanal, Longgu and Marau where Malaita people have settled. Traditionally, there was trade and intermarriage between Gela and certain parts of Santa Isabel and north Guadalcanal, with the four main Gela clans all having branches in the Bugotu district of Santa Isabel. Gela and north Guadalcanal were probably settled by Austronesian speakers about the same time, probably over 2,500 years ago, and south east Guadalcanal possibly earlier, according to some language scholars. People now speaking Bugotu probably moved to south east Santa Isabel from north Guadalcanal or Gela within the last 1,000 years and their language was influenced by neighbouring languages on Isabel. Gela is the Solomons language least affected by other languages, sharing over 30% of words with the languages of Polynesian outlying islands of the Solomons.

Some of these outer islands were peopled by Polynesians from other parts of the Pacific to the east, especially Tonga, arriving between 1200 and 1600 A.D.

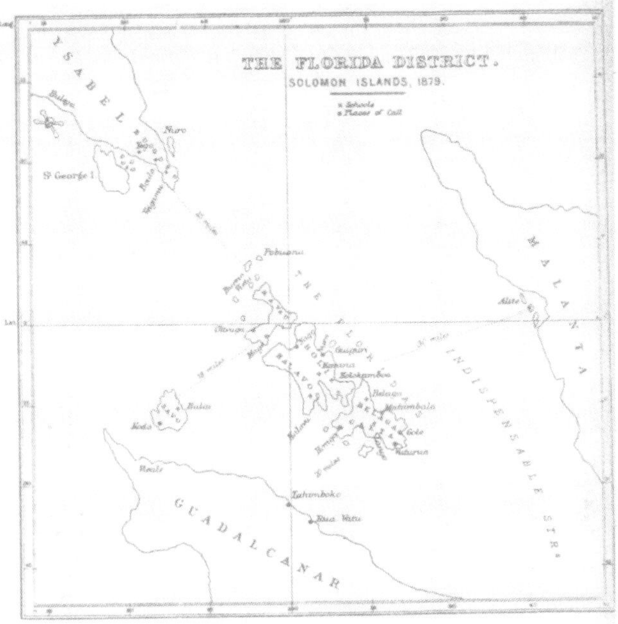

Figure 6 : The Florida District 1879. [Credit : The Melanesian Mission]

Figure 7 : [Credit : MM and MAA, Cambridge University]

CHAPTER 3

GELA CULTURE

Most people on Gela lived in villages by the sea, whereas in some of the mountainous islands like Guadalcanal, Malaita and Makira (San Cristoval) there were bush people, and they were cannibals. Cannibalism, however, was probably not practised in Gela or Bugotu. Relationships with other islands for trade – and sometimes for war or plunder -- were significant. Shell money was obtained from the Langalanga lagoon people 30 miles away on Malaita, megapode eggs from Savo, and the best canoes from Bugotu. Some chiefs organised great netting operations each year which brought in loads of fish of all kinds. Gela was a great market centre, as canoes from all the surrounding islands could get there, and Gela people could get to them. Voyages usually took place in calm weather, but sometimes canoes were lost in storms or heavy surf. People fashioned the base of their canoes from a large tree, using adzes. Planks were then added to form the sides. Holes were made in the hull and sides, to tie them together with fibre. A special nut was collected and cooked. It produced a soft red paste called 'tita' which was used for caulking the cracks between the hull and the planks. After a few days it dried hard and black. There was a high prow and stern, and, as these swept upwards, they were sometimes decorated with white cowrie shells and inlaid with nautilus shell. Although the canoes were usually paddled, there was sometimes a mast of bamboo and a sail made of matting, or calico when that became available. Seating was of bamboo or harder woods. Such canoes could be anything up to 120 feet long, the largest often being the war canoes. The number of seats determined the price of a canoe, if it was ordered from a professional canoe maker. Some of the most feared war canoes came from Roviana lagoon in the Western Solomons, where the chiefs were headhunters, and they targeted Bugotu, where the people would build small houses up in the trees to which they would escape when they saw the headhunting expedition approaching. There was also trade between the central and eastern Solomons and the Santa Cruz and Reef Islands. They got temper for pots from part of Gela.

Because of raids by people of other islands, or enemies closer at hand, some villages were surrounded by stockades of large tree trunks up to twelve feet in length, placed upright close together. The narrow entrance would be closed at night with heavy timbers. Visitors were expected to leave their weapons outside before entering. Sometimes just the chief's house would be protected in this way, and villagers could all go there if an attack was feared. Villages were therefore sometimes limited in size, and gardens also had to be guarded, as they might be raided and coconut trees might be destroyed.

On Gela, some people specialised in fishing, exchanging fish for garden produce. Various methods were used. Kite-fishing was practised by attaching a small palm-leaf kite to the stern of a canoe. From its tail would hang a ball of cobweb, bobbing along on the surface of the sea. This was bait for the "guard fish", and the cobweb would jam in its jaw. Other fish were caught by hook and line. Sometimes a live fish had a hole bored through its jaw and was then returned to the water. It attracted other fish of the same type, who were then scooped up in a large-mouthed landing net.

People's houses were either built on the ground or on posts raised on piles. A large house might require 3,000 screens of sago-palm leaves doubled over a reed six to eight feet long in order to cover the roof. Where there was a floor, this might be made of thick outer bark, flattened out. The bark of the betal nut tree was sometimes used, and this might be covered with a platted layer of long palm leaves, and then matting woven with small split bamboos whose joints had been carefully chipped away.

Gardening was a constant activity, especially for the women. The ground was first prepared by the men, before the women planted. Undergrowth was cleared, and, when dry, was burned round the base of large trees. The trees were then cut down, and the branches used to make a fence, while the trees themselves might be consumed by fire. The men then broke up the ground with long sharpened pointed poles. When shoots appeared, canes would be stuck in the ground for the stems of the yams to climb up. When sweet potatoes (kumara) were introduced from New Zealand, planting was done by hand in raised mounds. After the second or third year, the ground was left fallow for many years to enable it to be restored in energy. There was clear knowledge of ownership, even when land was covered in bush. Food and pigs were traded with other islands. People from Langalanga, who were expert fishermen, brought the red and white shell money they had made to trade for pigs, yams and coconuts. Their canoes were big enough to carry two or three tons of cargo. A fathom string of the beads ground from red shells – "red money" – could purchase 50 yams and 100 coconuts. A string of white shell money could only purchase half of that. The Langalanga people insisted on their money having a high value, so with it they normally obtained a good number of pigs, which they tended to value less, so they obtained a bargain. They also dived on the Gela reefs for a white shell, and paid a fee to the local people. When circulating in Gela itself, the shell money usually purchased less! Within the last 2,000 years most Pacific island communities have given up pottery manufacture and, for cooking purposes, imported pots and pans were later adopted, although wooden vessels continued to be used for some purposes.

Other things were used as money also, especially the teeth of porpoises and dogs. As there were not many dogs and only two teeth of a dog's lower jaw were extracted, dog teeth were five times more valuable than porpoise teeth; these dogs' teeth were pierced and strung into necklaces and handed down from generation to generation as treasures. A porpoise tooth could purchase ten coconuts. Chiefs and rich people might have tens of thousands of dogs' teeth which showed the antiquity of the custom, and indicated how long the people had been resident there.

People sometimes got into debt, or compensation was demanded for loss or injury. If the chief and people considered that there was a fair claim, then a party of women might sit all night outside the debtor's door. Messages would pass between the chief and the debtor, and a professional pleader of high social standing might be employed by the debtor – but he cost money! If the debtor did not pay up - and they usually paid what was demanded – then the women returned for a second night. On the third night men would arrive to burn the house, take the debtor's pigs and destroy his property. The skill of the pleader inspired by his 'tindalo' (spirit) would sometimes lead to a modification of the debt, it was believed.

MARRIAGE

Wives were more expensive to obtain on Gela than on Santa Isabel. Just as the pleader, acting on behalf of a debtor, was thought to be guided by a spirit, so a similarly inspired tattooist had to be employed to tattoo a girl. It was thought that the spiritual power (mana) of the 'tindalo' enabled him to operate painlessly. Like the pleader, he was thus able to earn a large fee. The tattooing took place at sunrise, but, before that, the girl had to be kept awake by friends while a company of professional singers sang throughout the night. There were soloists as well as a chorus, and, in the case of someone of chiefly rank, a new repertoire of songs had to be composed and paid for. The tattooist started by making tattoos, following a set work pattern, on the girl's face and bosom. She had to bear the pain, pretending that it did not hurt, so that his reputation and that of his spirit did not suffer! When the tattooing was finished, the girl was allowed to sleep, and, on waking up, she felt only smarting and stiffness. Thereafter, she was allowed no joking or familiarity with men or boys, as she was now considered a woman, eligible for marriage. People would have been invited to subscribe to the cost of the tattooing, and anyone seeking her in marriage would have to refund with interest what had been subscribed. The amount due would depend on the girl's rank, and the number and social position of her subscribing friends. A chief would demand a considerable amount before marriage could be considered, if the girl were his daughter. Money could be borrowed from rich friends, or a girl might have to wait for years while a young man worked to raise the remainder of the money after he had paid a 'deposit'. If the father died and the girl was still unmarried, a smaller amount might be required, which meant that a poorer person might be able to marry her. Sometimes it might be a widower, or a man who had other wives. Women were therefore, in practise, treated at the father's 'property'. The prospective bridegroom's family would, at the appropriate time, hand over the 'bride price' of shell money and the girl would go to live with her mother-in-law.

Customs regarding marriage varied from island to island; in parts of Malaita the bridegroom would go and live with the bride's family. Traditionally, land was key. In Malaita it passed through the male line, in Gela, Guadalcanal and Santa Isabel through the female line. After receiving the bride price, the bride's family would give a feast for those who had subscribed to the bride price, which was followed later by a return feast given by the subscribers. Thus, the two families were publicly and symbolically associated, and new relationships with accompanying responsibilities were established. An example of this was that, if the wife quarrelled with her husband and he refused to eat what she had cooked, it was the responsibility of her friends to send him a present to appease him. On one occasion, Takua, the chief of Boli, demanded a large sum of native money in compensation when one of his wives accidentally set fire to his new canoe house, with his new canoe inside! Her friends had to pay up. In some islands, including Santa Isabel, men were not allowed to have direct communication with their mother-in-law. It was said to be 'out of respect'. However, on Gela this did not apply and a man could speak with his mother-in-law. It was therefore important to understand the customs of other islands when visiting them, or meeting people from there, and still is. On Gela, if a couple wanted to marry, a custom developed called 'lavi bongi' ('taking by night'), a kind of elopement. This would affect the bride price paid – if the couple were allowed to marry as a result.

DANCING

In addition to feasts of various kinds, another occasion for contact between people of different villages (and sometimes of different islands) was and is through dancing. It was also another way of raising money. There were different dances from island to island, and those of the Santa Cruz group and the New Hebrides (Vanautu) had their own very distinctive features. In some islands only men danced. Solomon Islander dancers were paid more than those in the New Hebrides. In Gela, the initiative was taken by the chiefs, who got up dancing parties. A local chief would choose a particular dance, select dancers from those applying, and start rehearsals. There were five or six dances in common use. One called 'Soniruka' was danced by 36 men and boys, the biggest in front. The dancers themselves played the music on bamboo panpipes and trumpets. Changes in the music indicated when to change the movements in the dance. There was even syncopation in the deep notes. The dancers would wear coloured waist cloths and necklaces of dogs' and porpoises' teeth and other decorations. The chief would arrange for white cockatoo feathers to be held like plumes in the dancers' free hand. Women traditionally wore short skirts made of coconut fibre. The dancing party would then go on tour, usually by sea in the calm season. They were placed under the protection of a tindalo (spirit) as it was believed that this would improve their performance all round. This meant getting the approval of the representative of a particular tindalo. A tour could last three months and dancers would be provided with food by the spectators, and the local chief, who had received them, would pay them at the end according to the general approval accorded to the performance and the social status of the performers. After the tour, the money raised was divided among the performers and a large fee – the size of which depended upon the success of the expedition - was paid to the representative of the tindalo.

RELIGION

All life before the coming of Christianity was related to a belief in spirits and the power of dead ancestors. It was felt that the tindalos had the power to heal or destroy, to kill or revive, to bless or to curse. On Gela, there was a hereditary class of sorcerers who were able to make sacrifices to the tindalos. They could also refuse to sacrifice, but in that case, a member of the sorcerer's family might be prevailed upon to do so. People believed that the tindalos had the power to cause illness or calamity of any kind, and that there must be an explanation for any unfortunate event. They did not have a concept of 'accidents' without a 'spiritual' cause. Periodically, sacrifices and feasts were also celebrated on special occasions, such as the inauguration of the eating of first fruits from certain trees, or the making sacred (taboo) of certain places. These celebrations were associated with secret societies, of which there were many on Gela and in other islands. They had their special houses and admittance to the societies was gained by paying a large sum in native money. Certain privileges went with membership. For example, those initiated into the societies could land in certain places, or walk on certain paths. If non-members did so, they had to pay fines in food and money, and part of the fines would be shared among the members. On special occasions, usually only members could attend and participate. For the first-fruits celebration, a space would be cleared of undergrowth and a fence erected. Within that area, a small group would crack the large almond-like nuts (ngali), pounding the kernels into a mash with which they made cakes on a fire, using firewood provided by others outside the pen. The tindalos presiding over the nut trees were then invited to eat the baked cakes or puddings. When they did not do so, the general reaction was "The tindalos will not eat, so we will!". Thus, the ceremony became a feast.

The tindalos had symbolic objects, by which they were represented, usually large clubs of ebony or ironwood, some with the name of the tindalo inscribed on the club. They were kept concealed in special houses and only shown to members of the society over which the particular tindalo presided. Other ornaments might include a large shell carved in a circle, or an amulet made from a stalactite. There was also sometimes native money which was never used but kept in a basket. If that basket became worn, the money was transferred to another basket. The shell money could be dated, as its style varied over time, and so it was possible to estimate that it could be 200 to 300 years old. The clubs could have been even older. They were never used in fighting, due to their size and weight. There were also shields and bowls associated with the spirits, and kept in the special houses. In addition there were sacred groves where some of these objects, together with sacred stones, were stored and where sacrifices were offered.

There was a custom that, when a chief's garden was planted, the planters had to sleep near the fence in shelters made of boughs or other local materials, and in the morning they would not be able to eat until the planting was finished. This was to ensure that during the process nobody provoked the anger of the tindalo by treading on sacred ground, for that would have ensured that the crop would be a failure. After all the planting had been completed satisfactorily, a feast was held for the labourers.

Members of the secret societies tormented others, relying on their fear of the tindalos to trick them. A man claiming to represent the tindalos would say to non-members: "You must prepare a feast for the tindalos , tonight they will come!" The society members would then cover the windows and fasten the door of the chosen house from outside and warn those inside: "If you look out or stop working till all is ready you will die." So the frightened people would have to break nuts, scape coconuts and pound yams in the stifling, dark sweaty atmosphere which was full of dust. At night the society members would arrive, covered in leaves, screaming, whistling and hissing. They would be handed bowls of food through a hole specially left above the door. They were both feared and hated!

Sorcery was also greatly feared. It depended on obtaining something associated with the person whom the sorcerer wanted to bewitch, either because he himself wished to harm him or her, or because he had been asked or paid to do so. It was believed that the objects which had been associated with the person (or used or consumed by him or her) represented and contained the vital forces of that person, which could then be brought into contact with a tindalo and its power. These objects could include food, a lock of hair or even a piece of roll tobacco used to fill that person's pipe. The sorcerer would place the item inside a shell and put it in a place associated with the tindalo, and call upon him to consume the victim. If he had been employed to do this, he would be paid a fee, and the person being bewitched would then be informed. That person usually fell ill, and was told that he or she would need to pay to be delivered. If payment was made, the person normally recovered! If the sorcerer had however been paid to kill, or himself wished that person to die, then he or she would not recover. So there was fear of death, not just because of traditional enemies, but from the activities of sorcerers, within the local community or further afield.

At Boli, a chief called Savui, second in power to Takua, became ill. People believed that a particularly powerful sorcerer had bewitched him, but no-one dared confront or punish him in his own area of influence. The people gathered, expecting Savui's death. He had refused to pay the large sum demanded by the sorcerer as Savui was known to be rich. However, eventually Savui did pay a sum in native shell money which was enough to buy six or eight large pigs. The charm used by the sorcerer was then recovered – it was just a fragment of betel nut. Savui recovered his health in just over a week. He had probably been suffering from remittent fever. But the people believed that all sickness was explained by the existence of angry tindalos, and that it was often caused through the influence of sorcerers. People were therefore very careful to try and dispose of any personal items which might be used by sorcerers, but they did not always succeed.

There were classes of tindalo for different activities, and also tindalos 'possessed' by certain individuals such as chiefs, warriors, orators, healers and other significant people, from whom it was believed they derived their power or 'mana'. An individual might go to a chief seeking success for an enterprise, and, if this occurred, the reputation of the chief and of his tindalo was strengthened. With continued success, the reputation would become well established – but failure led to a loss of reputation and possible obscurity.

The main classes of tindalo on Gela were 'Keramo' (for fighting), 'Bagea' (meaning 'shark', for anything to do with the sea), and 'Luvaolu' (for success in 'love'). A chief might taunt his opponent by saying "Put petticoats on your keramo (tindalo)!" Some native tindalos were thought to live in sharks. If a tindalo was believed to haunt a spring, then a women's lock of hair or part of her clothing could be dipped in it, to make her more responsive. If a woman wanted to make herself more attractive, she might decide to bathe there herself. At another place it was believed that a tindalo played his flute, and if any woman could be persuaded to wander within hearing, she might cease to be unresponsive....

Traditional life held much of interest for the people of Gela,with the seasons and celebrations of planting and harvesting, the fishing expeditions, the dancing and feasting, the trade with other islands, such as Isabel, Malaita, Guadalcanal and Savo, but it also included conflict between neighbours and between people in different parts of the Gela group of islands who were rivals for influence. Gela however, was spared the head-hunting and slave-taking raids from the New Georgia group of islands to the north-west, which were experienced by the neighbouring island of Isabel, and the Gela people claimed that they had never been cannibals. However, the fear of the tindalos and those who claimed to have mana of one kind or another and used it for good or ill constantly affected their lives.

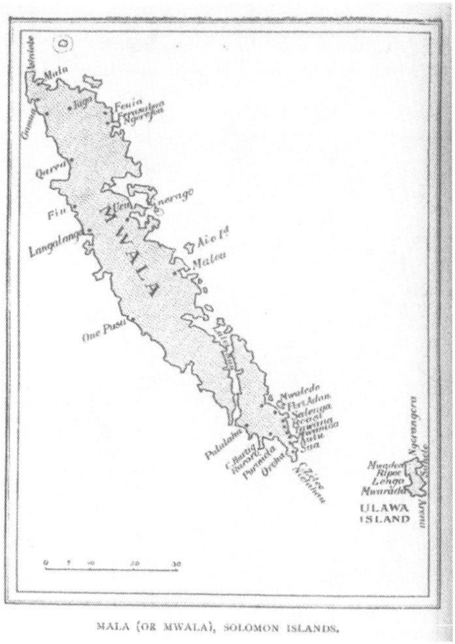

Figure 8 : Mwala or Mala. The island of Malaita is also known as Mala or Mwala, depending on the local language being used. [Credit : The Melanesian Mission]

Figure 9 : Women from Langalanga, Malaita island, makers of traditional shell money. [Credit : The Melanesian Mission]

CHAPTER 4

WHITE MEN

Thousands of years ago, people in Africa, Asia, the American continent and Europe made tools out of wood and stone and shell if available, just like people in the Pacific Islands. Then, in some places, they discovered that there were metals of different kinds in the rocks which could be melted down and made into tools and weapons and ornaments. Two of these were copper and tin, which could be melted together to form the strong, shiny metal called bronze. Then iron was discovered which was easier to work. But the metal which attracted people most was one which shone most brightly and constantly – gold. This could be used for personal ornaments of all kinds, and to decorate buildings and furniture. It could only be found in certain places, and, being rare in some parts of the world, it became very valuable. People in the Middle East knew it well, and it is mentioned a number of times in the Bible. At first, it was used as a kind of currency, being measured by weight, until coins were invented. Although not found in Palestine, it was present in Arabia, and the Bible records its use in Egypt, Jericho (one of the oldest cities in the world), and in the land of Midian, on the border of Edom, south of Palestine. It was mined in Arabia at Havilah and Sheba, and in Western Europe in Tarshish, which was probably a place in Spain. How the metals were mined underneath the ground is described in the Book of Job, chapter 28. King Solomon, the ruler of the people of Israel in Palestine in the tenth century before Christ, was especially keen to obtain gold from all these mines, especially to decorate the Temple he had built in Jerusalem in honour of the God of Israel. The Israelites believed that God had delivered them from slavery in Egypt and brought them into the "promised land" of Palestine, a land "flowing with milk and honey". However, the gold which Solomon appears to have prized most highly was that from the mine at Ophir, but it is not clear where that place was, except that it was somewhere east of Palestine. King Solomon had a fleet of ships based at Ezion-Geber in Edom at the head of the Gulf of Aqaba, near Midian on the Red Sea. Every three years this navy brought gold, silver, ivory, apes, sandalwood and peacocks to the court of King Solomon, as we learn from the First Book of Kings in the Old Testament in chapter

10, verse 22. The peacocks were birds found in India or further east, so if Ophir was the source of the gold, it was probably a place far to the east, although the navy probably called at many ports on its voyages there. Its location is still uncertain!

There were not many gold mines in Europe, so Europeans went in search of this precious metal wherever they heard (or believed) it could be found. When they crossed the Atlantic to the American continent in the fifteenth and sixteenth centuries, they found much gold and made search for more, exporting much of it back to Europe, where it was sometimes used in the decoration of churches and other public buildings. When they arrived in Peru in 1532, the Spanish 'conquistadors' (conquerors) heard stories from the Inca people about a great leader called Tupac Inca Yupancui who had over-run the city of Quito (now in Ecuador). He heard stories there of merchants on the coast who had ventured into the Pacific Ocean and had found islands "where there were many people and much gold". Because of that, Tupac himself, the Spaniards were told, had sailed into the Pacific with a large fleet of balsa rafts manned by 20,000 men but it was not clear what land he had reached. The story then told of his return with black people, gold and a chair of bronze after a voyage of nine months. Some think the expedition reached the island of Mangareva in what is now French Polynesia in the south eastern Pacific. There grew up a conviction that there were "Western Isles" in the Pacific where gold could be found. Were these the site of the fabled King Solomon's mines, which perhaps could be reached from the east across the Pacific? Was Ophir to be found there at last?

Early Greek philosophers from the time of Pythagoras in the sixth century before Christ had suggested that the world was round, a perfect sphere. They knew of Europe and north Africa and much of Asia, and they believed that this great land mass in the north had to be balanced by another land mass in the south. Writers thereafter described this "southern continent" as Terra Australis (the southern land) or Terra Incognita (the unknown land) or the Antipodes (the land on the other side, or upside down!). There was some speculation in the Middle Ages that there was land south of the Indian Ocean or further east. In the 16th century it even began to appear regularly on maps! When Christopher Columbus arrived in the island of

Espaniola or "Little Spain" (now called Hispaniola) in the so-called "West Indies" on Dec 6 in 1492, he believed he had reached the eastern end of Asia, where Ophir was to be found. In 1501 Amerigo Vespucci was sent with three ships by King Manoel of Portugal to discover new southern lands. He followed the coast of Brazil and, in 1502, reached the southern tip of mainland America, the continent which is named after him. Further south he also reached Tierra del Fuego (the land of fire) and described it as a 'Terra Australis'. Ferdinand Magellan went further, passing through the Straight between the mainland and Tierra del Fuego (with some small islands to the south of it) into the Pacific Ocean. The Strait was, therefore, named after him. He did not find the southern continent, but he was the first to cross the Pacific and to name it. He was killed in 1521 in a battle in the Philippines with the islanders there. 'Terra Australis' on some sixteenth century maps was even called Terra Magellanica, thus recognizing the significance of his voyage. Although Portuguese, he had been commissioned by the King of Spain to reach the "East Indies" by a westerly route. The way was thus opened for other voyages and explorers to cross the largest expanse of water on the earth from the east – but neither the 'western islands" or the "southern continent" had definitely been located, and the search for gold was still on. It was the Spaniards who took it further.

MENDANA

In 1550 the King of Spain, Charles I, who was also Holy Roman Emperor, was urged by Gomez de Solis to send an expedition to discover certain islands which were believed to exist in the "mar del sur" (south sea). He was therefore entrusted by the Judges of the Royal Tribunal in Peru to discover "various large rich islands from which it is told that they brought much gold to traffic with the nations of this coast". That expedition never materialised, and, in 1565, the Governor or Peru was approached by a merchant called Pedro de Ahedo, who offered to send an expedition at his own expense. However, that was cancelled when it was discovered that it might be used by some who had agreed to serve on it for piracy.

Governor de Castro, in writing to the King about the proposed expedition, said that its aim was the discovery "of some islands, called Solomon, which lie opposite Chile, towards the Spice Islands" – these islands were the Moluccas in the East Indies,whose ownership had been in dispute between Portugal and Spain. This is the first reference to the "Western Islands" being given the name 'Solomon' but it indicates that the search for gold was still a primary motive of the expedition. [8] Further expeditions took place but their destination was the Philippines, which were conquered in 1565 and settled by some Spaniards. They now had a base on islands in the Pacific, which they could use as their centre in the Far East for commerce, industry, administration and evangelism, establishing a powerful Roman Catholic presence which largely displaced Islam, except in the south of the archipelago. Manila was founded in 1571, and the University of Santa Tomas de Aquina [9] the first in the Far East, was established by the Dominican Order in 1611 and entitled at first "The College of Our Lady of the Holy Rosary".

When Ahedo's project failed, the Governor decided to take the initiative. He informed the King that he had decided to appoint his nephew, Alvaro de Mendana y Neyra as leader of the proposed expedition to "certain islands and lands which lie in this part of the equinoctial between New Guinea and this coast (Peru) and ..... are held to be very rich." It was believed that land discovered by the Portuguese Jorge de Meneses in 1526 and known as "Os Papuas" (possibly meaning the "fuzzy-haired") was in fact New Guinea. The north coast was seen by the Spaniard Alvaro de Saavedra in 1528 and 1529, and he named it "Nueva Guinea" (New Guinea) and when reports of it were received in South America and Europe, some speculated that it might be part of the great southern continent, Terra Australis. The generally agreed location of the "Western Isles" (or "some

---

[8] Maybe this was done to distinguish them, because by 1541 some officials had begun to call the Philippines "the Western Isles". In 1543 the expedition led by Guy Lopez de Villalobos called them 'Las Felipinas',named after Felipe (King Philip II of Spain from 1556) who was then heir apparent, and things were thus clarified.

[9] The University of St Thomas Aquinas in English.

islands called Solomon") was by now thought to be somewhere near New Guinea.

The purposes of Mendana's expedition were various. All the Spanish expeditions were intended to lead to the discovery of new lands, the expansion of the Spanish empire, and an increase in trade and wealth. But the Chief Pilot of the expedition, Herman Gallego, wrote later that the primary motive of the expedition was the conversion of the heathen. The Roman Catholic Church had been threatened by the Reformation in Europe and it was determined to establish itself in the Americas (both north and south), in East Asia and in the Pacific. This aspect of Mendana's expedition is made clear by the presence on board of Franciscan friars, including priests, the importance given to prayer and the celebration of Mass, and the giving of saints' names to many of the places they discovered. The importance of the religious motivation was underlined by a Spanish viceroy who wrote: "in each friar the King had in the Philippines a captain–general and an entire army". There was little distinction between the religious and the political – "service to God was also service to the King-Emperor .... State and religion, faith and civilisation, were one in those days". wrote Salvador de Madariaga in 1942. Gallego said that one object of the expedition was "the discovery of certain islands and a continent," probably meaning the "Western Isles" and the "southern continent."

Two vessels were prepared for the expedition and they were re-named the 'Capitana' and the 'Almiranta' (in English the 'Flagship' and the 'Admiral') at Callao, the chief port of Peru, which had been founded in 1537. The expedition set out on December 19, 1567, and on board the 'Capitana' were Mendana, Gallego, Sarmiento de Gamboa (in charge of policy and navigation) and Catoira, the Chief Purser. On board the 'Almiranta' was Pedro de Ortega, the Maestro de Campo, in charge of the military aspects of the expedition. There were members of the Order of Friars Minor (Franciscans) as well, with their 'Vicar' in charge of them. The members of the expedition were known in the Spanish language as 'expedicionarios'. On December 30 the ships sighted an island which they called Ysla de Jesus, which may have been Nui in Tuvalu (formerly the Ellice Islands). Weather conditions prevented a landing, but some contact was made with the people, who presumably came off in canoes – possibly the first contact of

Europeans with Polynesians in the islands of the south Pacific. On February 1, they came upon extensive shoals, with no sign of human habitation, and that meant that they had probably arrived at Roncador Reef – they were therefore in the Solomon Islands! On February 8 they arrived at a high island which they named Santa Ysabel, after the patron saint of the expedition, and found a bay on the north central coast which was one of the very few safe anchorages in that part of the island. They called it Puerto de Santa Ysabel de la Estrella (the port of Saint Ysabel of the Star). Roncador Reef they had named 'Los Bajos de la Candelaria', as they had discovered these shoals on the Eve of the Feast of Candlemas, the Purification of the Blessed Virgin Mary.

The Spaniards were fortunate, Kesuo Cove in Estrella Bay was a safe anchorage during the season of north-west winds. They were able to land and take formal possession in the name of the King of Spain. Contact was made with the inhabitants, possibly the first contact between Europeans and Melanesians. There was mutual suspicion. However, Catoira was able to note down some words from their language and this enabled Charles M. Woodford, first Resident Commissioner of the British Solomon Islands centuries later, to confirm that the Spaniards had been in the Estrella Bay area. Some of the crew worked on constructing a smaller vessel, a brigantine, while others went on two expeditions into the interior, which were resented by the inhabitants. Mendana and the Vicar in charge of the Franciscans gave advice to the 'expedicionarios' about how to behave with restraint, as they were reliant upon the local inhabitants for food and water for their survival. One expedition reached the high central ridge of Ysabel, a considerable enterprise. Other expeditions set out to explore the coast of the island in the brigantine, a light two-masted vessel. From April 7 onwards, the coast south of Estrella Bay was explored, and on April 9 the north-west tip of the island of Mala was seen. The Spanish asked what it was, and were told "Mala ita –Mala over there". The Spaniards recorded it as being named Mala or Malaita – and they gave it the Spanish name Ysla de Ramos (Isle of Branches) as it was Palm Sunday when it was seen. On April 15 they reached the northernmost island of another group. As it was shaped like a ship, they called it La Galera ('the galley'). It was the island of Pombuana[10] which they reached at night and where they found anchorage. The following morning the ship was approached by many local people in canoes, probably attracted by the sight of a 'canoe' which was different from anything they had seen before. The skins of the Spaniards by now were probably well-tanned by their exposure to sun and wind, but their use of clothing to cover their bodies must have seemed strange to the islanders. The expedicionarios were invited to a large island about three miles away, which was surrounded by smaller islands. This was probably Vatilau, which they named 'Buena Vista' (meaning "attractive sight") "because it appeared very fertile". Gallego estimated its circumference at thirty-six miles. Mendana reported to Governor de Castro that it was a land of "bare mountains and 'sabana' (covered with grass or low vegetation) and with many clearings sown with 'panaes' (a local root crop)".[11] They probably moved the brigantine to the good harbour in the passage between Hanesavo and Vatilau, the best one when the south-east trade winds began. Although the descriptions given by the Spaniards point to the island they called 'Buena Vista' being Vatilau, Gallego says that it was called Pela, and Sarmiento that it was called Gella, which seem to be forms of the name now used for the whole group – Gela.

On Easter Day, the brigantine sailed along the south coast of Buena Vista and crossed a few miles to another island which some of them called 'La Florida' or, as Mendana stated, 'Isla de Flores' (Island of Flowers). This name was later used as an alternative to 'Gela' to describe the whole group, but it seems that its first use was as a description of the island of Olevuga. Islands to the east were seen, one of which they named San Dimas. Others beyond it and not visited they named San German and Ysla de Guadalupe. San Dimas was probably Big Gela (Gela Sule). Before landing there, they passed through a small group of five islands, the largest of which they called Pascua Florida (Floral Easter), as it was Eastertide. It is possible

---

[10] Called, appropriately, 'North Island' in the British Admiralty Chart of 1911.

[11] Probably pana, a species of yam with thorny vine. Kumara (sweet potato) probably arrived later from New Zealand via Norfolk Island.

that, from a certain viewpoint the Spaniards had guessed that the largest land they had observed was, in fact, three islands – which they called San Dimas, San German and Guadalupe, based on their observations of the mountains and hills. What, however, they were probably observing were Gela Sule and Gela Pile – but they did not discover the Boli Passage between them.

Leaving Gela, the Spaniards passed Savo, which was producing smoke, presumably from its volcanic crater, and they called it Sesarga, after the island of that name west of Coruna in Galicia, northwest Spain. They arrived at a large island which they had seen from afar, which they named Guadalcanal, the name of the place in Valencia in Spain where Pedro de Ortega had been born. He was on the brigantine. Gallego gave the native name as Guali. They approached the coastline at the mouth of a large river, which could have been the Mataniko (Matanikau) or the Lunga (Betikama). The present capital of the Solomon Islands is by the Mataniko. After a return visit to Ysabel on the brigantine, during which they discovered the island of San Jorge (St George), the two main ships arrived in Guadalcanal on May 12, having left Ysabel on May 8. They found anchorage near a point on the coast where there was some shelter in the lee. They called it El Puerto de la Cruz – Point Cruz today – and the Mataniko River nearby they called Rio Gallego. That suggests that the Lunga River was the one they called Rio de Ortega. From there, the Spaniards investigated the north coast and parts of the interior of the island, before sailing further east, giving Spanish names to the islands as they went. They were still looking for gold and silver, and a place to settle, according to the instructions which Mendana had received. They found neither, and Gallego persuaded the expedition to give up the search, as the ships were in a bad state, the islanders were mainly hostile, food and water were an increasing problem, and they were unlikely to find New Guinea – or that part of it called by discoverers ‘ Cabo de la Cruz’ (Cape of the Cross) -- or the southern continent. The Capitana and Almiranta left their anchorage on San Cristoval island (Makira) on August 11, 1568, having taken six hostages, and the Capitana arrived three months later off the coast of California on December 20, having been separated from the Almiranta. The two ships did not get back to Callao in Peru till September 11 1569.

Their return voyage had been one of extreme suffering and hardship, but that did not deter Mendana. Immediately on his return, he made a report to the king, giving a glowing account of the possible products of the islands, including gold, and of the number of "souls awaiting salvation". He wanted to establish there a base for further exploration, and to justify what had been achieved, although there had been no settlement. He was supported by his uncle, Lope Garcia de Castro, who had returned to Spain in 1569 on ceasing to be Governor and Viceroy of Peru. Mandana was successful. In April 1574 he received official appointment as "Governador de las Ylas de Salamon", permitting him to colonise them at his own expense. He returned to the Western Pacific with four vessels, accompanied by his wife, Doña Ysabel de Barreto and her brothers. The Chief Pilot was a Portuguese, Pedro Fernandez de Quiros, who had a burning desire to discover the southern continent. The ships left Callao on April 9, 1595 but, in spite of de Quiros's skill, the fleet did not reach the Solomon Islands, but instead found the Santa Cruz group to the east of them. There they established the first European settlement in the Pacific Islands south of the Philippines in Graciosa ('Thanksgiving') Bay on the island of Ndeni or Santa Cruz ('Holy Cross') – as it was named by the Spaniards. It did not last long. On November 7, the site was abandoned, as it had been found unsuitable, the islanders had become hostile, disease was rife, and the vessels were becoming increasingly unseaworthy. Amazingly, Doña Ysabel took command as her husband had died and the fleet set sail for the Solomons, which Quiros thought were to the west, but, as no land was sighted, Doña Ysabel gave the order to sail for Manila in the Philippines.

It would be many years before the people of Gela saw another 'white man', and only the people of Santa Cruz had seen a white woman! In spite of the failure of the expedition, it was de Quiros who was not deterred this time. Longing to find the southern continent and to convert its inhabitants to Catholicism, he managed to obtain the support of the Pope and the Duke of Sesa, the Spanish Ambassador to the Holy See. The fleet of three ships left Callao in Peru on December 21, 1605, with Torres on the ship called Almiranta, being the second in command. The idea was to use Santa Cruz as a base for further exploration, but, on their way there, they discovered various islands across the length of the Pacific. They sighted Taumako island and also visited Tikopia island in the area nearest Santa Cruz, having also heard of Sikaiana island further north. From Tikopia they went on to discover the Banks Islands and then the large island which de Quiros thought was the southern continent, and which he named 'la Austrialia del Espiritu Santo' – the island known today as Espiritu Santo, or just Santo. De Quiros described his discovery as 'Nueva Mondo' – the New World. But what he had actually 'discovered' was later called the New Hebrides, the country now known as Vanuatu.

He tried to establish a European settlement in Big Bay on Espiritu Santo but had to abandon it within 35 days and sail to Mexico, then on to Spain. Torres returned by a different route and discovered that there was a passage between New Guinea and Australia, establishing that New Guinea was in fact an island, and not part of the great southern continent. The passage was named after him, the Torres Strait. It was later revealed that the small islands in the Strait were inhabited by Melanesians. So there emerged a clearer picture of what the Spaniards had simply known as 'The Western Isles". They were not just the "Isles of Solomon", and the Solomon Islands were not on the edge of a great continent. Most of Australia had yet to be discovered!

Further visits by white men to the Solomons hardly affected the islands of the Gela or Florida group. The Dutch did not reach the central Solomons, seeing only outlying atolls en route to the East Indies via New Guinea. On his voyage in 1699 the British explorer William Dampier found some of the islands north of the Solomons and east of New Guinea, and named them collectively as 'New Britain'. The islands of 'New Ireland' and 'New Hanover' were later named in honour of the other kingdoms of the British monarch. In 1770 Captain Cook mapped New Zealand, the New Hebrides (which he named), and the east coast of Australia (known then as New Holland), which he named New South Wales. in 1767 Captain Philip Carteret, RN, 're-discovered' Santa Cruz and Malaita, and a group of islands north of Bougainville was named after him. Whalers started to arrive in the area in 1798, and sandalwood traders were active in the western Pacific from the 1840s to the 1860s and traded fire-arms and other goods with the islanders. The British interest in the South Pacific had begun! This would eventually lead to the establishment of a number of Colonies and Protectorates. Admiral George Anson had been sent on an exploratory voyage around the world by the British Government in 1740, but Dampier had already been round it three times! The Pacific was being opened up to the world, by a succession of naval explorers from different European countries, and this would have a lasting effect on the whole region.

Figure 10 : The Melanesian School (St Andrew's College) at Mission Bay, Kohimarama, near Auckland, with canoes on the beach and Maori houses along the fence line, probably associated with fishing. [Credit : Crombie, John Nicol, 1827-1878. Scene at Kohimarama, Auckland, with Bishop Selwyn's Melanesian Mission station. Ref: PA1-q-250-17. Alexander Turnbull Library, Wellington, New Zealand. https://natlib.govt.nz/records/23063366]

Figure 11 : Anglican Church in a village, possibly on Guadalcanal (1933). [Credit : MAA, University of Cambridge]

CHAPTER 5

CHRISTIANITY

There were very few Europeans in the Solomon Islands between the re-discovery of some of the Solomon Islands by Commander Philip Cartaret in 1767, and by the Frenchman, Louis Antoine de Bougainville in 1768, and the middle of the 19th century. They did not recognize them as the islands discovered by Mendana. Gradually traders arrived, usually from Australia, and in some islands of the Pacific there were white 'beachcombers' who had either been thrown off their ships for unacceptable behaviour or who had opted to go ashore and not return on board for their own reasons. The reputation of some of the Solomon Islands for cannabalism and head-hunting deterred most white people! At first, contact with islanders had sometimes been cautious, even friendly, as the islanders were curious about these strange people with their big ships appearing over the horizon from nowhere that they had heard of -- but their attitude soon changed, especially when the Europeans stole food or used guns to intimidate or kill people. The islanders soon realised that their bows and arrows and clubs were no match for the armed intruders. Europeans began to be feared, especially if they were armed, but they arrived with many goods the islanders themselves wanted, including iron tools, calico and guns. The people also enjoyed smoking stick tobacco. Sometimes Europeans were attacked or killed because they were feared, or just because they were foreign, sometimes because it was an easy way of obtaining the trade goods. Some of the powerful head-hunting chiefs of the Western Solomons, especially in New Georgia and nearby islands, actually wanted to attract traders and give them some protection, in order to secure the supply of the goods they had on offer, especially guns and machetes. Some of the traders even settled and married local women, and so survived and sometimes prospered.

The other people who ventured into these islands were representatives of the Roman Catholic Church. The early explorers, Mendana and de Quiros, had, as one of their main objectives, the "conversion of the heathen" to Catholicism. The friars on their voyages had conducted the first Christian acts of worship in the Solomons, but that was only for the 'expedicionarios'. At the end of their voyages, they had taken some of the islanders hostage in the hope that this would excite interest in Peru and Mexico and lead to further evangelistic expeditions, but also so that these 'natives' might be the first to be instructed and baptized. However, such stealing of people led to further suspicion, and certainly did not commend the Christian faith. However, the Church did not give up. Starting with Hawaii in 1825, the Vatican gradually established missions across Polynesia and, in 1836, a Vicariate Apostolic of Western Oceania was established. The French Religious Order, the Society of Mary or Marist Fathers, was asked by Pope Gregory XVI to be responsible. Father Jean-Baptiste-Francois Pompallier, a Marist Father, was chosen to lead the Oceania Mission. The Pope was particularly interested, as he had been the cardinal in charge of the 'Evangelisation Congregation' (Commission) at the Vatican before becoming Pope. A Vicariate Apostolic is an area without a normal diocese (in other words, a mission) but it is led by a bishop. So Pompallier was consecrated. The area entrusted to him was vast – all the Western Pacific and Micronesia as well. The Pope's plan was to start off with two Vicariates Apostolic of Eastern and Western Oceania, and then to divide these into smaller areas with their own bishops. Pompallier established his base in 1838 in New Zealand and concentrated his efforts there, so another Vicariate was established in 1842 for Central Oceania, based on the island of Wallis (Uvea) north of Fiji. Then in 1844 a Vicariate Apostolic of Melanesia was established to cover New Guinea and the Solomon Islands, with Father Jean-Baptiste Epalle as the first Vicar Apostolic. He had been deputy to the Vicar Apostolic of Western Oceania. He also took charge, temporarily, of the Vicariate Apostolic of Micronesia. He even had a plan to make the Solomon Islands a Vicariate with its own bishop. On December 1, 1845, the ship carrying the missionaries sighted San Cristoval, and investigated the possibility of their establishing a mission there. However, Bishop Epalle wanted to see if the island of Santa Ysabel, which had been significant during Mendana's visit and was considered to be more central, might be a better choice. On the way there, they decided to pass by Guadalcanal and drop anchor at what they called "Cape Hunter", although this was actually a name given by Lieutenant John Shortland to a place in the Western Solomons in 1788. Apparently, they reported the local people called it 'Ghela'. The islanders surrounded the ship in their canoes, looking ferocious. Their faces were painted white and their lips were red with betel nut juice. The captain feared that they might climb aboard and fixed a rope barrier several metres high around the deck. As their numbers increased, he ordered his sailors to load their guns, and also place a small cannon on the poop deck. At the sight of that, the islanders disappeared. Apparently, they were familiar with European ships and knew what the firing of a cannon might mean. Other ships had probably used them to fire at islanders and their villages, when the Europeans had felt threatened. The ship, the 'Marian Watson' departed for Santa Isabel and arrived on December 12 at Astrolabe Harbour in Thousand Ships Bay at the southern end. There again the ship was surrounded by canoes, but the islanders wanted to barter. Hoping to find a place to settle there, the captain exchanged hatchets (small axes) for yams, sugar cane and pigs. The islanders tested the hatchets by swinging then over their heads, and rejecting them if they were too heavy. By signs, they indicated a village with which they were at war and, banging their heel with the other hand, they communicated the message "If you go there, they will kill you."

A party of priests and seamen went out each day to seek a suitable place to set up a mission station. On December 16, they went further, out of sight of the ship, and saw a large group of men standing motionless, silent and armed, on the shore. Leaving their own weapons in the boat, to show their peaceful intention, the party went ashore. The leader of the group of islanders was a man called Londo. The Second Officer of the ship offered him pieces of iron, which did not please him much, then a hatchet, which he accepted eagerly. Then he saw the bishop's ring, which the bishop refused (with a smile) to remove from his finger. Londo gave an order, and one of the men brought down a hatchet on the head of the bishop from behind. The other white men tried to escape, and one sailor managed to reach the boat and to fire two shots with his pistol. Hearing that, the attackers dispersed. The Second Officer and one of the priests were badly wounded. The bishop's body was recovered; the ring was missing, and he was nearly dead. The area was later called 'Martyr's Bay', as the bishop did not recover consciousness except to utter a few words and, before his death, to clutch a crucifix. He died on board, surrounded by the kneeling priests and with their doctor and the captain standing nearby, at 4.00 pm on December 19. Before his death, all the priests had insisted that the captain take no action against the islanders, although they acknowledged that one of his officers had been wounded. There was a funeral Mass on board the next day, the priest remarking that it was the first Mass he had celebrated in the Vicariate of Melanesia. The bishop's body was buried with no marker on St George Island, although a careful drawing of the spot was made. They did not know it, but St George was the island to which the people of Santa Ysabel believed that the spirits of the dead went. The people who had killed the bishop came from the Maunga tribe.

After his death, the question was whether those remaining should still try to find a place for the mission on San Cristoval, continue further north to New Ireland, or return to San Cristoval. Because the anchorage would have been far from any suitable place for the mission station on Santa Ysabel, it was eventually decided to return to San Cristoval. Amazingly, there was a man called Loukou on that island who had been a cabin boy on an English ship, and the missionaries were able to contact him and get him to act as an interpreter. Completely naked, he accepted the captain's gift of a shirt. He told them of a good anchorage, Makira Bay, which they found and named Port-Sainte-Marie, in thanksgiving to the Blessed Virgin Mary. After establishing their mission station, some items were stolen and one of the priests was attacked with a spear, but that was after the attacker's wife had been raped by one of the white sailors. It was six months after it had sailed from Sydney that the first ship, the Marian Watson, eventually returned there. It carried the sad news of the death of Bishop Epalle. There was one priest on board who had had to go back to Sydney to buy necessary provisions for the new mission station. The bishop's body was eventually found on October 18, 1900, and the grave marked. When that area of Isabel became Christian, it was Anglicans who cared for it.

Bishop Epalle was replaced by Bishop Collomb, who found that the Marists on San Cristoval were all suffering terribly from fever, and were physically weak and unable to develop the work, so on September 3, 1847, the entire mission staff, with all their supplies, were moved by ship to Woodlark or Maria Island, off the east coast of the island of New Guinea. They left behind the grave of one of the priests who had died of fever one month after arriving at San Cristoral, aged twenty-three. There were now no

Christian missionaries in the Solomon Islands, and hardly any others in northern Melanesia.

It was their situation which exercised the mind of Bishop George Augustus Selwyn from England. Queen Victoria had appointed him first Bishop of New Zealand in 1841, and he had arrived there in 1842, after his consecration in England. His "Letters Patent", appointing him, had included many of the islands north of New Zealand in his diocese -- which was unusual, as they were not in Her Majesty's domains! However, the Archbishop of Canterbury had encouraged him, in a letter written on behalf of the Colonial Bishoprics Council, to regard New Zealand as "a fountain diffusing the streams of salvation over the islands and coasts of the Pacific." This was not unlike the intention of the Roman Catholic Church in setting up first the Vicariate of Western Oceania, then another of Melanesia. Bishop Selwyn saw New Zealand, which had become a British colony in 1840 after the signing of the Treaty of Waitangi by many of the Maori chiefs, as the base for furthering these aims: the development of the Maori Church, the care of the white settlers and the conversion of the Melanesians. As part of this plan, he set up St John's College at Waimate North soon after his arrival, in order to train Maori and Pakeha (European) students, especially for ordination, to which he hoped he would later add the training of Melanesians for missionary work among their own people, if they accepted the Christian faith. The College moved near Auckland in 1844. In 1849 he made an exploratory visit to see the methods of the Wesleyan Methodist missionaries in Tonga and the London Missionary Society (Congregationalist) missionaries in Samoa. He was aware that the pioneer missionary in Samoa, the Reverend John Williams, had been killed during his first missionary visit to Melanesia on the island of Erromango in the New Hebrides in 1839. He was informed that the L.M.S had, nonetheless, sent Polynesian missionaries to the Loyalty Islands near New Caledonia, and to the Southern New Hebrides. He also met in Samoa two missionaries from a Presbyterian Church in Nova Scotia, a British colony which later became part of the Dominion of Canada in 1867. Bishop Selwyn was impressed that a British colony was sending out missionaries to the Pacific, just as he hoped New Zealand would. He wrote: "This was a striking lesson for our New Zealand Church, for I believe that this was the first instance of any Colonial Body sending its own Mission to the heathen, without assistance from the mother country." He persuaded the L.M.S to transfer the work they were doing in the Loyalty Islands to the care of the Bishop, who then decided to concentrate his initial efforts on the Loyalty Islands, New Caledonia and the north of the New Hebrides, respecting the 'rights' of the other missions working already in the south of that country. The work of the Marist Roman Catholic missionaries in New Caledonia had ceased in 1848, when they were attacked and withdrew.

ANGLICANS

Bishop Selwyn made his first missionary journey to this area in August 1849 in his first mission ship, the 'Undine', which he navigated himself for parts of the voyage, having studied navigation on his way out from England. This date is recognised as the beginning of the "Melanesian Mission", as he brought back four Loyalty Islanders and one New Caledonian to New Zealand. The plan was for them to spend the summer in New Zealand and be returned to their homes before the winter arrived in New Zealand. On this voyage, the bishop discovered that the work would be complicated by the fact that, in that island area, there was a flourishing trade in sandalwood which 'European' ships were taking to China. Most of the foreign contacts of the islanders were with the traders, who had been operating since about the 1820's in collecting shell and beche-de-mer, as well as sandalwood. There were also whalers in the area. In order to communicate with the islanders, with their multiplicity of languages, a trade language had gradually developed, based on English but with some elements of Melanesian grammar. This was sometimes called "sandalwood English", but, in the New Hebrides, it came to be known as Bislama, from the Portugese for beche-de-mer, as the traders had contact with the Portugese trading colony of Macao near Canton in China. In the Solomons, it was known as Pidgin (Pijin). As only a few of the islanders were involved in trade with the Europeans, the Anglican missionaries had to acquire as many of the local languages as they could, and the young men brought to New Zealand had to try and acquire some English. Bishop Selwyn saw most of the traders as a bad influence, and believed that his task was to bring about a better relationship between Europeans and Melanesians, and to encourage all his students to acquire and practice "true religion, sound learning and useful industry." In 1852 the Mission voyage reached the Banks Islands (north of the New Hebrides), Santa Cruz and then San Cristoval, 3,500 kilometres north west of Auckland.

In 1850 the first Solomon Islander, Didimang from Mwata on San Cristoval, had been brought by a naval ship to Selwyn, and he was baptised on board the Mission ship moored at his home village in 1852 as the first Solomon Islander Christian. When he returned home however, he did not do the teaching of the Christian faith to the people, as the Bishop hoped he would. As the only Christian teacher in the Solomon Islands, with no support, it must have been very difficult for him, but it was deeply disappointing for the missionaries who had taught him in New Zealand. By comparison, the work in the Loyalty Islands prospered with missionary support.

In 1853 the Bishop returned to England for two reasons : to raise the finance for the purchase of a Mission ship, the first of a long line named the "Southern Cross", and also to obtain a priest who would gradually take over responsibility for the Melanesian work. He succeeded in getting funds for a vessel of some size, and the services of a young man who had recently been ordained, John Coleridge Patteson, son of a judge, whose mother's uncle was the famous poet, writer and thinker, Samuel Taylor Coleridge. Patteson had been at Eton College where Selwyn had also done his schooling, and he had done his university degree work at Oxford, where he was made a Fellow (senior member) of Merton College on graduating. There is a fine memorial to him in the Chapel there. Sir John Patteson, the father of 'Coley' – as he was known in the family – was a friend of Selwyn. He agreed that his son should go, as Coley truly wanted to follow the Bishop who had inspired him by a sermon preached at Windsor, while he was still at school. Selwyn had certainly found the right man. Patteson took over the Melanesian School at Mission Bay at Kohimarama near Auckland.

They set out for New Zealand in 1855, Patteson learning something of navigation and the Maori language on the way. He showed a remarkable ability to learn new languages which was a valuable gift in the islands. The Southern Cross made exploratory voyages in the 1850's, and in 1856 the first large group of Solomon Islanders was taken to Auckland, seven young men from Marau Sound at the eastern end of Guadalcanal and the coastal villages of north western San Cristoval. From 1859 the Melanesians no longer went to St John the Evangelist College on the top of a windy hill, but to St Andrew's College, Kohimarama, in a bay on the southern shore of Auckland harbour, which came to be known as Mission Bay. By the 1860's Selwyn was convinced that the time had come to establish a "missionary diocese" linked to the Church of the Province of New Zealand, which had become an autonomous Anglican church in 1857 with the adoption of a new constitution. It became known as the Diocese of Melanesia, but many continued to refer to it as the Melanesian Mission, with its boundaries not clearly defined. Patteson was consecrated as its first bishop. He continued Selwyn's system of collecting young men and boys from the islands who were willing to go to New Zealand, with the agreement of their parents and communities.[12] In 1862 the bishop wrote:

"The most distant point we reached was the large island of Ysabel in the Solomon Archipelago. From this island a lad has come away with us, and we have also a native boy from an island not many miles from Ysabel, called Anudha, but marked in the charts (though not correctly) as Florida."

Anudha (or Anuha)[13] island was a small island off the north coast of Big Gela, which could be passed on the way to Ysabel. For this voyage, Patteson had chartered a schooner, a vessel of 70 tons, a little larger than the old "Southern Cross", for four months. It was called "Sea Breeze".

On this voyage, Patteson thus reached 'Florida' island, which he described as 'beautiful', for the first time. He landed twice there. He wrote: "There is here a regular town, 102 houses in one place, and many large villages." Some eighty men, young and old, stood all around him on the reef and he was astonished when one of them returned with him to the boat and

---

[12] Between 1849 and 1860, 152 Melanesians were brought to the mission school near Auckland. Some died there, and are buried at St John's College.

[13] Called 'Alligator Island' on the British Admiralty chart of 1911!

“without any opposition from the people quietly seated himself by my side and came away to the schooner.”

It is not clear in these accounts, taken from Patteson’s letters, whether Anudha and Florida are the same island. It seems likely that the ‘lad’ he mentions in two accounts is the same person, and that, for a while, until the group of islands was better known, the names ‘Anudha’ and ‘Florida’ were used inter-changeably for Gela as a whole. On that voyage, Patteson eventually had on board thirty islanders, including two from Norfolk Island, probably part-Tahitian Pitcairn Islanders. The others came from eighteen islands and spoke twenty-eight dialects or languages!

Patteson had introduced a new system - a summer school in New Zealand and a winter school at Mota in the Banks Islands north of the New Hebrides. There were, in 1862, fifty-one Melanesians from twenty-four islands at the summer school and forty at the winter school. Regarding the Solomon Islanders, the bishop wrote “All can read a little, some pretty well.”

A new Diocese of Melanesia was established in 1861 and Patteson became the first Bishop. In 1866 it was decided, after negotiations with the authorities in New South Wales and London -- which had been going on since the 1850’s -- to base the new diocese in the small British territory of Norfolk Island. This had first been used as a British convict settlement and then it became the new home of the Pitcairn Islanders, who had been moved there in 1856. By 1867 all was nearly ready to receive the staff of the Mission and the Melanesian scholars for the new St. Barnabas’s College on the island, which was still being built by an advance party to replace the Melanesian school called St Andrew’s College, Kohimarama,in New Zealand. On March 23, 1867, Bishop Patteson wrote :

“On Monday, only two days hence, the ‘Southern Cross’ sails (weather permitting) with our first instalment. Mr Atkin and Mr Brooke, with their classes of thirteen Mahaga, Anudha and Savo scholars, and fifteen Malanta,

Guadalcanar, Ulawa and San Cristoval scholars,[14] George Sarawia also, and his wife, and Walter Hotaswol, who again has been spitting blood, form the first party. Mr Palmer has got his house up and they must stow themselves away in it, three whites and forty-five blacks, the best way they can ….."

This "first party" was going to join the one already on the island, so that the 31 Melanesians would be joining the fourteen already there in the work party. There was much work to be done by them all on arrival. The teachers were Joseph Atkin, a New Zealander, who would be teaching those from the 'eastern' Solomons – that is Malaita (which Patteson called Malanta), Guadalcanal, Ulawa and San Cristoval – and Charles Hyde Brooke, an Irishman who would have the care of those from the 'central' islands, namely Ysabel, Gela and Savo. George Sarawia and his wife, Sarah, came from Mota, in the Banks Islands, where he would establish the first Christian village in Melanesia (called Kohimarama) in 1869, having been ordained deacon – the first Melanesian clergyman – by Patteson in 1868. Charles Bice, an Englishman[15] taught scholars from the New Hebrides, and the language of instruction was Mota, used by everyone.

During the annual voyage in 1867 the ship called at Savo and the Bishop "slept ashore at Florida and left Mr Brooke there to the hospitality of three old scholars for a few days, by way of making a beginning." The Bishop commented that Brooke "speaks the language fairly; and his visit will, I hope, do good." He "stayed four days and came back on the ship with three former pupils and four new ones, one of them grown up, a relative of the leading men of the island." It was probable that Mr Brooke, by using Gela language, was able to communicate not only with the people from that island, but with those from Savo and southern Ysabel as well. Sadly, in 1868, John Keble Barau, a baptised boy from Ysabel died from typhus. The

---

[14] Gela was known as 'Anudha' by Selwyn and Patteson, and 'Ulaua' was later spelt 'Ulawa', 'Malanta' was 'Malaita.' 'Mahaga' indicated Ysabel.

[15] Bice was ordained deacon at the same time as Sarawia.

Bishop described him as "our most hopeful Ysabel scholar." In 1868 he baptised Taroaniara (whose name he spelt 'Taroniara') from San Cristoval, and described him as "a young man full of promise." He was the only Solomon Islander confirmed and able to receive Holy Communion by 1869.

From 1869, plans were made to place Charles Brooke, then a deacon, at Florida, and Joseph Atkin at Wango on San Cristoval, with the aim of encouraging "native self-supporting Melanesian churches." Brooke spent ten days at Florida with his scholars. In 1869 the Bishop also ordained Joseph Atkin and Charles Brooke as priests. In 1870 at Epiphany on Norfolk Island, the first Christian marriage of a couple from Ysabel took place – Capel Oka and Sekahave. The clergy were expected to learn at least one of the languages of their scholars. The Bishop knew best the languages of Mota, Bauro (San Cristoval), Mahaga (Ysabel) and Nengone (Loyalty Islands). However, he expected Joseph Atkin to acquire a good knowledge of Bauro and Charles Brooke of the language of Florida. In 1870 Charles Brooke was again dropped at Florida and made his base at Boli (Mboli).

Charles Brooke had a greater facility in learning languages than Joseph Atkin. The Bishop reported that "Brooke knows and speaks the one language of Anudha very well. For there is but one language, with a few dialectical varieties of course." Brooke spent ten weeks there, while Atkin was at Wango on San Cristoval. Brooke was accompanied by two Gela youths, Dudley Lankana and Richard Maru, who actually spent a lot of time with their relatives, leaving Brooke to do what he could without their constant help. They, however, did not go back to 'heathen' ways and expressed their intention of returning with him to Norfolk Island after their home stay. A small house was built for Brooke at Boli, which the Bishop considered a very healthy place, as the coral grit and sand ran a long way in shore under the coconut trees, and there was no very dense undergrowth. When the easterly wind was blowing, it was drawn upon the shore there. To windward, there was the good harbour of Sara, two miles distant, where the Mission ship could anchor. In Brooke's house, raised five feet on poles above the ground, the floor was of bamboo, woven like basket-work. He had a table, two benches, a cane chair, a cork bed, a harmonium, boxes and plenty of food. Nearby was the great boat house, the 'kiala', about 180 feet long, and about 42 feet in height and breadth.

This was used by Brooke for services on Sundays with the small band of Christians, wearing his surplice. They sang hymns and chanted psalms in the presence of a large number of people, which varied from 150 to 300 and sometimes even more. He usually spoke twice during the service, to avoid giving one long sermon. The Bishop was aware of the value of these extended visits by missionaries in getting to know the people, who usually discussed everything at great length and in some detail. It was only by being among them, listening to them and establishing relationships with them, that the missionary would gain any real influence and respect – that was the Bishop's conviction. Brooke however had to face two big challenges. The first concerned his relationships with the local 'big men'! Three brothers were the principal men at Boli – Takua, Savai and Dikea. Takua and Savai wanted to control Brooke's activities, seeing him as their tame white man. Brooke, who had a strong personality and could be quite outspoken, even dramatic, would have none of that. Brooke had been all over the group of islands and did not see himself as only serving Boli. He made it clear that he had come with a message for all the people of Gela, not just for those of Boli. The chiefs objected when he made up small parties of boys from different parts of the island. They feared that they might lose the advantages for trade which they had with a white man (mane pura) like Brooke in their midst. Brooke was firm, friendly and kept his temper. At the end of his stay, he had gathered thirteen young men and boys from different parts of Gela, including Dudley and Richard, to go to Norfolk Island. Brooke hoped that Takua would also send his two little girls, as, increasingly, the bishop felt that the girls should be educated as well as the boys, not least so that the baptised boys could have Christian wives. In the end, Takua, feeling that his views had not been respected enough, refused to let them go. On the voyage back, however, Taroniara's little girl of seven years, called Paraitaku, was allowed to go by her relatives at Wango. The second problem was the nature of the islands of Gela. They were not as fertile as the neighbouring volcanic island of Savo. There was much less bush than on other islands, and instead of coral crags, the rock, often of a reddish colour, had little soil on it. The people sometimes found it hard to grow enough food. However, the work done in 1870 was considered by the Bishop as "the nearest approach yet been made to regular missionary operations there."

Tragically, at the same time as the evangelistic work appeared to be progressing, recruiting ships, knows as 'blackbirders' arrived in the central Solomons, having already been operating further south. Bishop Patteson had already written to his Primate, Bishop Selwyn: "The Banks Islanders are very shy now of the vessels sent to carry off men to Fiji or Queensland. They will find their way into the Solomons soon. One indeed, a cutter, has taken about twenty men from Ulaua." The people believed that the Bishop would somehow be able to bring them back. When Brooke returned to Gela in 1871, two chiefs confronted him, because over a few months previous to his arrival, over 50 men had been taken, and there was a report that eighteen had been killed. They angrily said: "Why does not Bishop take us on board and take us to these places so that we may kill these killers?... You two Bishop have deceived us: you came and told us not to kill – and then these vessels come and kill us."

The voyage of 1871 started off with the Bishop feeling unwell and somewhat depressed. The activities of the blackbirders were often questionable. There were some responsible recruiters but many of the ships followed no rules and treated those they attracted on board, or captured on land or sea, with little consideration. There was much resentment among the islanders throughout Melanesia. The Bishop was not completely against people being taken away to work for a period, unlike the Presbyterian missionaries in the New Hebrides who were totally opposed, but he wanted them to be treated properly and work under good conditions and be returned at the end of their service abroad. He was planning to visit Fiji himself to see what the conditions were like for the labourers who had been recruited to work on the plantations there. However, he was cheered by the fact that Edward Wogale of Mota, the brother of George Sarawia, had volunteered to go and work on Gela, hundreds of miles away, with his friend Charles Sapinamba of that island, to aid him in his work among his own people. He was older than Charles and knew more than him. They could talk together using Mota, but the Bishop wrote; "Edward will soon have to speak the tongue of Anudha when living there." On Easter Day, April 2, a day after his birthday, he had confirmed three girls and two Solomon Islands boys, his last confirmation. Charles actually became a sailor on the 'Southern Cross'.

The voyage began on April 27. At Pentecost Island he learnt that a 'thief ship' had carried off people from that New Hebridean Island. He stayed at Mota while the ship carried Charles Brooke on to Gela, where he learnt the details of the incident when the 'snatch-snatch' vessel had carried off the fifty men. Some of them had gone on board to trade, but were clapped down under the hatches, while tobacco and a hatchet were thrown to their friends in the canoe. A rope noose had been used to upset some canoes, then a gun had been fired, and the islanders had jumped into the water. The swimmers had been picked up by the ship's boat and taken aboard. A white man on board had held up two fingers, which a man called Lave, who escaped by jumping overboard, thought meant two months. It actually meant two years, but who was to know? However, on that Mission voyage ninety-seven children from four villages on Mota were baptised, along with the separate adult baptism of a man, the first public baptisms on the island. A coral-lime building had been erected as the first Church, and it was where the Holy Eucharist was celebrated on June 25.

The 'Southern Cross' then toured the New Hebrides, and Charles Bice heard on Aoba (now Ambae, called also Leper's Island) that a recruiting vessel at Espiritu Santo had been attacked by the local men, and that the crew had been killed and eaten in revenge for some men stolen by another ship earlier. Charles Bice had been ordained priest the previous Christmas, and was becoming an increasingly valuable and respected member of staff. The Southern Cross had then gone back with Atkin and Brooke to Norfolk Island to collect the 24 Solomon Islander scholars there. It then picked up Bice at Mota, as the Bishop wanted him to see something of the work that the others had been doing in the Solomon Islands, as he had been involved in teaching the New Hebridean boys and girls. A recruiting vessel had been at Savo and other places trying to get men. Brooke was the farthest north of all the missionaries but the Bishop was also planning for a new station on Savo and the Loyalty Islander Mano Wadrokal of Nengone (Mare) with his wife Carry and daughter Jemima were left there. There were a few baptised people with him, including a married couple, "and three other very good lads, to start with", according to the Bishop. Some Ysabel people had fled there from the head-hunting raids, as expeditions came over to Santa Ysabel from the New Georgia Group, seeking heads and slaves. By the 1870's the central coastline of the island was almost depopulated, as there were also raids within Ysabel itself. Many had fled to the southern district of Bugotu, where the people built tree homes on platforms up to 30 metres above the ground. Increasingly in the 1870's the raiders came armed with rifles, so even the tree-houses were ineffective as places of refuge. Wadrokal started a school on Savo for refugees from Ysabel and boys who had been at Norfolk Island. He was a man of great energy but with a violent temper and proud manner. However, it was significant that a Melanesian missionary from the Loyalty Islands, a fruit of Patteson's early work there, was now spear-heading the Mission's work in that part of the central Solomons.

On this voyage, the Bishop noticed the effect of depopulation on islands in the New Hebrides and Banks Islands, and increasingly in the Solomons, because of the 'blackbirding.' It had reached the Santa Cruz group, as well as the main Solomons group. Records show that between 1871 and 1903 30,000 islanders were taken to Fiji and Queensland to work. Joseph Atkin on San Cristoval had spoken with the master of a recruiting ship based in Fiji called the 'Emma Bell', which was on its way towards Santa Cruz. Bishop Patteson was not just concerned with the activities and behaviour of the recruiters; he was equally concerned with the behaviour of the returning labourers. He wrote: "They bring guns and other things, which enable them to carry out with impunity all kinds of rascality. They learn nothing that can influence them for good. They are like squatters in the bush, coming into the town to have their fling. These poor fellows come back to run riot, steal men's wives, shoot, fight and use their newly acquired possessions to carry out more vigorously all heathen practices."

The redoubtable Wadrokal had to face all that on Savo, where ships called regularly, and the island's chiefs were often acting as agents for the traders. In 1870 the first permanent trading station in the Solomons was based there, and the way of life of the people thus became closely linked with warfare and trade. Savo men returning from Fiji and Queensland with Snider rifles terrorized the coastal people of western Guadalcanal. Some missionaries later described Savo as "the Sodom of the district." Even Wadrokal found it too much and soon moved to Isabel.

The Southern Cross had left Mr Brooke and Edward Wogale, George Sarawia's brother, at Gela. The island group was also experiencing the recruiting ships of all three kinds – the ones with Government agents on board, recruiting fairly, but also the 'snatch-snatch' and the 'kill-kill' . On July 11, a 'Sydney vessel' was on the west coast, and nine islanders had been killed. On the 13th a 'kill-kill' vessel had anchored four miles from Boli. Takua asked Brooke what he should do, adding : "How was it that you and Bishop came first, and then these slaughterers? Do you send them?" Brooke advised Takua to stay on shore, but to fight if the recruiters attacked them with the intention of killing or burning. Takua replied: "Your words are the words of a chief!" On August 13 another ship came and canoes went out to it. Dudley Lankona returned to report that they had not been able to sell their fruit, and that the men on the ship had said that the Bishop and Brooke were bad, but that they themselves "were good, and had pipes and tobacco for those who would go with them." They also reported that a becalmed ship nearby was a 'killer'. Brooke went on board, and the captain thought he must be a maker of coconut oil. The man was a Scot, who had settled on Tanna in the New Hebrides, but was a recruiter as well. "If I get a chance to carry off a lot of them, I'll do it, but killing is not my creed." Brooke pointed out that he might be attacked by angry Gela people. The man then pointed to six muskets he would use, saying : "That's only a few of them. Let them come. We'll give it to them pretty strong." When Brooke revealed that he was a clergyman, he observed: "Well, wherever you go nowadays, there's missionaries. Who would have thought you would have got so far down!" (He meant, so far north from the southern islands). Seeing this party of islanders in the canoe which had brought Brooke out to his ship, he said : "Ah, my fine fellows, if your friend was not here, I'd have the whole lot of you – what a haul!" Meanwhile, on shore, Takua and Dikea were preparing old guns which had been given them by somebody on the ship 'Curacao', and were disappointed when they found out that there was to be no attack on the vessel. So, she left safely – Brooke's intervention had been successful.

However, at the other end of the island at Vara, four out of five men were killed by the crew of a ship's boat in a horrific manner. Sorova, the survivor, had gone out with a companion in one canoe and three men in the other. They saw four black men on the vessel, whom he thought were

Ysabel men. The ship's boat had a white man on board who came and sat in Sorova's canoe, then stood up and capsized both canoes. He caught at Sorova's belt, which broke, and he was able to escape by swimming away, but another boat then appeared. Those in it, whose race he could not distinguish, beat his companions with their oars, then attacked them with tomahauks and cut off their heads. Their bodies were taken on board and then thrown into the sea to the sharks. A later enquiry at Sydney came to the conclusion that the vessel was probably a tortoiseshell trader, commanded by an American. It was suspected that the actual killing was done by Pacific islanders working for the men-stealers, and that they had probably also assisted their chiefs in head-hunting. In spite of all this, on July 26, five men went out in a canoe to another ship, even after they had been warned not to trade. Two boats were lowered, either side of the canoe. A great crowd on the shore saw it, and cried out. A war fleet was launched with Dikea standing in the leading canoe, brandishing a long ebony spear – but the ship went off under full sail and escaped. In 1871, during five months recruiters had taken over 50 men from Gela and reportedly killed eighteen. These tragic events led to widespread anger and wailing. People wanted revenge. Takua said; "Let not their pigs be killed; we will give them to Bishop, he will avenge us." His brother Dikea added; "My humour is bad because Bishop does not take us about in his vessel to kill-kill these people!" Two days later, the "Southern Cross" appeared and Takua declared; "Let Bishop only bring a man-of-war and get me vengeance on my adversaries, then I shall be exalted like-like-like our Father above!"

It was clear that the Gela people had confidence in the Bishop for a number of reasons. Brooke had been settled for a time among them, so they could distinguish between good white men and bad. They therefore knew that the Bishop was not on the side of those white men who were against them and they had also had good reports about the way of life on Norfolk Island, where islanders had been well treated. There was less head-hunting on Gela than on Santa Isabel and no cannibalism as on Malaita or San Cristoval. There was also no established white trader. Gela seemed to be the place where the Christian faith might take root and transform the lives of the people, and so become one of the centres of evangelization in the Solomon Islands.

The Southern Cross collected Brooke and Wogale and Joseph Atkin before setting out for Santa Cruz. Atkin wrote down his thoughts about Missions, and the speed at which the Bishop was trying to operate in the Solomons. “Why not be content to set to work to try that the conversion of those to whom you are sent may be as thorough and real as possible in that time, and not to fret at being unable to hurry the work some years?” The Southern Cross avoided calling at Santa Cruz island (Ndeni) for fear that the islanders would not be able to distinguish between that ship and the recruiting vessels. Patteson was also unable to communicate with them – because of their difficult language – in order to explain their purpose in coming. So, the ship sailed for the island of Nukapu where he was known and could communicate with the people, as the islanders there spoke in a Polynesian language close to Maori. Indeed, some of the people there he considered to be friendly to him, from his previous experience of meeting them.

Figure 12 : John Coleridge Patteson. [Credit : The Melanesian Mission]

Figure 13 : Patteson Memorial Cross. [Credit : The Melanesian Mission]

Figure 14 : Man of Nukapu. [Credit : The Melanesian Mission]

Figure 15 : Patteson Memorial Chapel. [Credit : The Melanesian Mission]

CHAPTER 6

DEATH AND DETERMINATION

Bishop Patteson knew the danger he was in because of the recruiting vessels. On September 16 he wrote: "The master of the vessel that Atkin saw did not deny his intention of taking away from these or from any other islands men or boys he could induce to come on board. I am aware that we may be exposed to considerable risk on this account." He was right. He insisted on going ashore alone at Nukapu. The ship's boat took him as far as the circling reef. When he reached there, six canoes eventually came to meet it, and the Bishop was recognised. Two chiefs, Moto and Taula, who had been very friendly to him before, invited him into their canoe. However, the tide was so low that they had to drag the canoes over the reef. Another canoe accompanied that of the chiefs. Those in the ship's boat, Joseph Atkin, Stephen Taroniara, James Minipa and John Nonono, saw the Bishop land on the beach, then he disappeared from their sight. The remaining canoes remained near the boat, then, after about half-an-hour, a man stood up in one of them and called out "Have you anything like this?" while he shot off one of the arrows, a yard long. The others then shot too, calling out as they did so: "This for New Zealand man" (meaning Atkin), "This for Bauro man" (Taroniara), "This for Mota man". Only James escaped completely, by throwing himself back in the boat. Regaining the ship, Atkin said "We are all hurt". Three of them had actually been struck by arrows and it was Charles Brooke who extracted, as best he could, the six arrows in Stephen's chest and shoulders. Atkin said to Joseph Wate, his godson, and to the Gela man Charles Sapinamba (Sapibuana): "We are going to look for the Bishop, are you afraid?" Wate answered: "No, why should I be afraid?" – in spite of the fact that his godfather had just had an arrow in his left shoulder. With Mr Bongarde, the mate, who carried a pistol – for the first time in the records of the 'Southern Cross' – the four of them rowed to the reef to wait for the tide to rise high enough to carry them across it. There were people standing on the beach, and they then saw two canoes rowing towards them. One cast off the canoe it had been pulling, which had a heap in the middle of it, and returned to shore. Wate said to Atkin: "If there is a man inside to attack us, when he tries, we shall see him." Then suddenly Charles Sapinamba said: "Those are the Bishop's shoes." As the crew lifted the body, wrapped in a mat, into the boat, there was a shout from the shore. Four other canoes came out, probably to recover the drifting canoe, and the boat rowed swiftly back to the ship. As it was lifted up, two words were said: "The body!" It was placed on the skylight, with the mat open, and just five wounds were discovered. One was to the head, shattering the skull at the back, probably caused by a blow from a club. Another was to the top of the head, and the body and both legs had been pierced with arrows, apparently after death. He was naked, except for his boots and socks. The five wounds were probably of great significance. Just before the arrival of the Bishop, a recruiting vessel had arrived at the island and carried off five young men; later it was discovered that there were five Nukapu men in Fiji. Under the mat was a palm frond with five knots in it. It was September 20, and next day, the Feast of St Matthew, the Bishop's body was committed to the Pacific, to whose people he had dedicated his life. The burial service was read by Joseph Atkin, his "son after the faith". Following that, Charles Brooke and Edward Wogale became sick with malarial fever, but Brooke was well enough to take English and Mota morning prayers the next day. Atkin also celebrated Holy Communion, but began to stumble over the words of administration of the consecrated bread and wine, and realised that the end would soon come for him and Stephen. The arrows had been poisoned. He died in agony on September 29, after Stephen, who had died the day before. Bauro had lost both of its missionaries. They were buried at sea, as their leader had been.

Bishop Patteson had hoped that Stephen would be the first Solomon Islander priest and that the work on San Cristoval would go forward under his leadership, with the support of Joseph Atkin. It was not to be. The 'Southern Cross' reached Norfolk Island with news of the deaths on October 17, having called at Mota on the way. Brooke went ashore first and broke the news. The Reverend Dr Robert Codrington was in charge of the College and Charles Bice was with him. The Bishop's will provided that the senior priest should take over the running of the Mission if anything happened to him, so Codrington became the leader until a new Bishop could be chosen, which took some years. Bishop Selwyn's son, John Richardson Selwyn, offered himself to serve as a priest in the Mission from 1873 in response to the need for more clergy and other workers to fill the places of those whose services had been lost, both European and Melanesian. When the news reached England on November 29, the Society for the Propagation of the Gospel (SPG) petitioned the Archbishop of Canterbury to appoint an annual Day of Intercession for Missions, which was first held on December 20, 1872. In the month before the news reached England, HMS 'Rosario' had arrived at Norfolk Island and Capt Markham was given the news, and decided to investigate the circumstances of the Bishop's death at the island of Nukapu. The staff at Norfolk Island had requested that the captain should not avenge the Bishop's death, but after three attempted landings had been repelled by arrows, the crew fired on the islanders, who believed they were only defending themselves. Some may have been killed, houses were burnt and canoes destroyed. For the Christian islanders, however, the greater tragedy was the death of their Bishop. The memorial cross erected in 1884 to his memory on the island had this inscription; "In memory of John Coleridge Patteson whose life was here taken by men for whose sake he would willingly have given it." As the 150th anniversary of the Bishop's death drew near, the people of Nukapu, who had gradually embraced the Christian faith, started to make enquiries about how they might be reconciled with members of the Patteson family.

In Queensland, the Polynesian Labourers Act had been passed by the State's Legislature in 1968, in order to monitor the activities of the recruiting ships and control the trade. However, after the death of Bishop Patteson, Queen Victoria raised the question of the kidnapping of the islanders with her Government, and the Lord Chancellor read what she wanted to say to both Houses of the British Parliament on February 6, 1872. After referring to 'practices scarcely to be distinguished from Slave Trading ', the statement continued : 'In the South Sea islands ,the name of the British Empire is even now dishonoured by the connexion of some of my subjects with these nefarious practices, and in one of them the murder of an exemplary Prelate (Patteson) has cast fresh light on some of their baleful consequences.' A Bill was then passed to deal with the 'trial of offences of this class in Australasia'. The extent of the challenge becomes clear when one realizes that between 1863 and 1904 about 20.000 islanders from the New Hebrides and Solomon Islands were taken to Australia to work on plantations, nearly always as labourers.

On October 12, 1871, Lt. Albert Hastings Markham had been appointed as temporary commander of the Royal Navy vessel the 'Rosario' by Commodore Frederick Sterling, the Senior Naval Officer on the Australian Station, and he had been given the special mission of investigating alleged cases of kidnapping of Pacific islanders. The commander was not aware at the time that the bishop had been killed. Markham left Sydney on October 18 and twelve days later arrived at Norfolk Island and was told of the bishop's death at Nukapu. The missionaries begged him to make no reprisals if he visited the island to investigate, although they also thought it unwise for him to visit there, especially if he had no interpreter with him. However, he felt it was his duty. After touring the New Hebrides and places further east, the ship arrived at Nukapu on November 29 – the same date as that later assigned by the Church of England, inspired by Bishop Patteson's martyrdom, as the Day of Intercession and Thanksgiving for the Missionary Work of the Church, as it is now called. The islanders initially waved leafy branches, apparently as gestures of welcome, but when members of the crew attempted to go ashore, they were twice met with a hail of arrows. Markham felt that he had to respond to the hostility shown to him and his men, and decided to burn the village nearby, as he had done in a similar incident on the island of Nguna in the New Hebrides. This was done after the firing of warning shots from the 'Rosario'. The incidents were later investigated by a Court of Enquiry set up Commodore Stirling, and a report was sent to the Lords Commissioners of the Admiralty in London. Markham was criticized for acting carelessly on both occasions, and not taking enough care to avoid bloodshed. However, the Court of Enquiry found that probably the natives of Nukapu had not suffered any casualties in the encounter.

Captain Markham was soon promoted to Commander, and eventually became an admiral. He left the Pacific in 1872, but it is greatly to his credit that before leaving the area he advised Commodore Stirling about the need for greater control of the 'blackbirding' ships, in these words:

"The only way I see to put a check, for I believe that it is almost impossible to put a stop to this traffic as it has now assumed such gigantic proportions, is by men-of-war (Naval vessels) repeatedly visiting the different islands, and for them to be empowered to seize all such ships as are unlawfully kidnapping the islanders, or are in any way infringing the rules laid down in the 'Merchant Shipping Act'...."

The Gela group for a while became the most important centre of operations in the Solomons, especially after the death of Joseph Atkin. Dr Codrington observed the signs of progress there, writing, "They are a lively, energetic people, and when they begin to move they will move quickly." There was the prospect of protection for both missionaries and Christians being provided by several chiefs (vunagi) who had gained their positions of influence by their personal qualities and success in fighting. However, there was also internal unrest as the peoples of Boli and Honggo were at war. In 1872 seven of the crew of the ship 'Lavinia', trading for beche-de-mer , were killed at Matevago near Boli by a group led by Bishop Patteson's first scholar from Gela, on the orders of chief Kalea. Takua was Brooke's protector. He collected a fee from anyone who entered the missionary's house, and any boys who passed through Boli on their way to Norfolk Island and back were taxed, paying in iron, tobacco or beads. Brooke distributed trade goods generously all over Gela, but Takua was unable to control that, much to his annoyance. Brooke was active in writing about his experiences in English religious papers, and he preached fluently in the Gela language on Sundays to congregations (or audiences) of hundreds. His colleagues and the Gela people were impressed. Unfortunately, he began to behave in ways unacceptable to the Mission, but this was only discovered in 1874. He had been having close physical relationships with some of his male pupils. He found the whole of his situation rather romantic and even wrote; "There was I, the only white man on the Island, without so much as a pop-gun to defend myself with, dwelling amidst that crowd of eager bloodthirsty savages, but without the slightest fear or misgiving ..... The romance of the life appealed to me strongly."

Figure 16 : Chief of Ngore Fou, Malaita Island, and a child listening to a gramophone. [Credit : BMM and Photo by Beattie of Tasmania for the Melanesian Mission https://nla.gov.au/nla.obj-141085807 (nla catalogue record 6343514) National Library of Australia]

Figure 17 : Native men of Savo Island. [Credit : The Melanesian Mission]

CHAPTER 7

THE CHURCH ON GELA

The Christian Church was now established on Gela, with its outreach to Bugotu and its hope of reaching out to both Guadalcanal and Savo. It increasingly seemed to lend itself to being developed as the centre of operations of the Anglican Church in the central Solomon Islands. It had many advantages. Its people were increasingly becoming Christian. There was little head-hunting there. It was a centre of trade, as ships felt safer there than elsewhere in the Solomons, and it basically had only one language, unlike Guadalcanal or Ysabel. It had a splendid passage through the island where ships could safely pass, with care -- even the 'Southern Cross' -- and its northern exit near Siota was sheltered by a reef. The island, like that of Malaita, had probably been fractured by volcanic activity, thus creating the Boli Passage, 16 miles long, with an average width of 100 yards and a depth of seven fathoms – although one stretch of 200 yards had only three fathoms. At its narrowest, it was 60 yards across. It had one of the finest harbours in the Solomons, situated near the small island of Tulagi off the south coast. At certain seasons of the moon, the Passage had a 4-knot current. All this was very different from Guadalcanal, which had some rivers navigable by canoes, but few safe harbours, except at Marau Sound. Gela had however few rivers and fresh water could be a problem. Where there were swamps and mangroves, as in parts of the Passage, alligators flourished. There were opossums in the bush and large beetles which were called 'tabevatu' (stone-holders), as they could grip stones as well as human limbs at night. Other than mosquitos (and so malaria), and sand flies biting during the night, there were comparatively few other hazards. From Savo, megapode eggs could be obtained, as these birds laid their eggs in the hot volcanic sand. Penny and others called them 'sand-fowls'.

The Gela chiefs sometimes organized great netting operations which would bring in fish of all kinds, including the box fish with its four-sided shape and tender flesh. The local people used the Gela word for the fish to describe the traders' bottles of the same shape. The 'boila' fish with large green scales could weigh over 30 pounds and had nippers instead of teeth, with which it battered the coral to make small crabs appear. The island group could therefore provide safe waterways, good anchorages and varied sea food, as well as plentiful coconuts. By the end of the 19th century it was estimated that Gela had 3000 to 4000 people, whereas Guadalcanal probably had 25,000, Malaita 60,000 (the most populous island) and San Cristoval 10,000. Until almost 1900 there were very few white settlers, except for traders and a small band of missionaries who were all Anglicans. In 1898 the Roman Catholics returned and settled at Rua Sura island off Guadalcanal, and the Methodists arrived in the Western Solomons in 1899. At that time, some believed that Melanesians might die out because of internal divisions, armed conflict and European diseases. However, the evangelistic, medical and educational work of the Churches were to prove them wrong.

In 1872 Brooke spent three months on Gela after the attack on the 'Lavinia' and visited Honggo on the west side, where no white men had been before. He was assisted by two men from the Banks Islands, Walter Ulgau of Mota and Walter Woser of Mota Lava. In 1873 he again spent three months there, visiting many villages. He had built at Boli an elaborate schoolhouse 18 metres long and 13 metres wide, but the school only operated when he was there. Alfred Penny later reported that this was "because there were no teachers old enough and reliable enough to carry it on themselves, and no native converts to Christianity to rally round them and back up their efforts." The chief, Takua, used to attend these classes when they were held for the instruction of both the boys from the College on Norfolk Island and others who wished to attend, but he eventually became unconvinced by the missionaries' insistence that "the people would be much better for the new religion." Takua had five or six wives and one of these was the sister of Charles Sapibuana who had trained at Norfolk Island. He and his sister were not from Boli, but from Gaeta district. Sapibuana or Sapi[16], was

[16] He appears to be the same as the islander called 'Sapinamba' in earlier accounts.

the name by which he later became known. He was named 'Charles' after Charles Brooke.

Brooke described Gela life between 1867 and 1874. He said that infanticide was common, so there were few children. If a chief chose to dismiss one of his wives, she was considered a harlot (rembi). During the services conducted in Takua's canoe house, people would smoke and chew betel nut. Kikoa, the chief of Belaga village, would sit in the canoe itself under a large white umbrella; he was a little man with a bald head. Dikea, Takua's brother was a head-hunter and used to visit Mala (Malaita) to get heads. Returning with four heads he found four visitors at Boli and promptly added four more to his collection. The people of Gela were distinguished by having their heads shaven, except for a tuft on the top of their heads. The heads of the Mala people were not shaved.

Brooke worked on the Gela Prayer Book and wrote some Gela hymns. After his departure from the group, he wrote a novel, praised by Dr Codrington for its accurate details of island life. Its hero was 'Percy Pomo' of Pombuana (meaning Gela) who was taken on a mission ship ('Aurora') to 'Happy Island', and then kidnapped as labour for New Caledonia, from where he was rescued by his beloved missionary teacher, 'Percy Wakefield'. This was the first novel about the Solomon Islands. In spite of Brooke's dismissal in unhappy circumstances, he had laid the foundation of the Gela Church and his influence was considerable. His work was carried on by his favourite pupil, Charles Sapi, who established a school on his final return home from Norfolk Island. This was not in Boli (Big Gela) but in Gaeta. The Gela Prayer Book, on which Dudley Laukona and Sapi had worked, was printed in Auckland by William Atkin in 1871. Dudley had a school at Boli in 1873.

The Reverend Alfred Penny came out to serve in Melanesia and took over the oversight of the work in Gela and Ysabel in 1875. Sapi became his key fellow-worker. Penny,who was from England, was an impressive figure. He was a big, bearded man who, like Brooke, learned to speak the Gela language well. He made sure that the four Gospels and Acts were translated into Gela. He also closely studied local customs, both in Gela and

Ysabel. Being a good boatman, he regularly visited Ysabel, forty miles away, as well as the Langalanga Lagoon on Mala. His book, written after his return to England, entitled "Ten Years in Melanesia", gives a good picture of Gela and its customs, as well as the work of the Mission in the area he covered. He also wrote an adventure story of Ysabel, although he entitled it "Head-hunters of Cristobal"! On Ysabel, the attacks of the head-hunters from the islands of New Georgia, especially around the Marovo Lagoon, in the Western Solomons had caused the people to move south into Bugotu from other parts of Ysabel island. This was the part of Ysabel closest to Gela, and it was where Penny would take over from Mano Wadrokal in 1878; he had been ordained deacon in 1875. Wadrokal's Ysabel students had returned there from Savo in 1874 and put themselves under the protection of Bera, a notable head-hunting chief. The situation on the island was generally dire. Penny wrote: "These constant raids have so demoralised the people that they live in constant dread, and have no sort of unity among themselves or trust in each other." Bera had established himself at Thousand Ships Bay and, by assisting labour recruiters and traders in beche-de-mer, he had been able to obtain more than a hundred rifles and revolvers and also ammunition. Wadrokal had with him two companions from his home island of Nengone (Mare) who unfortunately killed two of Bera's followers. Bera was furious, and Wadrokal had to be removed by the Bishop. However, he had managed to establish three schools, the largest with one hundred pupils. Bera himself tolerated the Mission, but went on head-hunting. Penny regarded him as the chief obstacle to the spread of Christianity in Ysabel.

On Gela, Penny had to use Mota at first, which was translated into Gela by an interpreter who had studied at Norfolk Island. Then he acquired Gela and Bugotu languages, Although he was able to preach in these languages, his message was difficult for the people to understand. It seemed part of "a white man's strangeness". They were also puzzled why he and other missionaries were there. Their questions were like: "What does he come for? He does not buy coconuts or ship men, so what does he want? He says his country is good, better than ours, so why did he leave it?" Penny felt that preaching to people with questions like these was ineffective. He relied instead on teaching the children, hoping that their influence would extend to their parents, and also on the moral power and authority of the teachers from among themselves who had gone away to train, and so had already lived in a Christian community. In 1875 he found no permanent school on Gela or Ysabel, but at Boli, and also at Nuro on Ysabel, 'schools' for young and old were conducted by Norfolk Island scholars on their visits home to their own villages. The word 'school' came to be used to describe the Christian religion. Boys and sometimes girls from these 'schools' were then selected to go to Norfolk Island. There were problems in keeping schools going, especially if a teacher was ill, weak, fearful, lazy or lacking the support he felt he needed. The local community sometimes required people for dancing parties or working projects during school time. Penny tried to visit the schools, and get to know the people of the villages as well.

Sapibuana eventually returned to settle at Gaeta, Small Gela, in 1877. He had been taken by Bishop Patteson to New Zealand in 1866 when he was probably twelve years old. He started learning at Kokimarama, then moved to the College on Norfolk Island. He had a holiday on Gela every two years. During his last two years at Norfolk Island he married and they had a child. His people at Gaeta were largely untaught, and at first he was opposed and his life was sometimes in danger. However, he persevered and, in 1878, his brother (who had previously raided a ship) and his brother's wife were baptised and this was a turning-point in the gradual acceptance of the Christian faith in Gela. A great questioning arose. People wanted to know more. Classes for catechumens were organised in the evenings, and men and women came to question Penny and the teachers late into the night. This was in spite of the displeasure of some of the chiefs, who threatened death in some cases when people gave up heathen practices, refused to attend sacrifices or trod on sacred ground. This change of heart on the part of the people of Gaeta happened partly because of their reaction to a tragic incident. In 1879 a visiting white trader had been killed on Guadalcanal. The chief of the place was a 'brother' of some kind to Kalekona, the chief of Gaeta. Penny came with a group of people to visit Kalekona, who received them. Penny warned them that a man-of-war, a British naval ship which patrolled the islands dealing with matters of law and order, would be sent to investigate, under the authority of the High Commissioner of the Western Pacific, representing Great Britain. The captain of the vessel to which the trader belonged had insisted that the Naval Commander in Sydney, Australia, take action. So HMS Danae, a naval ship, arrived and imposed a fine of pigs, which was then usual in such cases. Then another trader was killed on the Russell Islands, about 50 miles from the place where the previous victim had been killed, and this time he was the captain of a trading ship flying the British flag.

In 1880 HMS Sandfly was touring the Solomons, commanded by Lt. Bower. He set out in a whale boat from Guadalcanal, where the ship was anchored, on a surveying exploration. They reached the small uninhabited island of Mandoliana, about three miles off the coast of Small Gela. Kalekona, the chief of Gaeta, was feeling furious at the time as precious custom money had been stolen and he was having problems with his son and son-in-law. He demanded a head, but the people did not have the money to obtain one. Penny and Sapi were away at Norfolk Island for the consecration of the Patteson Memorial Chapel, and for Sapi to be prepared to be ordained deacon. Vuria, Kalekona's son, had seen the naval party land on Mandoliana and realised that he could obtain a head to restore his father to his "accustomed equanimity", and restore the family's reputation. He took three others with him and crept up on three of the men and then killed them, cutting off their heads. Their leader hid in a tree, but was later found at night and also killed. One man escaped and swam ten miles to Honggo, where a villager took care of him, and also persuaded the chief to spare his life. The sailor, called Savage, stayed with this man Pitia until the 'Sandfly' found him, and the sailors on board then discovered and buried the headless bodies of his former companions. A shore party destroyed Kalekona's canoe house and houses, and the 'Sandfly' returned to Sydney to report to Commodore Wilson. Later, HMS Emerald arrived, and canoes, houses and coconut trees were destroyed throughout the Gaeta district -- to the outrage of some in England. However, Sapi had already established a new Christian settlement of about 100 people at Langgo with a schoolhouse, school bell, slates and books, and there was also a grave marked by a cross – and that was all spared. In 1881 HMS Cormorant arrived to investigate officially, and the Southern Cross was also there with Bishop John Richardson Selwyn, who had been consecrated as Bishop of Melanesia in 1877. The Bishop was able to act as a mediator between the naval officers and the chiefs of Gaeta. Kalekona and Vuria were spared, but three of the other murderers were tried and executed. However, one man escaped into the bush and was never caught. It was an unsatisfactory compromise, but it saved the island from bombardment by the ship, and it also showed the people the influence which the Bishop could have with the British authorities. Out of fear and respect for the man-of-war ships, warfare ceased and people felt free to move around, and the power of the chiefs who were not Christian diminished. The villages from which they had all fled were gradually restored, although Langgo had survived unburnt and continued as before.

Meanwhile, Penny had paid a visit to England. He returned in 1882. New regulations were brought in by the Colonial Governments, allowing recruiting vessels to carry only a certain number of guns, requiring the confiscation of other weapons, and prohibiting the trade in guns. Melanesians returning to the islands were not allowed to have them. Gradually, fighting grew less as the supply of guns ceased and the men-of-war also stopped using harsh methods to punish whole communities. The people began to appreciate their presence rather than fear them, as they gradually helped to establish peace and justice. In 1882 Sapi was ordained deacon at Gaeta among his own people. A threat to his life occurred after the tindalos started to be rejected. In 1883 Kalekona and some of his people had appeared at Sapi's school, saying that they had destroyed their charms and relics and wished to be taught. By then there were seven schools in the Florida group, about 250 people had been baptised and about 375 were in classes for catachumens or nearly ready to join. However, sacrifices continued and Sapi forbade the elder boys in the school to attend an important sacrifice which had previously been required of them, if and when any boy was ready to become a 'man'. Respect was gained by participating, but sacrifice to a 'tindalo' was involved, along with other 'heathen' practices. The chiefs threatened Sapi with death. He did not budge, and, although the threat was not carried out, his house and property were destroyed. By 1885 he was in great need of a rest and recuperation as the strain was affecting his health. However, on arriving at Norfolk Island, Penny found that a severe epidemic of a dangerous influenza was affecting people on the island. Instead of Sapi being priested there, as Penny had hoped, Sapi contracted the 'flu, which developed into pleuro-pneumonia, and he died on the 23rd Sunday after Trinity, deeply loved and respected. Kalekona had died in 1884 and Sapi had managed to hold the people together, although not himself a chief. He was only thirty years old when he died. His ministry had been deeply appreciated both by the missionaries and the people. The clergy considered all that was good in the Gela Church had their origin – or their adaptation and improvement – from him. He was also one who had been closely linked with Patteson, his beloved former teacher, whose body he had helped to recover at Nukapu. At Gaeta, when the news of his death reached the people, "there was a silence in the whole place; no-one cooked food." Dr Codrington was told: "The loss is felt throughout the island, but, of course, chiefly at Gaeta, where in fact for some time they had not thought of anyone else as a leader."

Dikea, the brother of chief Takua of Boli, Big Gela, had led a dancing party to Gaeta, Small Gela. Then there was a change in the wind, and Dikea found that they were stranded there. He sacrificed to his tindalos asking for a calm, so that his party could go home. He had to wait and wait, and when the wind eased he swore that he would never go to Gaela again with such a party "because the power of the new teaching was too strong there." The news of this spread throughout Gela, but the general reaction was that this power was only effective in Gaeta, and that if Kalekona and his party moved away from its influence and wanted to do something elsewhere, they would find a big difference. Before his death, Kalekona had taken some direct action when Rogani, a neighbouring chief, refused to pay back a sum of money which he owed Kalekona, when he heard that he had destroyed the emblems of his tindalos. He made all his possessions taboo, placing them under the power of his fearsome tindalos. Every scrap of food was eaten or burnt, even by infants, so that none could be used to bewitch people ,and, for the same reason, dancing parties would not bring food ashore to eat. Kalekona arrived, however, seized two pigs, destroyed the custom house by fire, shattered some of the emblems of the tindalos and carried others off as trophies. Rogani and his friends did not dare to resist. They thought their tindalos would take their revenge! But Kalekona told Penny afterwards: "There was not a man of us ill afterwards!" This action was seen all over Gela as a triumph for the "new religion." People began to walk over sacred ground, to use beaches formerly reserved for initiates of secret societies to walk or land on, to refuse to pay fines, to cease to offer sacrifices and to sell relics or emblems for cash.

There were various reactions to this increasing movement towards Christianity. When a baptised woman was taken by an alligator while gathering oysters in a lagoon and never seen again, the non-Christians said: “The tindalos are angry because they have been deserted, but their mana (power) is strong enough here to punish those who desert them. If the people are not warned in time, the same fate will overtake them all.” A year after, Penny’s life was threatened while he was visiting Halavo village. The Christians at Halavo had stolen pigs from the neighbouring district of Bonesi because they believed that they would not be punished by the tindalos. The Bonesi people had threatened to kill the Halavo Christians because they had given up their tindalos. Penny as well, if they were given a chance, might have been at risk from the Bonesi people. By then, however, every powerful chief on Gela was Penny’s friend, so he went to Bonesi two days later to confront the people there – but there was no-one on the beach. The Halavo people were not troubled any more…

People, however, still believed in the power of the tindalos in certain places. There was a dark pool near Boli which was thought to be haunted by tindalos. Nobody would go near it or bathe in it, so Penny invited a young man to go with him there. However, this man had been told that, if he bathed there, he would get sick. He refused to enter the pool on arrival there, saying to Penny: “I feel ill. I am going to have an attack of ague (fever). I shiver already. You go down and bathe, and I will light a fire and sit here till you return.” After Penny came back, he said: “When I have received baptism, I shall not be afraid to bathe there.”

One old man named Baulee who had been a high priest of the tindalos and the terror of Belaga District, Small Gela, approached Penny and told him that he wanted to be baptised. He told him he had given up the power (mana) which he had exercised for so long, but he wanted to be assured that there was ‘mana’ in the new religion which he could lean on and trust in. Christianity was beginning to be seen as a source of spiritual power greater than that of the tindalos, but Baulee wanted to know whether, if that power was indeed available, he could be baptised and receive it. Normally, a person would have a year of preparation before baptism, and Penny would have a “season of initiation” when he would check on the preparedness of people for baptism. In Baulee’s case, however he decided to act more swiftly. The old man was baptised, and when the time came for the yearly sacrifice to make the beach 'sacred' (taboo), he refused to perform and so the practice ceased, as others did not know how to "throw the sacrifice." The beach at Belaga was no longer 'taboo' and all could use it!

After Christian communities had been established at Gaeta and Boli, the most important challenge was at Honggo, where the chief was Tambukoro. Lesser chiefs would bribe him to kill somebody belonging to another chief, if one chief had a grudge against another. Being clever, he would inform the intended victim that he might be killed if he did not pay him the same amount – so he got paid twice over! From 1878 onwards, Gaeta people made efforts to establish a school at Honggo, but it did not become 'permanent' till 1883. In 1886, Penny's last year, there was a spiritual upheaval there, as there has been at Gaeta earlier. Twenty adults were baptised and there were visible "tokens of God's power" at work in them. The chief was deeply affected, and came night after night for teaching by Penny. If he was not there, he would go to Gaeta each weekend for teaching by Sapibuana. After the first baptisms, the 'Southern Cross' arrived and Captain Bongard asked Penny: "How is it that Tambukoro has not been off to the ship?" Penny replied: "Don't you see him now? He has been standing beside you for the last five minutes!" He took his time about asking for baptism, because it would mean giving up all his wives except one, which was the policy adopted by Bishop John Selwyn. This was hard on the women, if they lost the protection of a husband or the status of being married to a chief. However, many became Christians, and some were taken in by a family in exchange for the work each one could do in support of her adoptive family. They were available for young single men to marry, and having more women free to marry meant lower "bride price." The expensive tattooing process also became less important. People gradually came to accept marriage to only one woman as the Christian norm, even if you were a chief.

One of the young Christian teachers, however, aspired to marry the daughter of the high chief Takua of Boli in 1878. The young man was called Alfred Lombu, and Takua took his proposal to be an insult. He demanded that he pay a fine, because of his presumption. Alfred wanted to withdraw from his proposal, but Takua was having none of it. He felt Alfred had made a fool of him in the eyes of his people. He insisted on the payment of goods worth £400, including 600 strings of red custom money. In a dispute with a chief, a native orator was usually employed to argue the case on behalf of the accused. A famous orator called Piku was called up to speak on Alfred's behalf. In the end, Alfred had to pay ten pieces of 'red money' and forty dog's teeth and was laughed at as a fool, thinking he was fit to marry a daughter of a man of such high status!

When Penny took over the supervision of the work on Ysabel from the Reverend Mano Wadrokal, who had been moved by the Bishop in 1877 because of his rows with chief Bera – and with the Christian teachers! – there was already one established school, over a dozen people who had been baptised, and a second school which had been started at Tega. Both Wadrokal and Bera the chief were strong and volatile characters. Bera had by then become chief of a large area of the island. However, his son had died and he was determined that Kikola, his grandson, would not die in the same way. He attributed his son's sickness to the power of a tindalo, so he toured the bay, establishing new villages on each islet, away from the area where he believed his son had been bewitched. He then decided that was not enough. A human sacrifice was also needed. A young child was snatched from a woman working in her garden, placed beside his grandson Kikolo, and his throat cut. Bera prayed the tindalo to accept the gift of the child instead of that of Kikolo, who had tuberculosis – but Kikolo died that same day. He was transported back to Bera's main village to be buried as a chief, with people mourning and crying for the appointed number of days for one of his status. The Christian teacher offered to make a coffin and bury him. Bera agreed, but his powerful mother objected, and he was buried in the traditional way, upright. His head was burned by fire and his skull set up in the canoe-house so that he could be treated now as a tindalo. His wife and child were strangled and were thrown into the grave with all his possessions. Each person present then threw in a valuable item, and coconut trees and banana groves were cut down as a sign of public mourning. A heap of stones was piled over the grave. In spite of all this, the schools continued, and Penny visited the Christians there on regular visits from Gela. He had a house which he used while staying on the island, and was there when two labour-recruiting ships arrived in 1883; one was the 'Isabella' from Port Mackay, Australia, and the other the 'Hally Bailey' from Fiji. He was shown over the ship from Fiji, and was told that there were no women on board. However,after he had left the vessel, he was then told by his boat's crew that there were four women hidden under a sail! They probably had no idea that they might be carried off to Fiji, whether they liked it or not. Penny and others complained and the captain was sacked, which proved that Penny's regular visits to ships were sometimes worthwhile. He warned the ship's captains of the dangers of allowing armed men or women on board. Men with grievances might be seeking revenge. The 'Dancing Wave' had been attacked at Gela in 1875, the 'Ripple' at Bougainville and the 'Borealis' at Malaita in 1883. Captains often ignored his advice.

1884 was a memorable year. Bera died, and things began to change on Ysabel. A school was started at Boko, and, when Penny returned about six months later, he discovered that not only all the scholars but also men, women and children had been killed by visiting head-hunters, forty-five in all. The people had not organised a sufficient watch. Action was taken. Special men were appointed to guard the schools and settlements at the mission stations. Weapons and ammunition were purchased from traders or contributed by returned labourers. Watches were marked during the night by the ringing of the school bell. No raids came after this regular system was established. On one occasion, Hugo Gorovaka, a head teacher, had organised a rota which he led all night, after four large canoes had been sighted.

Penny tried to extend the work of the mission to north-west Guadalcanal, where the people spoke languages closely related to that of Gela. He found more opposition there than he found even from Bera on Ysabel. Kouna was chief of the district of Vaturanga. During the visit of the Bishop to the New Zealand Church's General Synod, Penny had the use of the 'Southern Cross' and went with it to install the Reverend David Ruddock as missionary there. The area had been constantly attacked by warriors from the neighbouring island of Savo, and attempts to establish schools had failed. It was hoped that, with the support of Kouna, there might be more acceptance of Christianity on Guadalcanal, where the tindalo religion was similar to that on Gela. However, as Kouna gradually heard about what had happened on Gela, with the increasing abandonment of the tindalos and their worship, he turned violently against the mission. Ruddock was collected two months later, and Kouna declared, "I don't want you or your ship. If you come, you will destroy my tindalos,and I shall have to give up my wives, the snatching of slaves and indiscriminate killing. I would rather remain as I am!"

At the end of Penny's time based in the Gela group of islands, there were 19 schools on Gela and Ysabel, with 53 teachers and an "aggregate daily attendance" of 753 children and young people. He gave oral instruction to adults two or three evenings a week. In the Christian settlements, the pattern of daily life was morning prayer soon after sunrise, an hour's school, then work or play. Evening classes were held before or after evening prayer, which was usually at seven o'clock. In the school there was reading and scripture instruction at least once a day, writing on two or three days a week, and arithmetic from time to time. Penny was not happy with the singing; he found the boy's voices harsh, and the girls too shrill – once they had overcome their nervousness ! He had a gramophone, apparently, and played recorded 'secular singing' of all kinds from various countries. The reaction from one old Gela man was "It sounds nice, but it will kill the songs of our country." He even taught a few boys to play the harmonium, but they only managed to learn some hymn tunes from 'Hymns Ancient and Modern'. The presence of a gramophone was rather remarkable as it had only been invented in 1877 in America by Thomas Alva Edison, who called it a 'phonograph'. It reproduced recorded sound on paraffin-soaked strips, using a steel stylus. He marketed it in 1878, replacing the paper strips with thin sheets of tinfoil. In 1886 a wax cylinder replaced the tinfoil in the U.S.A.[17]

Two years before Penny left the mission in 1886, there was a break-through (which he called the "crippling of the Heathen Superstition") with the 'break-up' of the tindalos. Two hundred adults were baptised, the next year more than two hundred, and, in his final year, two hundred and

[17] "Readers Digest Book of Facts" 1985, Surry Hills, NSW p.336

eighty-three, some with their infant children. The tide had turned. It had taken many years for the island group to accept the new faith, but the process had been according to a plan. People were usually under instruction for a year, and then became catechumens for about six months. They then could be baptised, if they were willing and considered suitable, and were deemed to be sincere in wanting to be Christians. Polygamists spent longer, as the consequences for them and their wives were more demanding. A few were able to express what it meant to them to accept the Christian faith: "It is true that we feared what did not exist, when we believed in tindalos, and we have been all our lives in bondage. We are free now, and we will remain so." For most people, Penny recognised that it would take time for many to be truly converted. He said: "The work cannot be complete till the mind, which has been all along imbued with the thought of the supernatural, finds rest and peace in the power of Christ." He added: "Only after the complete extinction of the tindalos would Christ's blessed influence be extended to the individual soul". "Superstitious fear and intimidation" would need to be gradually overcome. When he wrote of his experiences in the book entitled "Ten Years in Melanesia", published in England in 1887, he expressed his deep desire and longing for Gela: "May he whose Spirit has moved upon the waters in that distant spot among the islands of the Pacific, bringing light and life to Florida, complete the work by sending that light and life across the straits to the multitudes of Guadalcana[18] still lying in heathen darkness." He could look back to a moving farewell service for him and Sapi when they left for Norfolk Island in 1885, and from where neither ever returned. The service held in a large canoe house at Gaeta was attended by over 300 people, most of them "decently clad." They had listened to the farewell speeches of Penny and Sapibuana "with earnest faces and tearful eyes." They said their goodbyes and shook hands on the beach, before going aboard the 'Southern Cross'. Some people then sat on the sand and talked late into the night, while others went to sleep in the canoe-house

[18] Spelling of 'Guadalcana' is as in the original quotation

and woke up early to wave goodbye to the ship from a point jutting out into the sea. The people did not know that they would never see Sapi again.

When it became clear that Penny would be leaving before long, the Bishop of Melanesia wrote in his 'Journal' of 1883: 'We shall have to continue the work in Florida and Ysabel without his knowledge of the people – his perfect understanding of their ways and language – but above all, without that trust and confidence which he has won for himself. It will be a terrible loss to us, but God will direct us as he has hitherto.'

Sadly, after the death in 1885 of Charles Sapibuana[19], the first Solomon Islander to be ordained a deacon, there were no immediate successors to lead the Gela Church. One of the teachers, Alfred Lombu, had been ordained deacon in 1884, but had had a quarrel with the people at Halavo soon afterwards, and six weeks after his deaconing, had left his post. Unlike Sapibuana, none of the other teachers were trusted by both Melanesians and Europeans to provide leadership and a good example. Without Sapibuana providing such example and discipline, the infant church suffered for a while from newly-appointed village teachers who, with the lessening both of the authority and of the fear of the chiefs, took it upon themselves to become "lords over God's heritage", as the "Church Gazette" reported in 1886. The Reverend John H Plant succeeded Penny and continued the annual visits. By then, about 200 adults were being baptised each year, but Plant was disturbed to find that they were "extraordinarily ignorant", and he even wished that Christianity had not suddenly become so popular on the island! He felt the teachers should be providing better instruction for baptism, but instead he found on his visits that the people brought numerous accusations against them, including sexual misconduct, neglect of services and of their schoolwork, and misuse of their authority. Some were even banning people from attending school, and demanding fines before letting them come back. Those who refused to become Christians were sometimes abused, and one village and its

[19] 'Sapi' is commemorated in the Church of Melanesia Calendar on October 24

gardens were destroyed when the people refused to have a school. Christians were asking why there were not more leaders like Sapibuana.

Why then had Christianity (which people called 'school' or 'sikulu') become so 'popular?' One reason was deliverance from fear, both of the chiefs (vunagi) and their associated tindalos, and of their traditional enemies. There was freedom of movement. Dancing parties no longer had to pay respect to the tindalos in the places which they visited. People no longer feared sickness or death if they visited certain previously taboo places. There was some satisfaction in challenging certain traditional customs, especially among the young men. Formerly, in extreme cases, the priests and initiates of the secret societies would extort fines or kill a person by clubbing, or wrap the person's windpipe with a cloth and bite the neck, so that the teeth marks would not show – and then throw the body to the sharks. They would lie and say "The tindalos have killed him." These practices were brought to light and admitted after the 'break-up'. During a dispute about the "new teaching", one man said: "When I believed in tindalos I was like a woman carrying a load. I had to look where I trod and I moved slowly. Now I can go where I like, and I am as light as a dead leaf." There were other practical benefits which people came to appreciate. Former sacred land, fallow perhaps for centuries, was brought into cultivation. Some places however were barren points, where, as Penny wrote, "the winds howl, and the sea moans, or rocky caverns in which the waves dash with sudden roar, or some gloomy dell like the pool at Boli."

Bishop John Selwyn had done much on Gela when Penny was away in 1881, so he had made a direct contribution to the work there. He helped Plant start his work in the area in 1885 with the intention of also strengthening the work in Bugotu and reaching out again to Guadalcanal. Penny had hoped that Gela teachers, "with Gaeta as a base of operations", might one day be successful there. After Penny's return to England Bishop Selwyn baptised 56 adults at Honggo including the chief, David Tambukoro. A new kind of village life was emerging all over the island group. Those who had built their houses on the hilltops and ridges moved their dwellings to the shore, "where they could get their saltwater for cooking, and fish, and move about and see their friends." There were some "law and order" problems. Some hated people were killed by friends of their intended victims. Crime was said by Penny, according to local thinking, to consist of "being found out". Stealing was very common, especially from ships, and tricking visiting traders was widely practised, but things were also taken from the 'Southern Cross'. Sometimes coconuts would be sold to a trader, but a man would stand behind the buyer and pass them "back through several hands to their salesman." Christians and their chiefs pointed out that this was not "good business", as the people thought it was, but dishonesty, and would insist on the 'trade' they had stolen being returned.

The lessening of the power of the chiefs did however create a vacuum. Who was now to exercise authority, lay down the rules, and see that they were followed? The chieftainship system continued, and with the coming of Christianity there was a possibility of peaceful succession. Previously, rival claimants would often fight for the position. In Gaeta, the Christians decided who was the rightful claimant to the position when Kalekona died, and the Boli people, ten miles away, offered 100 men to help them if there were any trouble, but there was none. The old people thought it was a 'miracle' ! But how were the chiefs now to exercise their authority in a Christian way, and be respected? They would no longer levy fines as punishments for the breaking of taboos. Plant devised a new system, whereby chiefs and teachers together could exercise authority over the Christian areas of the island group. In 1887 he called a gathering of Christian chiefs (led by David Tabukoro), senior teachers and representatives of the male population of each 'school village'. It was named the 'vaukolu'[20], and was intended to be a kind of local government. Although it soon became an occasion for feasting rather than of law-making, it nevertheless made rules concerning fines for adultery and crimes which formerly were punished by death, for breaches of the Seventh Commandment[21], and for trespassing by pigs. People discussed

---

[20] 'gathering'

[21] "You shall not kill"

their concerns, including the recruiting of very young boys without their parents' consent.

After Plant's departure in 1890 and his death in 1891 in England, a "supreme council" of chiefs and teachers was added to the structure to guide proceedings and judge disputes. The great significance of this was that the local Christians were making the decisions and not the white missionary, although on matters where there was strong public feeling, he might be called upon to mediate or adjudicate, as in cases of murder or disputes over fishing grounds. In a significant way, the emerging church was attempting self-government, and the church and local government were seen as going hand in hand -- and the idea of a Christian kind of chieftainship with a special role was developed and accepted.

In each Christian village, a central feature was the 'schoolhouse', usually on the site of the kiala, the canoe-house where the large war canoes had been kept. In the 'Church house', the 'valekokoeliulivuti' (literally, the house of prayer), there were morning and evening prayers led by a clergyman or teacher. He would also catechise adults who were too old to learn to read, teaching them about the Creed, the Lord's Prayer and the Ten Commandments, as was laid down as a minimum of Christian instruction in the Book of Common Prayer. The prayers were conducted in Gela language according to the Prayer Book, led at Halavo by the Reverend Alfred Lombu "in the most grave and proper manner", according to the visiting naturalist Charles M Woodford in 1888. He was also "surprised at the manner in which all joined in responses and chanting the psalms." Sadly, in 1891, Alfred Lombu was suspended for three years on charges of adultery. Some of the complaints about the teachers were now being directed at the clergy too.... However, in that year another Gela man was ordained, Reuben Bula. He remained a deacon for life.

Alfred Lombu ministered as a deacon at Halavo until he was ordained priest in 1901. He served there for eighteen years, gradually gaining general respect, in spite of being very hot tempered, and was highly regarded by the time he died, the first Gela priest, in 1919.[22] Both Reuben and Alfred had been schoolboys travelling on the 'Southern Cross' when Bishop Patteson had been killed at Nukapu in 1871. Reuben had first been taken from Belaga village to Norfolk Island in 1869. From Belaga to Gole on the north coast of Small Gela, the people were under the control of a secret society called Tei Belaga. Once, on his return home for a break from schooling, and still learning about the Christian faith, Reuben was put to a severe test. He had spoken against the tindalos, although still a boy, and was told to climb a tree and touch a sacred emblem. Everyone expected him to fall down dead – but he did not. He thus became a true witness to the power of the Christian faith, as he had prayed inwardly before grasping it. He remained a zealous and humble man throughout his ministry, and the Tei Belaga gradually disappeared.

---

[22] Alfred Lombu is commemorated in the Church of Melanesia Calendar on June 21

Figure 18 : The Reverend George Sarawia and his wife Sarah and their family. [Credit : The Melanesian Mission]

CHAPTER 8

THE NEW HEBRIDES

While Christianity was gradually being adopted throughout the central Solomon Islands, the Diocese of Melanesia had been increasing its membership in the New Hebrides, especially in the Banks Islands to the north of the country. In 1867 a group of scholars from the small island of Mota, led by the teacher George Sarawia, had suggested to Bishop Patteson the formation of a separate Christian village on their island. Their idea was to have a place "where all live together, where we can let people see what our mode of life is, what our customs etc. are, which we have learned from you." It was established on land bought by the Mission and named Kohimarama, the name of the site of the Melanesian school in New Zealand which had just been replaced at that time by the one on Norfolk Island. Three couples who had trained there settled at the new Kohimarama, led by Sarawia and his wife in 1869. In 1871, a similar venture was started on the islet of Ra, attached to the larger island of Motalava, fifteen kilometres north of Mota, but integrated into the wider community. This had an impact on the neighbouring islands of Motalava and Vanua Lava, so that Ra, rather than Mota, then became the centre of evangelistic work in the Banks Islands. Initially, Kohimarama flourished, and it was given "all help to carry on the general work of religion and civilization," according to Bishop Patteson. It languished after the death of Sarah,Sarawia's wife,during an epidemic which followed a tropical cyclone in 1873,and this deeply affected her husband. The Kohimarama project had been one in which they were both much involved and the loss of her presence and influence -- as well as the effects of the epidemic -- contributed to the decline.

George Sarawia was ordained deacon by Patteson in December 1868, eleven years after he had gone from Vanua Lava to the Bishop's winter school on Lifu in the Loyalty Islands to learn about Christianity, and become literate. He was named after Bishop George Selwyn who had baptised him in 1863, and he was among the first group of Melanesians to be confirmed in 1865. He had then assisted the Reverend John Palmer in running a school at Mota for a few months each year, to which scholars would be brought from a wide area, including the Solomon Islands. His brother Edward Wogale was later ordained deacon in 1872, along with two leaders of the church on Ra, Henry Tagalad and his brother Edwin Sakelrau. Wogale played a crucial role in the translation work, working alongside Dr Codrington and John Palmer.

Sarawia was ordained priest by the Bishop of Auckland in 1873, as there was no Bishop of Melanesia at the time. He was thus the first deacon and the first priest in the Diocese of Melanesia, and probably the first ordained Melanesian minister of any denomination. He wrote of his experiences later. He and his brother had learned how to operate the mission press, and the Christian community on Mota needed the Prayer Book and the Bible in their own language, so Mota came to be accepted as the common language used by the Anglican clergy and the teachers of the New Hebrides, and then also of the Solomon Islands. It remained so until the general adoption of English after the Second World War in both the New Hebrides and Solomon Islands. Older clergy in the Solomons could still communicate with each other in Mota, at least until the 1960's. Then, with increasing contact with other denominations using other languages in both countries, Bislama (New Hebrides Pidgin) and Pijin (Solomon Islands Pidgin) sometimes became alternatives to English (or French in the New Hebrides), used by both Governments and Churches as more material was translated into both Pidgin languages in the twentieth century.

The gradual conversion to Christianity of the people of the Banks Islands had a link with what was happening on Gela. Edward Wogale, Sarawia's brother, was an outstanding pupil of Bishop Patteson, like Sapibuana, and they became close friends. He went with Sapi to Gela as a missionary in 1870 when Sapi was finding it difficult to work alone, and he paid another visit there in 1880. Thus, these two small groups of islands became the main hubs of mission work in both countries, largely carried out by Melanesians – the Banks Islands in the south and Gela in the north. However, both Mota and Gela went through a period of decline after the initial enthusiasm. The question was motivation. Were people being attracted to Christianity because of the benefits of peace, security, trade goods and to a lesser extent, education, or was there a real understanding and appreciation of the 'Good News' of Jesus Christ and the 'mana' of the Holy Spirit? It was significant that both the Banks Islands and Gela were smaller island areas with plenty of opportunities for people to gather together as Christians. In the larger islands with their mountainous interiors and warring groups, it was much more difficult.

Gela provided some missionaries to other islands, as did Isabel, but the remarkable fact about the evangelisation of the area of the Solomons where the Anglicans were then working was the number of Banks Islands missionaries. They went to the most difficult places – San Cristoval, North and South Malaita, Ulawa and Tikopia – and six of them were influenced by Henry Tagalad. He was ordained in 1883 as a priest and was the greatest influence in the Banks Islands until 1901, when he 'fell' morally, and as there was no other priest in the group to give him absolution, he died of grief. The pressures on some of the Melanesian clergy without other priests to support them were sometimes too great. His brother Edwin Sakelrau died young in 1883, greatly missed, after outstanding work on the island of Vanua Lava. He was trying to extend the work of the Church to the island of Ureparapara, and became ill. He was then carried back to Vanua Lava and died there, on the island where he had become like a father to the people. By 1881 the number of baptised Christians in the Banks Islands had already exceeded a thousand, about one fifth of the total population, and half of these had been concentrated on Mota, where the total population was about 870, although there was still one pagan district there then. The peak of enthusiasm had been in the early 1870's, and seven missionaries had gone out from Mota in that decade to other islands in the Banks and Torres Islands, and also to Pentecost and Maewo in the main New Hebrides group further south. The Banks Islands (and especially Mota) had a very important place in the development of the Church in the whole area of Melanesia where the Mission was working, even greater than that of Gela.

Figure 19 : Government Court House, Aola, Guadalcanal (pre-WW2). [Credit : MAA, Cambridge University]

Figure 20 : [Credit : MM and MAA, Cambridge University]

CHAPTER 9

GOVERNMENT AND CHURCH

Gela had become the first part of the Solomon Islands that was mainly Christian, at least in name, by the time that the British Government had decided that the British presence in the Western Pacific should be more than just protection of its citizens by patrolling naval vessels. Trade with the islands had become quite profitable, especially in coconuts, copra, beche-de-mer and shells of various kinds, and the local people now traded with neighbouring islands, visiting ships and resident traders or their Melanesian agents. However, the attacks on trading and naval ships and the killing of traders in some places, many of them being of British nationality – although often originating from Australia or New Zealand – required further action on the part of the High Commissioner for the Western Pacific, a post held by the Governor of Fiji.

In the case of the Solomon Islands, a significant book had been published in London in 1890, entitled 'A Naturalist Among the Headhunters: An Account of Three Visits to the Solomon Islands in the Years 1886, 1887 and 1888'. The author, Charles Morris Woodford, was a Fellow of the Royal Geographical Society in London, of the Royal Geographical Society of Australia and of the Linnean Society of New South Wales. Not only that, but he was also a Corresponding Member of the Zoological Society in England. Other than the white missionaries of the Melanesian Mission, he was the first British person to write with deep interest and discernment about the Solomon Islands. He had made his base at Aola on the north coast of Guadalcanal and had twice spoken to Bishop John Selwyn when the Southern Cross passed by there during the night. The Bishop had come near to the shore in the ship's boat to have a word with him. Woodford much appreciated his kindness, but wrote 'I had to wade out into the sea to speak with him, so that, although we conversed together, we should pass as strangers should we meet in the street'. His work of studying zoology throughout the archipelago was greatly assisted by trading ships and white traders[23], and he also studied native customs, geology, geography and local languages, giving the basic vocabulary of six of them, including the Polynesian language of Lord Howe Atoll, in an appendix to his book. He had valued the first deep study of Melanesian languages made by the Reverend Dr Robert Codrington – done mostly through his contacts with the boys and girls studying at Norfolk Island – which had been published by the Oxford University Press with the title 'The Melanesian Languages' in 1885. In the preface to his book, written from Gravesend, Kent, in England in 1890, Woodford wrote: 'That the Solomon Islands will one day be of great importance to the Australian Colonies I have not the slightest doubt. Any information about them should therefore be welcome. The object of my visits to the islands was neither political nor commercial, but the following pages .... will enable the outside world to form an idea of the state of affairs now existing'. However, the book led to both political and commercial developments!

Dr Codrington's book included references to the languages of Florida and Vaturanga, both of which would have been of interest to Woodford, as he included a list of Aola/Tasimboko words in the appendix of his book, and this language was related to those other two. Moreover, the trader to whom he was most grateful for assistance in his work was Mr Lars Nielsen, with whom he had stayed for three months in 1888 on the small island of Gavutu, off the south coast of Gela. Nielsen had bought the island two years before, in the hope of spending his 'declining years' there. As he had already been in the Solomons for eight years when he bought it, he thought 'after living so long in the Tropics, a colder climate might not suit him'. Woodford made collections of items on Gela and accompanied Nielsen on his trading voyages in his ketch, a vessel of about five tons. He also spent time identifying places visited by the Spaniards in 1567, surveying the north-east coast of Ysabel for about sixty miles, and visiting Savo and north-west Guadalcanal (which he called Guadalcanar). On his return to

[23] A list of some of these is on Page 82 of Fox: 'The Story of the Solomons' (revised edition 1975)

England, Woodford was shattered to learn that Nielsen and three of the Melanesian men working for him had been murdered. He assumed that Nielsen had been somewhere where he was not known, 'as a juster or quieter man in his dealings with the natives it would have been impossible to find. From his long residence among them ... he had acquired deep insight into the native character and a fund of information which he was always ready to impart.' He had also been presented with a gold watch by the President of the United States, as he had rendered assistance to the crew of an American ship 'wrecked upon Guadalcanar' a few years before Woodford's visit.

Woodford detailed in his book some of 'the long list of murders that have taken place in the Solomons'. He reckoned that out of a resident or floating population of less than thirty white men in the Solomons, eight had been killed in the eighteen months leading up to the time of the publication of his book, the latest being at Rendova Island in the Western Solomons, where the mate of a ship and three seamen (probably Melanesians) had been killed and eaten on October 29, 1889. Woodford claimed that the names of the murderers were well known and that 'so secure do they feel from punishment, the Rendova natives freely visit the white men's trading stations in the Rubiana (Roviana) Lagoon'.

Woodford recognised that the regulations of the High Commissioner for the Western Pacific rightly forbade any retaliation by the resident white men – presumably in order to prevent any further retaliation by the natives. However, he wrote 'the traders have therefore a right to expect that adequate protection should be afforded them in the pursuit of a lawful and peaceable calling'.

Having set out, in writing his book, with no political or commercial aims in mind, he was now appealing for protection for the traders, as well as for the local people working for them. He made his views explicit in a footnote added to the work just before publication: 'These (murders) will continue so long as England ignores her obligation to extend by annexation that protection to her subjects in the Solomons that she was at length forced against her will to extend to British New Guinea (December 1889). I know no place where firm and paternal government would sooner produce beneficial results than in the Solomons. The numerous small tribes into which the population is split up would render any organised resistance to properly constituted authority quite futile, while I believe that the natives themselves would not be slow to recognise the advantages of increased security to life and property. Here is an object worthy indeed of the devotion of one's life.'

Coming from a visiting naturalist, this is a remarkable plea. He is calling for people to devote their lives to establishing peace and 'paternal' government in a little-known island territory on the other side of the world from England. He probably realised, although he did not say so, that the experience of the coming of Christianity to Gela had eventually led to 'security to life and property', and that this could be established elsewhere in the Solomons by 'firm government'. The death of his friend Nielsen had led to this outpouring of feeling, as Nielsen was to him the ideal trader, and he also respected the work of the Anglican clergy, both white and Melanesian. Nielsen had established good relationships with the people of Gela. He only wanted to plant coconuts, build a comfortable home on a tropical island, provide a service to local people and live in peace. The missionaries had brought peace to Gela and, increasingly, to parts of Ysabel. Why could not the British Government do the same for the rest of the Solomon Islands?

Britain's interest in the South Pacific had been aroused by the voyages of Captain James Cook in 1769-71, 1772-75 and 1776-79, leading to his dramatic death in the 'Big Island' of Hawaii during his last voyage. This had led to an interest in the 'unevangelised' South Seas among the founders of the London Missionary Society in 1795. They sent their first missionaries to Tahiti in 1797. This island had also been associated with the voyage of HMS 'Bounty' which had sailed in 1787 to Tahiti to collect breadfruit plants for the West Indies. The attractions of the island had led some members of the crew to mutiny in 1789 near Tonga and return to Tahiti and disappear with some Tahitians to the uninhabited Pitcairn island, which had been wrongly situated on the Admiralty charts. The fighting there, probably over the Tahitian women, between the mutineers and the Tahitian men who had accompanied them, meant that only one mutineer was left alive when the community was discovered in 1808. What amazed the British reading public was that the mutineer, who called himself John Adams, had taught the Tahitians and mixed-race children about Christianity from the Book of Common Prayer and the Bible, salvaged from the 'Bounty', which had been burned.

The main activities of Cook which interested the British Government were the discovery of the east coast of Australia and its surveying by him. He named it New South Wales, whereas the whole of the Southern Continent had been named New Holland by the Dutch, who had first seen its western shores in the seventeenth century. Cook also discovered Norfolk Island and surveyed the islands of New Zealand, whose European discoverer was the Dutchman Abel Tasman – but the Maori settlers had reached there about 300 years earlier than he! The British wanted somewhere to send their convicts, and the 'First Fleet' bringing convicts arrived in Botany Bay near Sydney Harbour in Australia in 1787. Some convicts were sent to Van Dieman's Land, later renamed Tasmania, and some to Norfolk Island.

From Australia, Samuel Marsden, the second Anglican Chaplain in New South Wales, began an Anglican mission in New Zealand in 1814, and the increasing number of missionaries, whalers and other Europeans there led to the signing of the Treaty of Waitangi in 1840 with some of the Maori chiefs. That country was thus opened up to European immigration and to the establishment of the Anglican Diocese of New Zealand in 1841, alongside Roman Catholic and Methodist missions, and later a Presbyterian one as well. The colony of New Zealand appeared to be more fertile than New South Wales and had been exporting food to the early settlers there, which was another reason for British interest in it. In Tahiti, where the Protestants of the London Missionary Society (LMS) had been the only Christian Church, French Roman Catholic priests arrived in 1836 and requested the right to establish their form of Christian religion. Queen Pomare II at first refused, but was threatened with a French naval bombardment, and so relented. In 1843 the French established a 'Protectorate' which the British eventually recognised, in exchange for French acceptance of British 'rights' over New Zealand. George Pritchard, an LMS missionary, was appointed as British Consul in Tahiti.

Thus by 1840 European colonisation of the Pacific Islands had started, beginning with a rivalry between the British and the French. In answer to the annexation of Australia by the British, the French annexed New Caledonia in 1853 and set up their own convict colony there. French and British naval ships patrolled the New Hebrides, which had been visited and named by Cook, as missionaries and traders of both nationalities were operating there. The rivalry between them delayed any annexation, but there was some co-operation between the two navies from 1888. An Anglo-French Condominium[24] was eventually formed in 1906.

This left the status of the Solomon Islands unresolved. The French made no claim to the archipelago for their Empire, but the Germans did. In 1884, the rapidly expanding German Empire, which had been established in 1871, claimed the north-eastern part of the island of New Guinea, together with the New Guinea Islands of the Bismarck Archipelago and also the Admiralty Islands, and it began to show an interest in the Solomons as well. In Samoa, the British, the Germans and the Americans were all interested in establishing their influence and formed a joint administration between 1889 and 1899. So, the British were now challenged to decide what action to take in the Solomons, following both the German interest in the northern part of the archipelago and also Woodford's challenge to the British to do something to 'protect' the south of it.

The majority of returned labourers did not exert a good influence, according to the clergy and teachers. They conversed with each other in Pidgin, swore, told people that many in Queensland did not go to church, and questioned why their people had to give offerings of 'pigs, fowls, yams and breadfruit' to the Church. They also reported the attitude of white workmen in Queensland to clergymen – very different from the friendly relationships the white missionaries appeared to have with the officers of visiting naval ships! Increasingly, the white clergy had become associated with British power, as the Empire was extended into the islands. In 1887, the Reverend John Plant had organised celebrations with Christians in Gela

[24] A form of joint Colonial Government

for Queen Victoria's Golden Jubilee and spoke to them of 'our dear Queen, and the meaning of a protectorate and other matters on which they wanted information'. He wrote to a friend who was a member of the British Parliament and who had been a fellow student at Cambridge University: 'Why can't these islands be annexed? Guadalcanal and Florida would be very profitable possessions ...the people of Florida want annexation – they are afraid of the Germans and more so of the French.'

Because of the activities of many recruiters and traders, some of the white missionaries saw the advance of Christianity being helped by colonialism, annexation and increasing co-operation between Church and State – a very different attitude from that of Bishop John Patteson and Bishop John Selwyn who had opposed annexation by any power, unless there was full and proper consultation with the local people. Charles Woodford's assumption that there would never be sufficient co-operation between the disparate groups on the big islands to provide any real opposition to the colonial power was later proved wrong – partly because, having become Christians, people began to co-operate with one another in other ways. However, the white missionaries generally welcomed a 'protectorate'. When it came in 1893, there were only two white missionaries resident in the Solomons, the Reverend Charles Browning, and the Reverend Richard Comins on San Cristoval. Comins was actually taken on board HMS Curaçoa to advise on the best places to hoist the British flag, and to explain the significance of the event to the local people. However, on Gela, he made sure that the ceremony took place in both Christian and pagan districts, so that people should not assume that the new Government was only to cover those areas where the Mission worked.

On October 6, 1893, the British proclaimed a 'Protectorate' over the southern part of the group and this status was maintained until independence, whereas in Tahiti the 'Protectorate' was turned into a colony by the French in 1880, with nearby islands and other island groups annexed to form 'French Oceania' by 1882. It was later renamed 'French Polynesia'. There was also gradual annexation by the British and the Germans in the Solomon Islands. The Protectorate of 1893 included the islands of the Central and Eastern Solomons, including Gela, but not Ysabel or Choiseul and the Shortland Islands in the Western Solomons, or the large atoll known as Ongtong Java or Lord Howe. In 1886, the Germans and British had both declared 'spheres of influence' which included parts of the Solomons, but the boundaries of these areas were changed with the withdrawal of the British from Samoa in 1899. Then the present boundary was established, leaving just Bougainville and Buka in German hands, with the rest of the archipelago becoming the 'British Solomon Islands Protectorate'. Ysabel (later known as Isabel) and some other islands were then 'transferred' to Britain, so Gela and Ysabel found themselves under one administration, to the benefit of the Anglican Church -- although the British flag was not raised on Ysabel until 1901. So the strongest influence in local affairs on that island continued to be the Church. Things were rather different on Gela.

The British had to decide how best to administer the scattered islands of the central and eastern Solomons, together with the islands of Ysabel and Choiseul, and also the Santa Cruz group, annexed in 1898. The arrangement in 1893 brought the head-hunting islands of the New Georgia group under the control of the British, a great opportunity to improve the security of the people of Ysabel. It was decided to appoint a Resident Commissioner, who would come under the authority of the High Commissioner for the Western Pacific in Fiji. The obvious person for the position was Charles Morris Woodford. He had to choose a suitable place for his Residency, and he chose the island of Tulagi, with its splendid harbour nearby. He was appointed in 1896. His father had sold a mixture of rum and water (known as grog) in a shop in London, but the son had chosen a very different life for himself ! When he wrote his book, he apparently had no idea that he might be spending time in the Solomons again, although he had already shown his enthusiasm for the country, its wildlife and some of its people, including the Christians on Gela. The Reverend A I Hopkins of the Melanesian Mission described Tulagi as an 'islet rising to 300 or 400 feet'. It had been cleared for planting coconuts, and one could walk around it in 40 minutes. The Commissioner's house was built on the top of the island, with splendid views of the main islands of Gela and the offshore islets, as well as distant views of the Guadalcanal mountains when the skies were clear.

Gela was now at peace. Woodford divided the Gela group of islands into five districts, each under a chief, and officially recognised the Vaukolu, but with diminished powers. For Gela people, the presence of Government as a 'settled administration', steadily developed by Woodford, meant increasing contact with Europeans and more use of English, as well as a greater opportunity for trade. In 1899 a punitive expedition found and broke up the Roviana head-hunting canoes, which had been attacking Ysabel.

Having annexed Australia and New Zealand by different methods, and been forced to come to an agreement about the partition of eastern New Guinea by the actions of the Germans, the British Government was not keen at first to extend its responsibilities any further. Under pressure from Australia and New Zealand, however, the British had eventually accepted the cession of Fiji to Britain by King Cakobau in exchange for payment of debts to the Americans, caused by destruction of some of their property in the Fiji Islands. When the Deed of Cession was signed in 1874, there were already 4,000 'Europeans' in Fiji, twice as many as there were in 1840 in New Zealand when that country was annexed. Under pressure to care for expatriates in other parts of the Pacific, the Governor of Fiji was also appointed as High Commissioner for the Western Pacific in 1877, with consuls in New Caledonia, Samoa and Tonga reporting to him. There had been no such system in the Solomon Islands, but now, with the appointment of Woodford as Resident Commissioner reporting to the High Commissioner in Fiji, the latter's role increased in importance. The High Commissioner was now the person ultimately responsible to the British Government, not only for the proper administration of the Solomon Islands, but also of the Gilbert and Ellice Islands, which had been declared a Protectorate in 1892. Thus the British Solomon Islands Protectorate found itself related to Fiji and other Pacific islands in a new way, which would influence its future.

The Gilbert and Ellice Islands Protectorate was declared a Crown Colony in 1915 and more islands were added to it, so the Solomon Islands became the only British Protectorate in the Pacific, with Tonga being a 'Protected State' with its own monarch. Gela, with the capital of the Protectorate established at Tulagi, was at the centre of the new political arrangements in the

Solomon Islands until the Second World War, and it was also the centre of the Anglican Church there.

Meanwhile, there were developments on Ysabel. On Guadalcanal two brothers, Basilei and Gorovaka, had earlier been kidnapped from near Maravovo in the northwest of Guadalcanal and sold as slaves to Soga, the war chief of Ysabel. They later had the opportunity to go to Norfolk Island before returning to Ysabel and marrying local women there. They then became Christian teachers. In 1883 Soga had succeeded his father Bera. Soga was friendly to the Mission but refused a school until he fell sick. Bishop John Selwyn was visiting the village of Sepi at the time and was able to cure him of his influenza with a mixture of brandy and quinine. This gave an opportunity for the bishop to tell Soga about Cakobau of Fiji and his conversion to Christianity, and what he had been instructed by Cakobau in 1880 to tell other Melanesians: 'Go and tell them that I have fought battles and killed many men, but that this teaching is the true one.' As he had obtained the chieftainship from Bera his father by conducting a series of head-hunting trips to north Ysabel to prove himself more suitable than his brother, the words of Cakobau had an effect. Soga decided to embrace peace rather than war, and even tried to arrange a truce in the ongoing conflict between the island of Savo and Vaturanga, in northwest Guadalcanal, in 1888. He was not successful in that, but he refused to hand over heads to raiders from the western Solomons. Rather reluctantly, he allowed Hugo Gorovaka to begin a school at Sepi, having been persuaded to do so by the Reverend Robert Turnbull, who had become the first resident priest in Ysabel in 1886.

Turnbull's middle name was Monilaws, and when Soga was eventually baptised in 1889, after Turnbull had left, it was by that unusual name that he was known as a Christian. The Reverend Charles Bice, on a visit from the New Hebrides, was the priest who baptised him. From then onwards, Soga became the acknowledged Melanesian Christian leader of Ysabel, and he worked closely with Henry Welchman, who arrived on Ysabel in 1890 as a layman and doctor[25]. Welchman had been ordained in 1892 and married in 1896, but his wife died three months later at Siota on Gela.

Dr Welchman worked on Ysabel with no summer breaks on Norfolk Island till he died in 1908, in a leaf house, and two of his best loved young Melanesian helpers were with him. He was the first fully resident white 'district priest' in the Solomons and became a model for other white missionaries to emulate, living very simply in a Melanesian way and sharing the leadership of the church with the former head-hunter, Monilaws Soga. Ysabel thus gained the strong leadership which Gela lacked after the death of Sapibuana.

The Resident Commissioner, Sir Charles Woodford, who had been knighted by the time of Welchman's death, wrote: 'To the natives of Ysabel his death is an irreparable disaster. I admired and respected him, perhaps more than any other man I know, as a true follower of the Master he served, whose example he followed in every act of his simple, unselfish, self-sacrificing life.' Ysabel gradually became the strongest island church in the Diocese.

In 1883 the Reverend David Ruddock attempted to persuade the people of Vaturanga district to accept a school, with the help of Hugo Gorovaka and George Basilei, first at Savulei, George's home, and then at Maravovo, Hugo's home. They failed and withdrew to Ysabel, but the Melanesian teachers did not give up hope. When Soga became friendly to the Mission, he at last allowed George to go back with his wife Louisa to Savulei where they lived the Christian life among George's own people for three years without any response, until one day in 1896 a man came to enquire how they managed to live such a peaceful and amiable way of life!

The next year, Hugo Gorovaka and his wife joined them, and they started a school on Hugo's land at Maravovo, not far away. So Maravovo became the

[25] The first resident doctor in the Solomon Islands

first Christian village on Guadalcanal. The work there was encouraged by Welchman, who also managed to establish work on Savo and the Russell Islands, not far from Guadalcanal, and even attempted to start work on Vella Lavella and Choiseul in the Western Solomons. But the work in that part of the Solomons was soon taken over by the Methodists, after their arrival. Gradually the first Christian island, Gela, was able to work together with Christian communities established on surrounding islands, and to send out its own missionaries, notably to Malaita. Through the various activities of the new Government and the Churches, peace was beginning to spread through the Solomon Islands. An outstanding example of this was on Ysabel, where Soga ambushed a head-hunting party from New Georgia in 1897, but did not kill them. He fed them instead, and told them not to come again! He also made peace between Kia, 90 miles to the north, and its traditional enemies further south, so that all of Ysabel could live in peace. Kia then agreed to have a Christian school. Before he died in 1898, his message was: 'Keep peace in Bugotu. Make friends with the hillmen... Stick to the Church.'

Figure 21 : Boys at Maravovo School, West Guadalcanal. [Credit : The Melanesian Mission]

Figure 22 : The boathouse on the beach at Maravovo, West Guadalcanal. [Credit : The Melanesian Mission]

CHAPTER 10

A NEW CENTURY

By the year 1900 it appeared that progress in the work of 'evangelisation and civilisation' – according to Bishop George Augustus Selwyn's ideas of 'true religion, sound learning and useful industry' – had begun to take hold in the Central Solomons, although less so in other islands. This was sometimes blamed by the white missionaries on the influence of the less scrupulous traders. Before 1870, there had been no permanent trading stations in the Solomons, but ten years later they had sprung up on every major island except Choiseul and Malaita. Copra, tortoise-shell and other items were sent to Sydney and Auckland, and some traders had a chain of stations spread throughout the group. Islanders were able to obtain tools such as knives, axes and adzes as well as tobacco, pots, calico and clothes of various kinds. In many places, they could obtain these items easily, while also maintaining their native customs and customary dress if they so wished. The missionary could thus be kept at bay! However, it had become the custom on Gela and Isabel, especially on Sundays, for men to dress for Church in shirts and trousers (and even straw hats) and the women in petticoats and 'jackets' (neatly made by themselves), all to Penny's satisfaction. Where trading and employment as boats' crews or station labourers was available, people saw no need for the Mission, and this was particularly so on Savo and Guadalcanal in the Central Solomons, Ugi and San Cristoval in the Eastern Solomons, and Omba (Ambae) in the New Hebrides – all places where the Melanesian Mission was trying to establish its work. Some of the missionaries opposed recruitment for the plantations of Queensland and Fiji, but Bishop John Selwyn had a rather different view: 'Do what we will, we cannot keep those islands wrapped in cotton wool ... Our duty is to try and strengthen them morally and physically, that they may be able to resist (evil).' However, by 1900 the male population of Gela, where recruiting was easy and no longer dangerous, had been much reduced. Mission teachers had been unable to deter young men from 'signing on'. The population in 1895 was about 4,000, and it was claimed that 500 men out of that number were working in Queensland – in some villages that meant the absence of most of their able-bodied young men abroad. In 1896, six of the designated chiefs who were Christians signed a letter, drawn up by two deacons, petitioning the British Government to ban the recruiting on Gela. They summed up the reasons for their opposition, saying that when their children 'have grown big the ships that trade in men carry them all off to Queensland and other places, and not many of them come back here, and many of them die and many, too, stay there for ever.'

Many of those recruited from the Solomons were from Malaita and were still pagans, so there was the extra concern among the white missionaries about the influences that the Christians would face in the so-called 'Christian country' of Australia. The churches of Queensland were unwilling to do anything, partly because of 'the colonists' deep prejudice against missionary work among the non-Europeans in their midst, whether Aborigine, Chinese or Pacific Islanders'. The few 'schools' associated with the 'Church of England', from which some converts later went as missionaries to New Guinea, were soon outstripped by the work of the undenominational Queensland Kanaka Mission, founded by Florence Young in Bundeberg in 1886.This work led eventually, with returning Christian labourers, to the founding of the South Sea Evangelical Mission (later Church) in the Solomons.

The new century was therefore not a good time for the Church and people of Gela from a Christian point of view. Villages were languishing for the lack of young people, returning labourers were often a bad influence, unfavourable reports of the behaviour of some of the Mission's teachers circulated widely, the negative reaction of people on other islands to the work on Gela and Bugotu was strong, and the unexpected criticisms from colonial Europeans whose support had been expected led to deep heart-searching. Where had the Mission gone wrong? Why was there not more support from New Zealand and Australia? 'What's wrong with Gela?'

Bishop John Selwyn had had to resign in 1891 through ill-health, and returned to England. In 1893 he was elected Master of Selwyn College in the University of Cambridge, founded in 1879 (but opened in 1882) in memory of his father, Bishop George Augustus Selwyn, who had died in 1878 as Bishop of Lichfield in the Midlands of England. In the year he resigned the New Guinea Mission was founded, drawing most of its support – which was not very much – from the Church of England in Australia and Tasmania, formally constituted with a General Synod, and with an Australian Board of Mission as its official missionary agency, from 1872. However, help with confirmations and advice came from Bishop H H Montgomery, then Bishop of Tasmania. (From 1901 he was Secretary of the Society for the Propagation of the Gospel, based in London.) Bishop John Selwyn asked him to do a three-month tour of the Diocese of Melanesia in 1892 on the 'Southern Cross' and he wrote a book, published in 1896, entitled 'The Light of Melanesia: A Record of Fifty Years' Mission Work in the South Seas'. In it, he took the opportunity of doing an appraisal of the work of the Mission, challenging it to update its organisation, deploy its staff better between Norfolk Island and the islands to the north, establish Europeans at permanent stations, provide central schools in the major island groups (and in Fiji and Queensland), employ women missionaries in the islands and review the Mission's rather tolerant attitude to native customs. The book was re-published and widely read, as the Bishop was highly regarded in the Church of England and was an adviser to the Archbishop of Canterbury, Dr Randall Davidson.

Criticism came from other quarters. Although Charles Woodford had chosen Tulagi in Gela as his basis, and he respected the work of people like Dr Welchman on Bugotu, he became suspicious of the influence of the church on Gela, doubtful of the depth of conviction of the Christian converts, and determined not to give the Anglican Church a special position in the country as the 'Established Church of the Protecting Power'.[26] He was in fact carrying out the principle enunciated by Sir John Thurston, the High Commissioner for the Western Pacific, who had rejected missionaries' claims to 'particular and special protection' for Christians of any kind. Sir John had been furious when Bishop John Selwyn had criticised the way the Western Pacific High Commission operated, and he was not impressed with the way the races mixed so freely in the Mission. Probably comparing the Anglicans in Melanesia unfavourably with the Methodists in Fiji, he complained that 'the natives treated their

---

[26] As it was later described by a Melanesian bishop!

Pastors with scant courtesy'. Methodists in Tonga and Fiji had strict rules about dress and behaviour, and he found the people of Gela dirty in appearance, wearing 'ragged articles of European clothing' and smoking 'trade pipes'. He also found the teachers and church buildings unimpressive. He wrote in his diary: 'Little or no permanent effect has been produced anywhere.' Woodford agreed with him in so far as he privately recorded his view that there was not 'one genuine convert who, if the Mission were to retire for a year, would remain faithful to it.' A harsh judgement!

All this was a wake-up call, especially to the Church on Gela. John Palmer became Acting Head of the Mission from 1892 to 1894, when there was no Bishop. Cecil Wilson, an Englishman aged 33, was chosen by Bishop John Selwyn, Dr Codrington and the Archbishop of Canterbury to become the next Bishop of Melanesia, and he was consecrated in Auckland in June 1894. Although a quiet and cautious man, he took some significant actions. By 1899 the number of white missionaries had risen from eight to 14, and an office with paid staff had been opened in London. In 1903 an organising secretary was appointed in Australia, and the 'Southern Cross' did a tour of New Zealand with a group of 22 Melanesian schoolboys to drum up support there in 1895.

Suddenly new action was also taken on Gela. In 1879, the Reverend Richard Comins had suggested the establishment of permanently manned centres with European staff for Gela and Mota, but it was then against Mission policy, as laid down by Bishop John Selwyn. Under Bishop Wilson, however, he was free to purchase land for £10 at Siota, a former 'tabu' place, at Boli Harbour. St Luke's School there was to train more teachers, as the number coming out of St Barnabas College, Norfolk Island, was too few for the increasing number of village schools – only 20 teachers a year. Comins and Welchman were to be the European teachers, Welchman in 'summer', Comins in 'winter', with the aid of George Basilei. Siota scholars were to have a uniform – red shirts and blue trousers – and were to be taught some English as well as Mota. But Welchman's new wife, the first white woman in the Solomons, died after a few months there in 1897, and 11 boys died of dysentery in 1898 – a quarter of the school. With more sickness in 1899 and with heavy garden work, lack of food and the refusal of Christian villagers on Malaita to send them any, the Bishop closed the school and leased the land for planting coconuts. Moreover, Browning was discovering that the people, although nominally Christian, 'had retained their old ideas and motives': charms and sorcery were still being widely used, worship of the tindalos had continued in many places, and the people were adopting many immoral practices in their trading. Tragically, they were gaining a reputation as 'the biggest liars and thieves' among the traders in the Solomons. This came as a real shock to the gentle Bishop Wilson, who had assumed that Gela would be 'a fountain of life sending out missionaries to other islands'. It was indeed a real set-back. He also had to come to terms with the Protectorate Government's policy towards other Missions. No longer would the Melanesian Mission be the only mission at work, admired by naval officers on the Australian Station as the body largely responsible for the 'Humanising, Civilising and Christianising' of Melanesians.

Under Woodford, with a more peaceful environment established, other missions readily applied to enter the British Solomon Islands – the Roman Catholic Marist Fathers (Society of Mary) in 1898, the Methodists in 1902, a branch of the Queensland Kanaka Mission in 1904 and the Seventh Day Adventists in 1914, the last three all from Australia. About the same time, other Missions were entering the New Hebrides. Mission rivalry began to appear, especially among the Melanesian converts. Unlike the other Missions, the work of the Anglicans was very widespread, reaching to the outer islands such as the Santa Cruz group and some of the Polynesian outliers, but the work in the main part of the Solomons now had to be shared with other Christian churches. In 1900, the Bishop made an appeal to English supporters for a replacement for the 'Southern Cross' which was so necessary for its work in three countries, as the Diocese also included German New Guinea,which included the German Solomon Islands !

The policy adopted by Woodford echoed that of Thurston, who decreed that the Administration 'should protect and aid all Missions to the utmost of its possibilities, but lay itself under obligation to none'. In the Solomons, the Government declared in a circular: 'Christianity stands for all that is good, no matter by whom it is taught'. The Government saw Christianity, promulgated mainly through schools run by the Missions, as a civilising force, carrying out the overall intentions of the British as paternal colonisers. The government also had to raise money to run itself, which it did by inviting commercial companies to enter and develop plantations and other resources, thus providing at the same time employment for the indigenous inhabitants, but changing the nature of Solomon Islands society in significant ways.

A good example of the new Government's policy was the case of north-west Guadalcanal. George Basilei died in 1900, but Hugo Gorovaka carried on, although his school was weakened and surrounded by enemies, especially Sulukavo, a hostile warrior-chief who was opposed to all Missions. He tried to kill Hugo twice. He had also forbidden the children to go to school, and the Christians were constantly at risk. Bishop Wilson, however, took action. He asked one of the biggest and physically toughest priests of the Mission to go to the rescue. Percy Williams (known as PTW) was the grandson of Henry Williams, pioneer CMS missionary in New Zealand. He was blunt, courageous, and a natural leader, as well as being an outstanding rugby football player. He joined the Mission in 1895 and was sent to organise Anglican 'schools' in Queensland for the kanakas (Melanesian labourers). In 1900 Bishop Wilson called him back from Queensland to the school at Norfolk Island, where he was popular among the boys. When the call came to go to Guadalcanal, he managed to organise a group of young men willing to go with him – one from Mota, one from San Cristoval and two from Guadalcanal, Philip Rausale and David. Moreover, there were also five from Gela, who probably had no difficulty in making themselves understood in their language to the people of the north-west area of Guadalcanal. They were Hugo Toke, Ben Tumu, John Manevuti, William Songgo and Michael Terembutu. The Government was so concerned about the situation that CM Woodford lent rifles to the party and promised armed police to protect Maravovo if necessary! Williams reported that they had to force an entrance into the area, and Sulukavo was made aware of the fact that they were armed. This was the first time that the Mission had ever entered a place against the wishes of local inhabitants (except the Christians), and with Government backing. When the party arrived, Sulukavo did everything he could to prevent the work continuing, but Williams would not give up. The Christians had to be constantly on watch and even take rifles to Church, for they knew Suluvako intended to attack them there if possible. Williams reported: 'The people were so frightened it was impossible to go about. If we had left the village the school people and all the children would have bolted.' In the midst of all that, however, the party established a strong centre, being 'well prepared and letting them know it'. Williams was shocked by the brutal way in which unwanted children were killed and the way Sulukavo treated his wives, beating them and even killing one. He said: 'Those wretched women live their lives in filth and misery.'

The wretched condition of the people spurred Williams and his helpers on to do more and more. Williams even started another school five miles away at Komambulu, where the people were attacked and scattered, their houses burnt and a man hacked to death. But the number of Christians increased. Other schools were started at Tiero, 15 miles from Maravovo, and another at Honiara, near Point Cruz, the place which became the capital after the Second World War. He then brought the deacon Reuben Bula from Gela to start a school at Tasimboko on the Guadalcanal Plains west of Honiara, so there was a string of schools along the north coast for about 60 miles, with Maravovo as the 'mother school' of them all. One of the early pupils there, born about 1900, was Ini Kopuria, the future founder of the Melanesian Brotherhood.

Government policy was not just support for Christian schools in order to bring pacification to places like Guadalcanal and Malaita, which were considered wild and dangerous islands, but also to encourage the development of coconut plantations for copra production by overseas companies employing Melanesian labourers. Guadalcanal had more flat land than any of the other islands, some of it along part of the coast in the north-west of the island. Later, labourers were employed there, mostly brought from Malaita. Some of the people therefore retired from the coast and established villages in the bush. There was lingering resentment. An earlier attempt by Plant to establish a school at Tasimboko had been unsuccessful, and the schoolhouse had been burnt down, but when more teachers came from Gela the number of schools gradually increased from 1902 onwards, all along the coast of Tasimboko District.

Williams returned to Norfolk Island in 1903, and later became the Warden of St John's College, Auckland, where Melanesians had first been taught. Hugo Gorovaka was ordained and worked in Guadalcanal till his death in 1918, his two sons later becoming missionaries. John Steward followed Williams in 1903 and had the assistance of George Coats for a while in steadily increasing the number of schools. Steward learnt the local language, and in 1906 he moved to be the priest-in-charge of Gela, where the language was not too different. He remained there until 1911, when he returned to Guadalcanal. From 1913 to 1916 the second hospital in the Solomons was opened, named after Dr Welchman, at Maravovo.[27]

On Gela itself, there was much activity. In 1895 Siota became the Mission Headquarters, but the Reverend Charles Browning lived in the village on the other side of the Boli Passage, Boromole, on Big Gela. There were still some of the teachers from Brooke's time alive, including Monde and Takisi. Translation work was continuing. Herbert Kulai translated the Epistles and John Samu the Book of Revelation, the last book of the New Testament. Mostyn Vaguru, a pupil of Sapibuana, became the first teacher at the school at Honggo. Gela men were gradually coming forward for ordination. John Pengoni, who translated 'The Pilgrim's Progress' by John Bunyan into Gela, was ordained deacon in 1906, but had to wait till 1926 to become a priest. Ben Tumu, who had served with Williams on Guadalcanal, was ordained in 1909. In 1910 Gela had 20 missionaries at work. Hugo Toki continued his work on Guadalcanal for many years, and Toganiade also served there. So Bishop Wilson's initial fears were not realised – Gela continued to send missionaries to other islands.

Equally significant was the pioneer work on Malaita of Johnson Tome and James Ivo from Gela. Penny had obtained a boy from the Langalanga Lagoon in 1883 for Norfolk Island, but he was not baptised. It was only in 1903 that two more boys went, this time from Fiu Village in Kwara'ae, where two teachers from Motalava in the Banks Islands had been working

---

[27] The first hospital was established by the Methodists at Munda, Western Solomons, in 1903, and later named after Helena Goldie.

since about 1900. About this time some 'kanakas'[28] were returning from Queensland, most of whom were not Anglicans. At Fiu, the leader of the Christian community was Arthur Ako, who was killed by the non-Christians in 1904, the first Christian martyr of that area. In 1903 the Reverend Arthur Innes Hopkins arrived, a small man, not very strong physically, but with deep spiritual strength which enabled him to confront even the fiercest opponents. He was a scholar and theologian, and stayed for many years, writing an important book about the Solomons entitled 'In the Isles of King Solomon: An Account of Twenty-five Years spent amongst the Primitive Solomon Islanders', published in London in 1928. Walter J Durrad, a fellow missionary priest, wrote as follows about him and his work: 'It seemed like David essaying to go and fight Goliath. But the critics were all wrong.' This mildest of men seemed able to work effectively with rough and tough Malaita men, apparently without fear. At first he and his helpers, Johnson and James from Gela and Brian Menetela from Santa Cruz, were constantly at risk. Hopkins wrote: 'I could not take a step unguarded.' At Fiu, Hopkins replaced the two Motalava teachers with two from Gela. He was based at Ngorefou, north Malaita, where there were constant threats. He was sitting on his verandah there one day with Joe Sili when some men from the bush walked up and shot Joe dead. On another occasion, he was in a village with James Ivo. James had already nearly been killed when he had gone into the bush with a friend. However, the friend had seen the gleam of a rifle barrel and called out 'Ho there, don't shoot; it's a friend with me!' His life was thus saved. Apparently, the man concerned had been cursed by his wife and was looking for a victim 'to redeem his honour'. On a second occasion when a woman had uttered a 'bad word' against her husband, he also felt obliged to kill somebody to remove the disgrace. There had also been a report of a row in Queensland involving a Gela man, and there was money on offer to anyone who could take a Gela life. He therefore chose James as his victim, for both reasons. He was very clever. He approached James openly, bought a belt from him and left the house by

---

[28] This Polynesian word meaning 'man' was used to describe Pacific Island labourers working abroad, although the term 'bush kanaka' came to be used disparagingly of people living a more traditional uneducated style of life in the islands.

the front door. Hopkins was in a house nearby. The man then went stealthily to the back door of the house and shot James from there, before rushing into the bush and escaping into his own village. His 'mana' had thus been restored, and his wife's curse rendered harmless. James was a target because he was a Gela man, a 'foreigner', a Christian and an easy target. The man who killed him was called Gwaliasi, and he knew that, because James was a 'foreigner', no-one would strike back at him.

The death of James was another terrible shock for the Christians of Malaita and Gela and all the staff of the Mission, for in the same year a white missionary, the Reverend Charles Godden, was killed on the island of Aoba (Ambae) in the New Hebrides by a returned labourer with a grievance. James's death was one of a number on Malaita, although that of Godden was the only one in the New Hebrides. Hopkins wrote: 'The blow to us was, of course, very heavy, but I felt it an honour to accept this martyrdom, and we buried him with all honour that evening by the side of Amasia, the murdered founder of Ngorefou School.' In his written tribute to James he said: 'James was of Christian parents and from childhood showed a (natural Christian spirit), a gentle, cheery, loyal soul, of a quiet, well-balanced missionary spirit.' That seemed to be a characteristic of many of the Gela people, under the influence of the Christian faith. James became known as 'the Gela martyr'. He and other martyrs, Melanesian and 'European', are included in a special prayer for Bishop Patteson's day, September 20, where 11 of them are commemorated. It begins 'Almighty God, you have given to your chosen servants grace to give glory to you by their good lives, strong faith and holy deaths.' It then names Bishop Patteson, Joseph Atkin and Stephen Taroaniara; Edwin Nobbs and Fisher Young (young Pitcairners) and Thomas Peo, all three killed at Santa Cruz; Arthur Ako, Thomas Amasia and James Ivo, killed on Malaita; Charles Godden, killed on Aoba, and John Barge, killed in New Britain[29] - 'the army

[29] It was later discovered that his colleague in New Britain, a fellow priest, Bernard Moore, had also been killed by the Japanese. Both died in 1943.

in white of the martyrs' as the Melanesian Prayer Book translates that part of the 'Te Deum Laudamus' (We praise you, O God) in Morning Prayer.

George Moir came to Melanesia in 1907 from Aberdeen in Scotland. He worked first at Pamua on San Cristoval, then at Tasimboko, and he succeeded Browning on Gela in 1911 and worked there till 1916. He had a very deep knowledge of the Gela language and was greatly loved by the Gela people, whom he understood very well, unlike many other white people. He was very musical and taught singing. His knowledge of the people confirmed what others had detected already – the continuation of many non-Christian beliefs and practices among them. These included charms of all kinds – to procure sickness or death or 'love' or barrenness or fertility or fat pigs or death of others' pigs. They depended on certain charms for sun, wind, rain, calm or storms. There were 'good' charms used to obtain healing or escape from sharks. In other words, in many parts of Gela they were still depending on sorcery or terrified of it. It was indeed killing the Church. With the help of the teachers, he conducted a purge.

The arrival of other Missions did not affect life on Gela, except in so far as controversies on other islands reached the ears of Christians there, and led Dr. Welchman to give nine of the teachers a course on Roman Catholicism. He recorded in his diary that 'nine came, and were much interested in the Rosary, celibacy of the clergy, Confession, Mortification, the Inquisition and the House of Loreto.' This was considered necessary because of anti-Anglican propaganda, especially on Guadalcanal. From their base on the islet of Rua Sura off the north-east coast of Guadalcanal, the Marist Fathers gradually established schools along the coast until they reached those established by the Anglicans. There was tension, especially when the Fathers established a base at Visale in 1904, in the area where the Anglicans felt they had established a Christian presence after enduring much suffering – north-west Guadalcanal. That area therefore became of special concern to the Anglicans, who decided to consolidate their presence in various ways. Roman Catholics extended their work to San Cristoval in 1909 and Malaita in 1912.

The presence of French clergy permanently stationed in the Solomon Islands demanded a change of policy on the part of the overseas staff of the

Melanesian Mission. Significantly, after the arrival of the Roman Catholics in the Solomons and New Hebrides in 1899, Bishop Wilson made his appeal to Australia, New Zealand and England for more recruits. Fifteen responded, small European-style houses were built, and by 1907 there were 12 at various 'district headquarters' for the European district priests, who would live in the islands throughout the year and not return to Norfolk Island for part of the year to teach in the school there, as had been normal before. Instead, schools were set up in the islands along the lines planned for the original school at Siota. These schools were situated at Vureas on Vanua Lava in the Banks Islands (to serve that group and the northern New Hebrides), on the island of Bungana in 1910, near the southern end of the Boli Passage (to serve the central Solomons) and at Pamua on San Cristoval in 1911 (to serve the eastern Solomons).

The newcomers were sometimes left in their districts with hardly any advice about how to live and work in Melanesia, so W G Ivens compiled a handbook of advice. Mota was learned by all, as there were a Mota dictionary and grammar and some printed books in the language. Dr Codrington had completed the translation of the Bible into Mota, and that was printed in England and published by the the Society for Promoting Christian Knowledge (SPCK) in 1912. On Gela, they were fortunate enough to have the Gospels and Prayer Book in the Gela language, and Dr Welchman even gave a set to the Marist Fathers to assist them in their language studies. John Steward had good personal relationships with the priests at Visale, in whom he found a 'brotherly spirit'. The Christian converts, however, saw that the Churches were divided, and sometimes chose to join a denomination which was different from that of their traditional enemies or rivals.

Although the staff at the Mission increased, the turnover in personnel was great. On Guadalcanal there were eight successive white missionaries in 13 years. In 1916, C M Woodford accused the Mission of neglecting its staff and not providing for their needs. They were expected to 'rough it out' in difficult conditions. Between 1900 and 1920, twenty-three stayed for less than three years. A heavy responsibility continued to rest on the shoulders of the Melanesian clergy and teachers. As one white priest remarked: 'You cannot get at the people; you do not know their customs and difficulties as (a native priest) does, or their temptations… or the power that the old heathen customs have over them.' That was the Reverend Eccleston Graves on Gela in the 1920s!

The increasing numbers of 'European' (white) clergy and lay missionaries had both good and bad effects. The status and influence of the Melanesian clergy was diminished in some areas, if the white clergy insisted on their superior authority. Many of the converts to Christianity had been men, as they were the ones who tended to go to school, and only a few girls had been taken to Norfolk Island, where they had basically been trained to be the wives of teachers and priests. For most of the village women, the influence of the Church was much less; they simply got on with their traditional life and role, according to local custom. Bishop Wilson observed that the Methodists, the Anglicans in New Guinea, and the Roman Catholics were bringing in women workers who, according to custom, could more easily relate to the women and children. The Roman Catholics had Religious Sisters, especially the Missionary Sisters of the Society of Mary (SMSM)[30], who vowed to stay at their posts in the islands for life.

On Gela, Brooke had realised that the role of local women was powerful, but largely hidden from non-Melanesians, especially white men. They acted as 'messengers, mediators between enemies, and negotiators of loans'. On some islands, they were feared because of their perceived spiritual power, including the power to curse. Bishop Wilson responded by establishing with Miss Ruth Kitchen the first women's station on Gela in 1905 at Honggo,, where she worked with Miss Hardacre, both having previously worked with local women at Siota. The Mission magazine 'U Sala Ususur' of September 20,1905 (Bishop Patteson's Day), reported that at Siota 'they were very helpful to the sick people and good with the people who have sores and accidents,and their act of love and duty of care drew the people close to them, and made them want them to stay forever on that end of the island of Gela'. At Honggo 'they were so helpful to the school

---

[30] SMSM = Soeurs Missionaires de la Société de Marie, founded in the Pacific by a French woman tertiary of the Society of Mary.

and in care for the sick, and teaching the girls to be mature women in future'.(Translation from the Mota by Fr John Henry Wotlemaro in 2018.) Many of the five white women who successively came there learned only Mota, so could not communicate properly at first with the local people. What was taught to the local women was reading, writing, health, medical treatments, sewing, hymn-singing and Bible stories - all good in themselves but largely unrelated to village life as the women led it, with its emphasis on gardening and child care. Two of the women missionaries on Gela, Ida Wench and Gwendolen Child, realised that this was not enough, and bravely started the first Anglican girls' boarding school in 1916 at Boromole, although the Bishop warned them that they themselves would have to find the money to cover the extra expense this involved! By 1911 there were in the Diocese 21 white clergymen and 16 white men and women lay workers, compared with 13 mainly elderly Melanesian clergymen. In 1894, the Melanesian clergy had numbered slightly more than the white clergy. Now all was changed.

The Reverend Eccleston Graves, a former mining engineer, served on Gela for 13 years. In 1920, when he arrived, only 30 people out of a population of 4436 in the Florida group were not Christians. During his ministry, the remaining non-Christians were all converted to Christianity. 'He was a wise, sympathetic and courageous priest, a born fighter whenever and wherever there was any semblance of injustice to the native, ever on the lookout to conserve their rights and privileges.' He believed strongly in the need to ordain Melanesian clergy. He wrote: 'Where there is no native priest, something is missing... The most prosperous parts of Gela are those where there is a native priest'. In 1920, Peter Sukoku was ordained, followed by Reuben Sulu in 1927, Clement Kelo in 1928 and Daniel Parapolo in 1932. From 1933 the Church on Gela was in the hands of the Melanesian clergy, although from 1935 to 1937 Sidney Gething Caulton was stationed at Halavo. The 1920s were thus a period of stability in the Gela Church. The population there was not dwindling, as in some other parts of the Diocese, where European diseases such as influenza and pneumonia were causing many deaths.

What was happening on Guadalcanal would increasingly have an effect both on Gela and the whole Diocese. Charles Woodford and Bishop

Montgomery urged Bishop Wilson to move the headquarters of the Diocese from Norfolk Island, which he eventually agreed to. He resigned in 1911, so that a single man could make the arrangements – he himself was married with five children! He had served for 17 years, during a difficult period, and needed a rest from his episcopal duties. He had brought in many changes, most of them positive. Unfortunately, the staff at Norfolk Island, without consulting the rest, then delegated the choice of Bishop to the Archbishop of Canterbury and others in England, and Cecil John Wood was chosen. He introduced a more elaborate style of liturgy, by then accepted in many churches in England, but failed to make a decision about the transfer of the headquarters of the Diocese, or the use of English rather than Mota in schools. Soon after his arrival in 1912, the First World War intervened and the supply of recruits from England nearly dried up. The Mission's doctor in the Solomons felt that he had to join up, as a duty to the mother country, Great Britain, and by 1918 there were five fewer white members of staff than in 1908, and many of them were teaching in schools. There were only 15 active Melanesian clergy.

Robert Wilson had introduced English into his boys' school at Bungana in 1910 and its experimental use there was approved by the staff conference held on that island in June 1911. However, it was not approved for use anywhere else. Bishop Wood then re-imposed Mota there, so that the pupils could go on to Norfolk Island, but later changed his mind. The conference of 1916, held at Maravovo on Guadalcanal, approved of English being used in all the main schools, then it reversed that decision again in 1918. It took another 13 years to agree on English in schools ! Disssatisfaction with the ineffective leadership of Bishop Wood led to a meeting of clergy and lay workers at Maravovo in October 1918. They demanded that he in future should act on the advice of two counsellors, chosen by the staff. This was rejected by the Bishop and he promptly resigned. Robert Wilson became Administrator of the Diocese till the next Bishop could be selected.

The General Synod of the Church of the Province of New Zealand, of which Melanesia was a Missionary Diocese, appointed a special select committee to investigate the 'scandal' and reported that the staff 'had adopted the only course open to them to obtain an adjustment of their legitimate grievances'. The staff had been exonerated, but the state of the Mission was not good. The staff longed for a leader who understood the true nature of the work, and could possibly lead a revival. They exercised their right of nomination and this time did not refer it to the Archbishop of Canterbury, and so they decided to choose one of their own number, who had actually been involved in the revolt against Bishop Wood – John Manwaring Steward.

Steward had joined the Mission in 1902 from England, in the same year as Charles Elliot Fox joined from New Zealand. He had served as a priest on Guadalcanal from 1903 to 1906 and then on Gela from 1906 to 1911, so he knew the Central Solomons well. He returned to Maravovo in 1911, having attended the 1910 Edinburgh Missionary Conference as one of three delegates from the Melanesian Mission. He had therefore been influenced by international ideas of world mission, dreaming of a 'native church of the people' and a 'really strong native ministry', as well as Religious Orders. He even envisaged an eventual Anglican Pacific Province, including the Dioceses of Melanesia, New Guinea and Polynesia – a very far-seeing concept in the 1920s! Bishop Wilson had bought 320 hectares around the village of Maravovo to provide for the establishment of a coconut plantation to give employment to Melanesians and income to the Mission. By 1914, 40 hectares had been planted, but it was not a success. A women's station was established at Maravovo in 1913, and John Steward also ran a small training college there to train teachers and possible clergy from 1911 to 1919. In September 1919 he took up his duties as Bishop. At the end of that year, St Barnabas's College on Norfolk Island was closed. The headquarters, it was decided, would be at Siota, where land had already been used for a school which had closed 20 years earlier. It was within easy reach of Tulagi, and Gela would again become the centre for the Mission in the Solomon Islands.

Figure 23 : The Cathedral, Siota. [Credit : The Melanesian Mission]

Figure 24 : Bungana Island, Small Gela.
[Credit : The Melanesian Mission and MAA, Cambridge University]

CHAPTER 11

DIOCESAN HEADQUARTERS ON GELA

John Steward was an unusual missionary. Unlike many of his colleagues, who lived on a small income and 'roughed it', John Steward was wealthy and had private means. Bishop Wilson had not been impressed with his earlier work on Gela, but he had acquired much experience in district and other work on Guadalcanal and Gela since 1903 and he had a strong sense of humour, which endeared him to people. He took the beliefs of the islanders very seriously, recognising the power which spirits exercised over many Melanesian Christians, and advocating the use of exorcism and the laying on of hands for the sick. He stressed the importance of trusting in God's angels as his messengers and powerful agents. Like Brooke, he was something of a romantic. As Bishop, he marked the beginning of his episcopate by an 850 kilometre 'Primary Visitation' of the central and eastern Solomons by whale boat, during which he sang songs with his chaplain and dosed his crew with port wine and quinine, to cheer them and keep malaria at bay!

Although by the end of 1919 Norfolk Island's College had been closed, it was Steward's intention that its tradition should be continued, albeit in different ways. It had been the headquarters of the diocese, where the Patteson Memorial Chapel (erected in 1880 and richly decorated by Melanesian craftsmen) was in practice the pro-cathedral. St.Barnabas's had been a place for meetings of the staff, a school for boys and a few girls, a training centre for teachers who were also catechists (lay ministers) and a theological college for the training of the clergy, as well as the place where some of them were ordained. It was where agriculture had been important, where translation and printing had been done, and where Melanesians had learnt to play European musical instruments, including the organ. These various functions now had to be divided between various institutions, co-ordinated by the Mission's headquarters at Siota on Gela, although there were offices in Auckland, where the 'Southern Cross' was serviced, and in London. The training of the clergy from 1921 took place at

Siota for the Solomons, and from 1927 at Lolowai on Aoba (Ambae) for the New Hebrides.

Steward started a 'Sacred Synod' of the clergy of both races – rather than just a 'staff meeting' – which would meet every three years. The first one was held at Siota in 1921.The status of the clergy of both races in the Synod was equal, though the rates of pay were necessarily different, not least because the white clergy usually did not have land or gardens to grow their food, and some had to eat different food from their Melanesian colleagues, for health reasons. This was a significant shift in the way the Church was organised. Decisions no longer rested largely on the Diocesan bishop and his closest staff members, as had often been the case when the headquarters was at Norfolk Island, but on the whole body of the clergy, with the Melanesians being in a majority by 1928. In the other denominations it was very different, with their first ordinations in the Solomons being very much later – for the Seventh Day Adventists in 1935 and the Methodists in 1938. The Roman Catholics' first priest was ordained in 1966, and the Anglican theological college was invited to be represented at the ordination as priest of Michael Aike in the Roman Catholic Cathedral of the Holy Cross in Honiara.

The Reverend Arthur Hopkins was Warden of the College at Siota for training 'teachers' (and later clergy) from 1919 to 1925. The teaching was in Mota, at a level for 'village priests'. Education was also re-organised. The main school in the New Hebrides was based at Vureas on Vanua Lava in the Banks Islands, where the priest-headmasters were Walter Durrad from 1911 to 1918 and Harold Hart from 1920 to 1927. In the Solomons one of the feeder schools for Norfolk Island was at Maravovo on Guadalcanal. From 1920 to 1938 the headmaster was the Reverend George Warren, who had been at Pamua School on San Cristoval from 1913 to 1915. Maravovo served the central Solomons, and Pamua the eastern Solomons. The standards were not high, as unfortunately there was a low opinion among the European staff of the intellectual capacity of Melanesians, which was very different from the attitude of Bishops George Augustus Selwyn and John Patteson or Dr Codrington. However, the devotional life of the schools was strongly stressed, especially with the arrival from England of a number of Anglo-Catholic priests who had been influenced by the Tractarian or Oxford Movement in that country. Regular private confession to a priest was now encouraged in the schools. Durrad reported: 'It has helped much in checking the spread of evil'. At a staff conference held in 1926 it was agreed that the Holy Eucharist (or 'Mass') should be the principal service in the schools. However, not all clergy had the same way of conducting services, so Bishop Steward issued guidelines for ritual and ceremonial. Some Evangelical clergy in the Diocese had been supported by the Church Missionary Association of New Zealand between 1895 and 1919, but Bishop Steward brought that arrangement to an end. He also codified the canons (laws or rules) of the Diocese which were approved by his first synod, and these included a system of Greater and Lesser Excommunication for certain offences.

There were pressures on the Mission to provide something higher than the 'Senior Primary' education offered at Maravovo and Pamua in the Solomons for teenagers who arrived there from village schools. In 1924 the Reverend Dr Charles Eliott Fox became headmaster of the new school on a hilltop on the island of Ugi (Uki-ni-Masi) in the eastern Solomons. The Government then had no schools, so Pawa provided the nearest thing to secondary education available in the central and eastern Solomons. Fox had been born in England, the son of a priest. His parents emigrated to New Zealand, where he was brought up and went to university. He trained for the priesthood at St John's College, Auckland. He was basically a scientist, being especially interested in geology and conchology (shells), but on arrival in Melanesia he widened his interests to include anthropology and the study of language (philology). He taught first at Norfolk Island, then at Pamua School from 1911 to 1914, before becoming district priest on San Cristoval from 1915 to 1924. It was there that he studied the customs and life and language of the Arosi people, producing an anthropological study entitled 'The Threshold of the Pacific', which gained him a D. Litt. (Doctor of Letters degree) from the University of New Zealand in 1922. He also produced a dictionary of the Arosi language and, later, dictionaries of the languages of Gela and of Lau, on Malaita Island. From Pawa School his influence extended to many parts of the Solomons and the New Hebrides through his pupils, more than 40 of whom were later ordained. They usually went on from Pawa to become 'teachers', and then could be selected to go to the College at Siota for a basic theological education. It was only in the 1940s that a few began to be sent on for further studies in Australia at St Francis[31] College, Brisbane, or to St John's College,Auckland, the Provincial Theological College in New Zealand. Pawa School was named 'All Hallows' (meaning All Saints) after a parish of that name in England, which had originally offered it support. It was in Hampstead, London.

Bishop Steward needed a Cathedral, and it was built at Siota, using local materials, the largest 'leaf' building in the Solomons. It was built somewhat in the style of the old large canoe houses. The front of the building had woven panels, using bamboo and other strips to form different patterns all the way up to the point of the ridge. The roof was made of traditional panels of sago palm leaf, and in the front of the whole church there was a lean-to verandah. A small bell-house at ground level stood beside it. It was a striking and impressive building, and expressed his desire to have a truly Melanesian church building at the centre of the Diocese. On the altar some words were inlaid in shell: 'Rongo, Rongo, Rongo'. These meant 'Holy, Holy, Holy' in Mota language. Unfortunately, in the local Gela language the words meant 'Money, Money, Money'. The Cathedral was dedicated to St Luke, as the land had been bought on St Luke's Day in 1893, and it had been the name of the school there.

The house of the Bishop was also there, together with the other staff buildings and those needed for the College. The printing press however was at Hautabu near Maravovo on Guadalcanal. There was anchorage for ships at the Siota wharf, as the water there was quite deep, and the whole of the northern entrance to the Boli Passage was protected by a reef on which the waves broke, sometimes with considerable noise. The different functions of the headquarters on Norfolk Island had thus been dispersed to various places in the Solomon Islands and the New Hebrides.

One part of Bishop Steward's plan had, however, not yet been fulfilled. In 1910 there had been an experiment on the island of Santa Cruz in the form

---

[31] St Francis Theological College, Milton, Brisbane, Queensland

of a group of unmarried clergymen living together (rather than separately in districts) and forming a missionary brotherhood, like the later Company of Mission Priests in England from 1940, or the Bush Brotherhoods in Australia. One member died, and two others were withdrawn to work elsewhere, and so the experiment only lasted for 18 months. However, one of the three, Jack Blencowe, then a layman, returned and worked in the area of Santa Cruz and the Reef islands for a while with Guy Bury, a young English priest. Bury sadly died after a short time there, and was buried on Te Motu Island. Blencowe was later ordained in England and served as a chaplain in the Army in the First World War. The Santa Cruz people then were left with one small school and no resident missionary till 1925. Bishop Steward, however, hoped that something like a Brotherhood might still be possible elsewhere in the Diocese.

The Bishop's hope was fulfilled in a most unexpected way. A young man called Ini Kopuria had been born in the Maravovo area about the year 1900. He had been a member of one of the first Christian families on Guadalcanal, and had been given as a Christian name at his baptism Ini, the name of an early Anglo-Saxon King of Wessex in the south of England, who had been one of the first Christian rulers there. It was perhaps providential that 'Ini' sounded like a Melanesian word ! His people expected him to become a village catechist, but he wanted something more adventurous, and joined the Native Armed Constabulary of the Protectorate. He was stationed on Guadalcanal, and it was there that he injured himself while seeking to arrest someone in the bush on his island. In hospital in Tulagi he had an extraordinary vision which changed his life, and in time deeply affected the Church of Melanesia. He claimed to have seen a vision of Jesus, telling him that he was not doing what he wanted him to do. Bishop Steward had taught him as a small boy at the village school at Maravovo, and Ini went to see him, and after a time with Hopkins, his former teacher at Norfolk Island, he asked the Bishop if he could start a Melanesian Brotherhood, with his backing and support. The Bishop agreed. Ini made a life vow standing on his land at Tabalia, Guadalcanal, which he gave for the use of the Brotherhood, on the Feast of St Simon and St Jude, October 28, 1924. A large white cross now stands on the spot. He found others to join him the next year, especially from Pawa School, and Dr Fox, the Headmaster, later joined himself, the only white Brother at that time, serving from 1932 to 1943. This was the first time a 'European' had been under the authority of a Melanesian in the history of the Mission. Instead of having a Brotherhood of white priests such as he had envisaged for work in Malaita, Steward now had a Brotherhood of mostly Melanesian laymen instead, who were willing to work anywhere under his direction as 'Father of the Brotherhood'.

Steward now began to consider the needs of women and girls. He invited two Sisters from an Anglican Religious Order in Bombay to come and found an Order which Melanesian women could join. They called it the Community of the Cross. Sister Margaret was seen as its founder, and became known as Mother Margaret of the Cross. She was assisted by Sister Gwen, and they set up their first house at Siota in 1929, although by then Bishop Steward had returned to England. In 1936 four members took charge of the Mission's girls' school on the small island of Bungana, Gela, where they also trained Melanesian and Polynesian novices, especially from the outlying Polynesian island of Sikaiana, so that they could become Sisters. Their curriculum included the usual subjects, but also scientific food gardening. Sister Gwen wrote their story in her book 'The School Island'. After Bishop Steward's time, the Bishops became more autocratic and the Sisters insisted on their rights as a Religious Order, independently run – quite different from the Melanesian Brotherhood with the Bishop of Melanesia as its 'Father' ! Mother Margaret addressed the Melanesian Mission's Centenary Meeting at the Headquarters of the Mothers' Union at Mary Sumner House in London in 1949, then led her community into the Roman Catholic Church in 1950, having fallen out with Bishop Baddeley. Some of the Melanesian Sisters who left with her, including a few from the New Hebrides, joined the Roman Catholic 'Native Sisterhood' in the Solomons, called the Daughters of Mary Immaculate. The Roman Catholic Church did not allow the Community of the Cross to continue as a separate Sisterhood. However, the principle of having Anglican Melanesian Religious Sisters had been established, and was not forgotten. It was another example of how happenings on Gela could still sometimes lead the way in the Diocese.

After Bishop Steward returned to England in 1928, another Bishop had to be found. Steward had obtained a priest from England in 1925 to be consecrated as Assistant Bishop, responsible for the work in the New Hebrides. But in the Solomons there was a financial crisis, caused by Bishop Steward's lack of administrative control and financial diligence, as well as his illness. Among other problems was the 'Southern Cross', which from 1918 to 1923 had cost £50,000 to run, out of a total income for the Mission of £112,000. The General Synod in New Zealand appointed a commission of enquiry, and this recommended the establishment of a Finance Board, based in Auckland, with power to control the Diocese's financial administration. The New Zealand bishops also appointed Assistant Bishop Frederick Merivale Molyneux to be the next Diocesan Bishop in 1928, after nomination by the Melanesian synod. But he faced a formidable task. Debt mounted, as the 'Depression' in the world of finance and industry grew, affecting England and New Zealand, and so subscriptions to the Mission dropped. Molyneux proved unable to cope with the Mission's complicated financial situation, but he was well-off personally. The Finance Board demanded drastic cuts. Molyneux resigned in November 1931. He had not lived at Siota for very long! Indeed, he had had a breakdown, which was attributed by many to 'financial strain'. Actually, he had been accused of homosexuality, like Brooke on Gela before him. It was also like the originally much-admired A.E.C. Forrest, who had worked as a priest on Santa Cruz until he was dismissed in 1896 after nine years of service. Forrest, however, remained there as a trader until his arrest in 1901, and subsequent escape from custody in Sydney. He then fled to the Torres Islands in the New Hebrides, where he committed suicide in 1908. Men in difficult situations, whether European or Melanesian, were likely to 'fall' if they did not have the help, advice and support they needed, or were unwilling to accept it!

The higher standard of education at the Central School at Pawa meant that not all future clergy were expected to be village teachers before ordination. More and more Junior Schools developed in the 1930s, reaching six such boarding schools in the Diocese. More boys received an education in English, and from 1931 onwards some went on to study eventually at the theological college, and use the library there. However, whereas before, when Mota was used, Melanesians could be teachers in most schools, there was now a need for more expatriates who could teach in English. It was not until the 1960s that qualified Melanesian primary and secondary teachers returned from training abroad and were able to receive higher salaries at Government-set rates of pay. With the phasing out of the last European district priests in the same period, it meant that few expatriates had deep contacts outside Church institutions with local people, and most of them did not use any local language or Pidgin. The oldest clergy were still operating in Mota till the 1960s, when the last refresher course using Mota was held at the theological college at Siota.

Bungana School for boys had been founded by Robert Paley Wilson and his sister Ellen Wilson in 1910. It started with boys from other islands than Gela, but soon local boys were taken in as well. They used English at first, then Mota from 1913 to 1916. Because of illness, the Wilsons left in 1919, but returned to Gela from 1922 to 1926 to teach at the theological college at Siota. St Michael's School, Pamua, on San Cristoval, was founded in 1911, and it was established by Dr Fox as a boys' boarding school. St Mary's, Maravovo, came next, although it did not start out as a school. Bishop Wood had decided to start a theological college on the land of the former plantation there in 1913, but this did not happen till 1916. In 1920 the College moved to Siota on Gela, and the buildings were used as a technical college under Fr George Warren for two years. In 1922 it became the largest of the boys' boarding schools, eventually housing 200 boys under his control. He was helped by his wife and some fine European and Melanesian teachers, one of whom was his adopted Melanesian son. Bungana ceased to be a boys' school in 1920. St Mary's, Maravovo, took in the boys from Gela from then on. St Michael's School, Pamua, later closed, and so St Mary's, Maravovo, became for a while the one Junior School in the Solomons preparing boys for All Hallows School at Pawa, till St Barnabas School, Alangaula,on Ugi island, was started in 1936.

Girls' education had begun at Boromole on Big Gela in 1917; in 1918 the school moved to the hill at Siota. It was named after St Hilda's School in Dunedin, New Zealand, which gave it some help. The Siota station had a plain by the entrance to the Boli Passage, on part of which was a coconut plantation, and there was a hill behind. The sago palms had not been bought, but fortunately the Mission had the right to use the leaf. The first buildings had been erected on the hill in 1896, while the lower ground was used by the cattle – two cows and a bull, who were fenced in, and were the first seen on Gela. In 1898 a hill had been demolished to fill in a swamp, which made it a more healthy place. Nevertheless, there had been outbreaks of dysentery at the boys' school which had been on the hill from 1897 onwards. When the girls came they did not stay long, as they moved to the vacated school at Bungana in 1920. Sister Nellie Stead, a nurse trained in midwifery, mothercraft and district nursing, saw, however, a need for more instruction of Melanesian girls in these subjects. In 1940 she had 20 girls being specially trained in these subjects at Siota – then the Japanese came.

Eccleston Graves, who had worked so long and faithfully on Gela, became Administrator of the Diocese till the next diocesan Bishop arrived,after the departure of Bishop Molyneux. However, the Bishop had previously invited John Hubert Dickinson to become Assistant Bishop , after he had become the Bishop of the Diocese. Dickinson had been working as a teacher in Japan. After his consecration at Wellington in New Zealand in 1931, he went to Siota. However, his main role was meant to be as Assistant Bishop for Southern Melanesia, based in the New Hebrides. When Bishop Molyneux resigned, it was he who ordained a number of Melanesians, including Clement Kelo and Daniel Parapolo and his son Willie[32] from Gela, in 1932. Bishop Dickinson resigned in 1936 and returned to ministry in England, becoming a parish priest, first in Yorkshire and then in 1942 in Northumberland, where he became also Assistant Bishop of Newcastle Diocese. He was much respected for his spirituality and humility, and he continued to be a strong supporter of the Melanesian Mission in England, as his daughter Elizabeth Grande was.

[32] Willie Parapolo later became a Canon of All Saints' Cathedral, Honiara, although he was buried on Gela.

Figure 25 : The dining hall and clock, Siota, Gela, in 1935
[Credit : The Melanesian Mission]

Figure 26 : Mission boats at the wharf, Siota, Gela. The boats are the 'Gwen' and the 'Mavis'
[Credit : The Melanesian Mission]

CHAPTER 12

MUSCULAR CHRISTIANITY

After the departure of Bishop Molyneux in 1931, the process of selecting another bishop who would have his base at Siota began all over again. Under the system of appointment for the missionary diocese imposed by the New Zealand General Synod in 1922, the wishes of the clergy of Melanesia were carried by a small delegation for discussion with the New Zealand bishops, who had a bigger say in the appointment than they had had before that date. The delegation of two agreed that Dr. Fox should be invited to be Bishop, but he declined. He had not been the first person nominated – that had been a priest from elsewhere, whom the Bishops had not accepted. So it was to England that the Bishops looked again. They found Walter Hubert Baddeley, the Vicar of a large industrial parish in Yorkshire, and he accepted in 1932. He was tough. He had served in the First World War, having been born in 1894. As a combatant, he had been awarded the DSO (Distinguished Service Order) and the MC (Military Cross) and Bar. As Bishop, he enjoyed the company of planters and Government officials. He was a member of the Protectorate's Advisory Council, established in 1921, of which Bishop Steward had also been one of the non-Government ('non-official') members. By 1940, he was viewed as the spokesman of the 'non-officials' on the Council. In 1936 he declared that in 'no part of Melanesia is there justification for an opinion often popularly held that missions and governments are hostile to one another.' He brought with him from his parish his own lay assistant, Harry Bullen, and began to make it clear that he wanted to make new appointments in the Diocese – 'fresh blood'! There soon began an exodus of 'old hands', including Eccleston Graves, so he did not have the benefit of their experience and advice, although Dr Fox remained and became an enthusiastic admirer of his tireless energy and activity, and also of his respected Australian wife, whom the Bishop married in 1936. She was the daughter of the Bishop of Adelaide, and before her marriage was called Katherine Nutter Thomas.

Baddeley tackled some important issues – relations with the Government, education policy and marriage law, one result of which was the registration of Santa Isabel priests as 'marriage officers' in 1938. The Santa Isabel church had abolished 'bride price' and, although Christian marriage was available throughout the island, it was not recognised by the Protectorate Government unless performed by a 'European minister' - and there were none there, as Fr Hugo Hebala was now in charge.

Bishop Baddeley was concerned about the white settlers and planters, often Australians or New Zealanders, as well as the mostly British Government officers – that is, those from Great Britain. (Many of the other whites actually had 'British nationality'.) The Bishop collected money from many of them, including the companies of Levers and Burns Philp, and he erected a fine church in permanent materials at Tulagi, where he sometimes conducted services in English himself. Although not a linguist, he conducted confirmation services in different languages, and spoke some Mota. The Reverend John Pengoni, however, said 'I talk to him in English, which he does not understand, and he to me in Mota, which I do not understand.' The Bishop decided to move his headquarters from Siota to Taroaniara, still on Gela and not far from Tulagi, so the centres of the Diocese and the Government were even closer. For some Melanesians the relationship was too close!

Bishop Baddeley was deeply concerned about improving education in Church schools, providing a new hospital and a better medical service, and increasing the number of local clergy. He established 'district schools' taught by Melanesian teachers, trained from 1931 in English at Pawa School under Alfred Hill. He was a Master Mariner who had left the sea and worked in an East London Mission before offering to serve in Melanesia as Master of the Mission's vessel the 'Cecil Wilson' in New Britain, where Baddeley was keen to develop the work of the Diocese in the Mandated Territory of New Guinea.

Dr L M Maybury arrived in 1928 and set up a new hospital at Fauabu on Malaita. European nursing sisters were sent to Ugi (to serve the local people and Pawa School), to Lolowai on Aoba (Ambae) in the New Hebrides, and to New Britain. There was a leprosarium near Fauabu which closed in 1933 but re-opened in 1938. The people of the Kwara'ae area, where the hospital was situated, were somewhat suspicious of Western medicines, and often still trusted their 'custom' medicines and treatments more. The non-Christians objected to babies being born at the hospital rather than in the villages, where the women would be secluded in a special house for the final period of the pregnancy and the actual childbirth.Nursing training only became possible there from 1941. Attitudes were very different from those on the neighbouring Christian islands of Gela and Isabel. However, the general level of health gradually began to rise, especially with the progressive eradication of yaws, a terrible debilitating skin disease with open sores. However, since the death of Dr Welchman, there had been no regular medical work on Isabel at all, and the people there wanted more.

There was, however, a downside to all these developments, perhaps because of the Bishop's character and his custom of being in command. His contacts with Melanesian clergy were limited, partly because of his lack of enough Mota or of other languages, but also because he called no Synod during his time as Bishop! How were the Melanesians then to express their feelings to him? Even some of the Europeans felt that he exercised too much personal control. Fr Warren left in 1938 after serving for 25 years, Fr Albert Mason, who had done sterling work on Malaita, left in 1941 after 27 years. Dr Fox, although welcoming many of the long-needed developments, described himself as 'the ghost of a past generation'. He regretted that the white newcomers, many of them fellow New Zealanders, did not know the old traditions which he valued. The 'break' had been great, for, as well as a new Bishop, there was (eventually) a new 'Southern Cross'– the previous one having been wrecked before the Bishop's arrival – and a new Captain.

On the whole, the whites and the Melanesians did not now eat together on board, as they had done before. Not only had Norfolk Island gone, but so had Mota as a common language for all. However, Dr Fox admired the Bishop's support for the Melanesian Brotherhood, which he had joined in 1932. In 1936 Brother Charles Fox started a school at Alangaula on Ugi, on land bought by the Bishop for them to make copra. It became a Mission

Junior School and later a teachers' training college and a Franciscan Novitiate before being abandoned.

Theological education went ahead, and Stephen Hagesi, another Gela man, was ordained in 1934. John Steward had opened the College at Maravovo in 1912, and some European style houses were built there in 1916. The College trained village teachers and tested the vocation of the students for ordination. Under Arthur Hopkins, the College was moved to Siota in 1921 -- and six of the students were men who had been taught at the first school at Siota in 1896. About 60 men were trained in that period. Roger Tempest took over as Warden in 1926. The College closed temporarily in 1932 but re-opened in 1933. Fr Tempest stressed the traditions of the Mission and provided a solid training for the ordinands, but he resigned in 1935, and the College became a training school for teachers only. The training of ordinands moved to Maka in south Malaita, where Fr James (Jim) Edwards had opened a school for 'heathen' boys, and in 1935 he started to train men to be deacons. In 1939 the College moved to Taroaniara and remained there until 1946, although for two years it could not function because of the Japanese invasion. In 1947 it returned to Siota. In Tempest's time, the College had been called Selwyn College, with the agreement of Selwyn College, Cambridge. At Maka it was St Peter's College, and it kept that name at Siota,until it moved to Guadalcanal in 1970. By 1956 there were nearly 100 Melanesian clergymen. For the New Hebrides, there was training for some years at Lolowai on Aoba from 1927 onwards.

Bishop Baddeley saw in the long term that education of the islanders would lead to educated Melanesians going overseas – even to Oxford University -- and sharing one day in the government of their islands. 'Why should they not?' he asked. However, by 1941 only about a dozen islanders who had been pupils at Pawa had been sent abroad by the Protectorate Government, mostly to the medical college in Suva, Fiji, to qualify as 'Native Medical Practitioners'. Bishop Baddeley was hoping that there would also be training in Fiji or New Guinea in 'wireless' and agriculture, but little was done about that. His emphasis was on higher training which would lead to greater responsibilities being borne eventually by Solomon Islanders – which was similar in fact to the attitude of the Government, But it was all in the long term ! On some islands, the people felt that they had waited long enough to have a say in ruling themselves.

On Gela, Plant had established the 'Vaukolu' (parliament) before the arrival of the Protectorate Administration. It had been given some recognition by Mr Woodford for a while. On Isabel the situation had been different. Dr Welchman had led the Church, trained the teachers and provided medical services. The people there were industrious, growing coconuts and making copra, and diving for trochus shell to sell to Chinese traders. By 1937 there were 52 native-owned trading stores on the 100-mile-long island, supplying the needs of local people. Church collections were the highest in the Diocese. A Government District Officer had not been placed on the island until 1918, so the Isabel Christians had devised their own type of island-wide administration. Fr Hugo Hebala had taken over leadership from Dr Welchman and the District Officers found that it was he and the Melanesian clergy who had the greatest influence over the people.

Some representatives of Isabel had attended meetings of the 'Vaukolu' on Gela, including Soga and other Bogotu chiefs and some catechist-teachers. In 1888 the Bishop had attended the gathering and the Reverend Mr Plant had even organised fireworks! Matters discussed included the restraint of immorality, punishments for offences, and the prohibition of 'bride prices' demanded by those having a daughter 'available' to marry. The Bishop was even asked to take up with 'the authorities' (i.e. the High Commissioner) the wrong done by traders carrying off boys without the consent of their parents ; they knew that consent had nearly always been obtained by the Bishop before taking boys to New Zealand, or boys and girls to Norfolk Island. The 'Vaukolu' created a precedent for what happened later on Isabel. At Soga's death in 1898, Dr Welchman had challenged the Bugotu chiefs to to choose a successor. In 1899 they selected Eric Notere to be the Christian 'Paramount Chief'. Welchman sought confirmation of the election from the Resident Commissioner, and, on a visit to raise the British flag at the village of Vulavu in 1901, Mr Woodford appointed Eric Notere as 'Chief of Bogotu' in place of the chief Monilaws Soga, but he did not have the same power or influence as Soga had had. Notere was told to use a few 'trusted men' to help with arrests and punishment. He was also told to use money collected through fines for the benefit of his people, and Welchman advised him to buy medical supplies with it. The Government thus recognised a new Mission-based social order, with Christian chiefs in control. It established the close local link between Church and Government on the island, but it also meant that the Government provided hardly any services until 1918, when the first District Officer arrived with some police. Government Headmen were appointed without salary, mainly to act as arbitrators in disputes, which work was previously done just by chiefs and catechist-teachers. The Headman had the police to help him, and could send people to jail. In 1920 a poll tax of one pound per man was introduced, and enforced by the principal Government Headman, Walter Notere. Resentment grew. This was not the 'help' they had been expecting from the Government!

In 1921 four catechist-teachers complained to the Resident Commissioner about the 'white man', the District Officer dwelling among them, and made a list of their complaints. This was translated and passed on by Bishop Steward. They stated 'all Government laws seem unfair to us... we wish that our own chiefs should rule us, as did Lonsdale Soga formerly.' They objected to the 'white man' also because 'the owners of the land have not agreed to his living here.' When the District Officer left in 1925, he was not replaced for three years. It was found that he had not been superintending his Headmen properly. In the year 1923 there were three government districts in the island, with a Headman for each and 'village constables' (later called 'village headmen') in each village. In 1930 there were four 'sub-districts' - Bugotu, Maringe, Hograno and Kia, and their Headmen became key figures in island politics.

In 1929 an English priest, Richard Fallowes, born in 1901, took up residence on Isabel and remained there for much of the time for the next ten years. Unlike Dr. Welchman he saw the presence of 'Government' as threatening the influence both of the chiefs and of the clergy and catechists. Within a year, he had come up with a scheme to appoint a 'church chief' in every village, and the renewal of the office of 'Paramount Chief '. Thus the village headmen and principal Headmen were paralleled by the 'church chiefs' (something like English churchwardens) and the Paramount Chief. These 'church chiefs' were widely accepted, and in about 15 villages (roughly one third of those on the island) the church chiefs were also catechist-teachers or headmen. Thus some re-integration of roles was achieved in certain places at the really local level. Some of these men came from traditional chiefly backgrounds, where feast-giving and resolution of disputes had been part of their family's role. Lonsdale Gado was installed ceremonially as Paramount Chief, and in 1931 Fallowes went round the island with him ceremonially installing the 'church chiefs', who were given special certificates, which Fallowes called 'licences', at the Eucharist. In the evening they had a meeting at which they spoke to people about the authority of the church chiefs. Gado then organised a meeting of 'District Church Chiefs' appointed to be the church equivalent of the District Headmen. The church chiefs were considered to have exceptional 'mana', making the rivalry between them and some of those headmen who were not church chiefs as well all the more intense. Fallowes had a breakdown and left in 1935, but he returned, without the permission or 'licence' of the Bishop, in 1938. He then encouraged the leading men to organise a 'parliament' to discuss their needs and their grievances, and to submit the results to the Resident Commissioner.

The 'Parliament' met at Vulavu in Bugotu district and elected a 'Speaker' who sat in a carved wooden chair, presiding over the 'delegates' -so some Europeans and others called the movement 'Chair and Rule'. Fallowes acted as advisor. He and Lonsdale Gado had organised the event. Fallowes carefully explained to the District Officer some of the reasoning behind the calling of the assembly or 'Parliament', saying that neither Government nor Mission was furthering the natives' interests and that they were being exploited, stressing the lack of educational and medical facilities on the island. A second 'Parliament' was held on Savo in April 1939, with participants from Isabel, Gela, Guadalcanal and Malaita. A third was held at Halavo on Gela in June of the same year. A list of requests was drawn up to present to the High Commissioner for the Western Pacific, Sir Harry Luke, on his first visit to the Solomons soon after that. A Bugotu man working on San Cristoval also attended the 'Parliament' and took news of it back there. Sir Harry heard about it all and summoned Fallowes to Tulagi and lectured him on his 'dangerous and irresponsible' meddling in politics, and he was deported on the next steamer out. There were no more 'Parliaments' but, among his supporters, Fallowes was still held in honour, and his actions applauded. However, they had also seen their leaders summoned to see the High Commissioner and return dissatisfied and humiliated.

The response of both Government and Church authorities was, sadly, both unwise and counter-productive. It led to a stronger reaction later, with the rise of the Maasina Rule movement, more especially on Malaita. What the people were asking for, in one form or another, was equality with the whites, which they felt had been partly achieved in the Church in earlier decades, and which they were missing under Bishop Baddeley – however good his intentions – and the new 'white man' regime. The equality they sought was now economic, social and political, and there was a strong undercurrent of resentment at the lack of economic progress, limited sharing of resources and inadequate facilities, in spite of the taxes and church collections,and their frustration was expressed in words like these: 'We have only been taught the Gospel, but nothing yet about trade and commerce. We have been Christianised for 78 years now !' They pointed out that wages and prices were very low, and demanded higher wages for plantation workers and an increase in prices paid for copra and shell, as well as a Government technical school and manned dispensaries. Government saw their demands as representing a 'distorted Utopia' and all the white missionaries except Fox were not sympathetic either, forgetting that there was not then a Church Synod where these matters could possibly have been discussed. Bishop Baddeley was caught out by his own words, delivered in a radio broadcast in Sydney a few months earlier, when he said he was looking 'forward to the day when Melanesians will be able to take their part in the government of the islands'. Fallowes's supporters declared that 'clergy and teachers, chiefs and people' belonging to the Solomons had already said together: 'We follow Fallowes. Whoever is foolish will follow the Bishop and Hipkin, who desire to blind our eyes and shut our ears, and want us different from the people of England.' (Howard Hipkin was one of the Mission staff.) This statement was made by John Palmer Pidoke, 'Chief of Gela', in June 1939, and communicated by R P Fallowes to the High Commissioner. The next challenge for the Bishop, when he more notably and successfully rose to the occasion, was the Japanese invasion of the Solomon Islands in 1942.

Figure 27 : Members of Donald Kennedy's coastwatching group in training at Seghe Point, New Georgia island, Western Solomons, June 1943. [Credit : ANU Press]

Figure 28 : Mr Harry Bullen, Secretary of the Diocese of Melanesia, in military uniform as Lt. with BSI shoulder flash, and his wife Peggy. [Credit : The Melanesian Mission]

Figure 29 : Bishop Walter Baddeley with Armed Forces personnel and the Reverend Harry Reynolds. [Credit : ACoM]

Figure 30 : Bishop Baddeley addressing allied troops in a damaged church, probably St. Luke's Cathedral, Siota, Gela.
[Credit : Parrett & Neves, Ltd. Chatham | The Melanesian Mission]

CHAPTER 13

WAR AND PEACE

The earliest permanent trading stations in the Solomons were on the small islands of Savo in the Central Solomons and Ugi in the Eastern Solomons. When conditions were not propitious on Isabel, Deacon Mano Wadrokal had taught at a school on Savo in 1872, but it was for Isabel boys. Two Mota missionaries had started the school there two years earlier, but it did not attract Savo pupils. However, a young man from Savo, Albert Kuai, who had been trained at Norfolk Island, began a school again in 1879. Savo was renowned as a savage place, with formidable warriors who regularly attacked north Guadalcanal. They rejected schools and concentrated on war and trade! Labourers who went to Fiji and Queensland returned there with Snider rifles, making their raids even more terrifying.

In 1900 some Roman Catholic missionaries arrived, and in 1901 the Reverend Percy Williams transferred two of the indigenous missionaries working with him on Guadalcanal to the island. People then began to accept the Church, some villages becoming Roman Catholic and some Anglican. Wiliam Kenda from Gela worked as a teacher there for years. Eventually two Savo men were ordained -- Alan Tinoni, Fr Williams's adopted son, who established a boys' school on the island, and John Pita, who went as priest to Utupua in the Eastern Outer Islands. Fallowes and Hugo Toke visited Savo in 1932 and found 200 communicants. The position of that island was to have great significance in the Second World War, being situated between Gela and Guadalcanal.

In 1935 Harry Reynolds arrived from New Zealand and worked as a priest first in the New Hebrides, then in the Solomons, where he became the Bishop's right-hand man and the ideal person to be appointed as Archdeacon of the Solomons in 1946. He was fearless when war arrived in the islands. His character was marked by humility, dependability and loyal obedience, and he only retired to New Zealand in the 1970s. More Gela men were ordained in 1941, Frank Bollen Toke and John Bosamata, both sons of priests.

The Japanese attacked Pearl Harbor on the island of Oahu in the Hawaiian Islands on December 7, 1941, and so entered the Second World War, starting its Pacific islands' phase. They had already occupied French Indo-China (Cambodia, Laos, Annam and Vietnam) in 1940. They went on to occupy the Philippines in January 1942, then the Malay Peninsula and Burma (both British colonial areas) and the Dutch East Indies. The British Government had assumed, if it were ever necessary, that the Solomon Islands would be defended by the military forces based in Singapore. But Singapore fell to the Japanese in February 1942. Japanese activities in the Pacific had already been causing alarm in 1939, and by the end of that year all existing teleradio operators had been enrolled in Papua and New Guinea by the Australian authorities as 'coast-watchers'. The organiser, Commander Eric Feldt, then proposed to the Director of Australian Naval Intelligence that the Coast Watching Organisation's scheme be extended to the Solomon Islands, and the Resident Commissioner there gladly accepted the loan of several teleradios for use in the Protectorate. Each teleradio was fitted with a crystal, cut so that it would give a special frequency, which was known as 'X'. By August 1940 the teleradios were nearly all in place, in naval or private hands. There were teleradios throughout the whole Solomons archipelago, including south-east Isabel, north Malaita and Tulagi on Gela; and they were later placed in the New Hebrides as well. The Royal Australian Air Force arranged to keep an 'X' frequency watch at its Advanced Operational base on Tanambogo Island in Tulagi Harbour.

On January 4, 1942, Rabaul, the capital of the former German Territory of New Guinea, mandated to Australia after the First World War, was bombed from the air. Other towns were bombed on the 21st. A Japanese naval convoy approached on the 22nd and the town was evacuated. Administration of the Territory passed to the military at Lae. From January to May 1942 the Australian troops fought a bitter rearguard action,falling back towards Port Moresby. At the end of February 1942 the Japanese had occupied Lae and Salamaua on the coast of New Guinea and the Buka Passage,as well as the Shortland Islands in the west of the British Solomon

Islands on the border with Bougainville in the Territory of New Guinea. The Solomon Islands were now on the front line.

In late January 1942 the British Resident Commissioner left Tulagi Island and crossed over to Taroaniara, now the headquarters of the Bishop of Melanesia. The European and Chinese residents of the Shortland Islands had already been evacuated. The question for Mr (later Lt Col) William Marchant, the Commissioner, was whether the Government should leave or stay. But how could they abandon the Solomon Islanders, who were British Protected persons? British forces had been imprisoned in Singapore, and were tied down in air and sea conflicts in other parts of the world. There was only a small detachment of the Australian Imperial Force guarding the installation at Tanambogo and training the local Defence Force, which consisted of three officers, one British NCO, one warrant officer and 112 other ranks, who were all Solomon Islanders. Their Commander was Major Vivian Fox-Strangways, who was due to become Resident Commissioner of the Gilbert and Ellice Islands – but the Japanese had already arrived in part of the Gilberts. He was commissioned as an Army Officer instead, and arrived to review the situation in the Solomons. He made a report to the Resident Commissioner which pointed out the inadequacies of the Defence Force: 'For the defence of Tulagi there are available three Lewis guns (1914 issue), 113 rifles, six pistols' - with a limited amount of ammunition. He suggested that Tulagi should be held 'long enough to permit civilian evacuation and destruction of objects valuable to the enemy'. After that, he suggested that guerilla warfare be 'carried on, from and on Florida Island'.

Mr Marchant had been a soldier himself and he did not want to give the impression of running away, even if evacuation appeared to be necessary for most of the non-Solomon Islanders. He went therefore to have a critical discussion with Bishop Baddeley, conscious that he had been much decorated in the First World War for bravery. The Bishop stated: 'My own mind is made up. I am staying in the Solomons.' That helped Marchant to make up his own mind and confirm what he himself wanted to do. He would stay, with those colonial officers who volunteered to stay with him. Tulagi would not be defended, as the Government would move elsewhere. In early February the Australian vessel 'Morinda' (Burns Philp company) arrived to evacuate non-native civilians who wished to leave, and also some of the young colonial officers who had decided to join the Armed Forces in Australia and then return. From late January Japanese planes had been bombing Tulagi and Gavutu, and on January 27 the Bishop decided to move the Sisters and the remaining school-girls (who had been brought from Bungana to the college buildings at Taroaniara) to greater safety at Fauabu on Malaita. Miss Stead and her two assistants and some of her trainees would be moved from Siota as well. During the night of the same day, the Resident Commissioner woke the Bishop up and told him that his Headquarters staff were moving during the night to Auki on Malaita,although an expected raid had not happened as the Japanese had sustained many losses in naval battles in the waters of the East Indies. The Bishop then joined all the other staff at Fauabu. The Reverend Alfred Hill remained with 50 schoolboys at Fauabu while Mrs Sprott, the widow of the last white resident priest on Isabel, insisted on remaining there with members of the Mothers' Union, which she had started on that island. She stayed on in Meringe district. Some of the staff, including the Mission Printer, Mr Isom, had been sent off to Australia by the Bishop on the 'Morinda' -- after it had been strafed by a Japanese bomber while sheltering in the Boli Passage. The clergy staff at Maravovo School, Leslie Stibbard and Frederick Rowley, wanted to carry on, whatever happened, caring for 40 boys still there. The Resident Commissioner remained on Malaita, and five of his officers volunteered to be coast-watchers. Others who remained were the Bishop, priests and Sisters of the Roman Catholic Mission, Mr Norman Deck and five other expatriate missionaries of the South Sea Evangelical Mission, and some of the Methodist staff in the Western Solomons, as well as 16 of the white staff of the Diocese of Melanesia. A few planters and others stayed too – a grand total of about 100 'whites'. Some planters left their labourers to fend for themselves. All the Anglican staff stayed because they had decided voluntarily to do so, for the sake of the work they were doing and the people they served. Bishop Baddeley actually believed at first that the Japanese would not reach the central Solomons. If they did, he declared: 'The bush of Mala (Malaita) would provide quite adequate protection from the enemy, unless he deliberately set out to round up "whites" .' He was right about that.

Bishop Baddeley also met with Bishop Aubin, the Roman Catholic Bishop, who declared that he was sure that the Japanese, if they came, would respect the Fathers and Sisters, so they would be staying. His conviction was unfounded. Bishop Aubin sent a young New Zealand priest, Father Wall, to go and work at the Royal Australian Air Force base at Gavutu Island near Tulagi, and he organised the Gela people to help at the base, gathering news and boosting the morale of those stationed there – about 50 in all with the Australian Imperial military personnel. An immediate challenge was the repatriation to their islands of about 2,000 indentured labourers. They were taken back to their homes, using all small ships available, including those of the Anglican Diocese. Gordon Train and Harry Bullen, the Bishop's lay assistant, were in control of this operation, moving the labourers from Guadalcanal and the Russell Islands. Most of them were from Malaita. There was one District Officer involved, Donald Kennedy, who had a roving responsibility for Gela, the Russell Islands, New Georgia and the Shortland Islands. Another officer was stationed at Aola on Guadalcanal. They were all involved in making preparations for a possible invasion. Father Wall rescued the Government records which had been left on the wharf at Gavutu when the 'Morinda' had left, and they had got wet. There had been no space on the ship for them. One of the Government officers collected them at night and whisked them off to Vila, the capital of the New Hebrides. The Catalina flying boats at Gavutu would take off in the early morning to do reconnaissance flights, and so avoid the Japanese daytime bombing raids on Gavutu and Tulagi. The Japanese did not know that Tulagi was abandoned and empty!

A temporary headquarters had been set up in Sydney by the Solomon Islands Government, and a number of colonial officers from the Solomons were waiting there to be told what to do. Some wanted to join the military, but were not allowed to do so. There was then a Japanese air attack on Sydney Harbour, and everything speeded up. Some officers returned to the Solomons and were able to provide information about the islands to incoming US forces and act as their guides. The Australian Government station at Buka Passage, north of Bougainville Island, had been abandoned, and the officers there had moved to higher ground on Buka Island, from where they were able to keep in touch by radio with Port Moresby, capital of the territory of Papua, with the RAAF at Tanambogo, and with the

Resident Commissioner of the British Solomons on Malaita. All was in place by March 6.

The Japanese arrived at Buka on March 8. Between mid-February and mid-April, District Officer Kennedy visited all important villages on Gela, Savo, the Russell Islands, Isabel, and islands in the Western Solomons, with a simple message: 'These islands are British and they are to remain British. The Government is not leaving. Even if the Japanese come, we shall stay with you and in the end they will be driven out. We may have to endure dangers and discomforts, but they will be only temporary. Make every preparation for the arrival of the enemy. When he is here, avoid him if you can, and in any case do not help him.' The same message was delivered on other islands by District Officer Martin Clemens. Kennedy reported that 'The natives entered readily into all the plans and offered their services, their food supplies and their canoes without demur.' The general reaction of the people was: 'If they come, they will get nothing from us.' The islanders remained true to their resolution, whereas some Melanesians had co-operated with the Japanese in New Guinea, where they had established themselves and seemed intent on staying. Three hundred and thirty-three white missionaries and local Christians were killed by the Japanese in New Guinea, including two priests on the island of New Britain, which was then in the Diocese of Melanesia.

On May 2 there were five heavy bombing raids on Tulagi. The Bishop of Melanesia arrived in Auki on Malaita by schooner the next day with the news that the Australian Imperial Force detachment had got safely away in 'Balus', a ship of 50 tons. On May 3 and 4 the Japanese landed at Tulagi and on the neighbouring islands. They wanted to establish a seaplane base on Gavutu island. On Guadalcanal, District Officer Martin Clemens at Aola got more Melanesian volunteers for the local Defence Force, ready to do patrols if the Japanese landed on the island. When he had definite news of an imminent Japanese landing, he dismantled the buildings of the Government station and moved up with them into the hills, to the village of Vungana. Some heavy equipment was hidden in a tunnel dug deep into the hillside near Aola. From Vungana's fortified outpost, Clemens could see the beach below and vessels entering and leaving Tulagi Harbour. His people patrolled by foot and in canoes, observing all Japanese movements and ignoring the Japanese commander's threats to round up all Europeans of enemy nationality and intern them, and promising dire penalties for any people withholding information about them.

In late July, a Japanese raiding party set out from Tulagi to pay their only visit to Malaita. They found the Government station and the Melanesian Mission station, but they were both deserted. The Resident Commissioner and the Bishop had been warned of their coming and they had withdrawn into the bush. The Japanese were wary of going up there themselves, as they had been told that the bush people were head-hunters and cannibals! They ransacked the two stations before going back to their ship, which was probably one reported to have been bombed by an American plane passing overhead, a 'Flying Fortress'. The Bishop had been acting as Assistant Cipher Officer in the Commissioner's office, deciphering messages which came in from District Officers or the local Defence Force. One message read FORTRESSINSEASEASSESEARSGELA, which no-one could understand except him, because he knew the geography of the island of Gela.

The Bishop explained that the message meant that a Flying Fortress had come down in the sea south-east of the Asses' Ears -- a mountainous feature on the Gela coast ! The Bishop also toured the bush villages on Malaita and reported to the Melanesian Mission Headquarters, temporarily in Australia, that he was accompanied in his touring by a Melanesian man, Walter Vaitahi, who was also able to 'sew the soles on my shoes again at various halts along the wayside'.

Charles Fox had been in the Melanesian Brotherhood since 1932, and during this period he was a member of the Household of Brothers in the Tae Lagoon, near the north end of Malaita island. He volunteered to be a coast-watcher, and was given a written commission to show the Japanese (if he was captured) that he was one of the military. The idea was that he would then be treated as a prisoner of war with certain rights -- which he thought, however, would <u>not</u> have been observed. He had to report anything observed in that part of Malaita, but he had no teleradio, as there were not enough to go round. He had to send messages by runners across the mountains, some 2,000 feet high, which was not an effective method when speed was required. (When he had been on San Cristoval the people used to send messages quite quickly by drums.) His messengers took a day to carry the messages 30 miles over the hills. Japanese planes often flew overhead and when one crashed, the police came and arrested the crew, who were trying to commit suicide, as was the Japanese custom. They had been ordered not to allow themselves to be taken prisoner. On another occasion some Americans in a rubber boat were saved when they crashed into the reef nearby, having drifted from an aircraft carrier which had been attacked 200 miles away, off Santa Ana Island. The Japanese later established a camp on Malaita, 15 miles from Dr. Fox, and everyone had to be wary of their patrols. However, the Resident Commissioner was still receiving messages, and on July 27 the High Commissioner for the Western Pacific, Sir Harry Luke, received this message from the Secretary of State for the Colonies: 'Please wish Marchant and his colleagues, on behalf of His Majesty's Government, the best of luck in the difficult and valuable work in which they are showing such spirit.' This cheered them up, especially as they had received another message a few days before from elsewhere, stating 'It won't be long now!'

On August 7, 1942, the American counter-attack began, by land and sea.The 1st Battalion of the 2nd Marine Regiment landed on Gela. The American Marines also went ashore on Guadalcanal, assisted there by three Solomon Islanders then training in Fiji for the Protectorate civil service, who acted as guides and interpreters. The Marines were led by General Vandergrift, who received Clemens's offer of help with gratitude, although he was surprised to find that there was still a British District Officer at work on the island, with native soldiers trained by him in guerilla warfare! Clemens had actually passed through the Japanese lines to reach the Commander.

The Japanese were intent on constructing an airfield on Guadalcanal for their planes, and had forced the local people to assist in its construction. The airstrips at Munda in the Western Solomons and at Lunga on Guadalcanal were later of great use to the Americans. The Japanese had also landed near Maravovo, and the staff and students had all moved up into the bush. Of the usual 200 pupils, only 60 remained, because that was the only number the school could feed, as the boys were all boarders. When they fled, the stores of food were already almost exhausted and the

Headmaster, Leslie Stibbard, and the second master, Frederick Rowley, decided to cross the island with 13 senior students to try to get to the Americans at Lunga, to obtain food and also help with the evacuation of the boys to a safer area. They had great difficulty in avoiding the Japanese patrols. The eventually made it to Lunga, but one boy was killed on the way. Rowley then accepted a commission in the Defence Force, while the priest at a nearby Roman Catholic mission shared with them his limited stocks of food.

At Maravovo the Japanese set up a command post in preparation for an attack by the American Marines. When that was over, all that remained of the buildings there was the cement foundation of the sanctuary around which Rowley had built a large church. Frederick Rowley, a deacon, returned there later to rebuild the school, after it had temporarily been relocated to Fiu on North Malaita, under Deacon Harry Maabe.

At first, the Marines themselves had limited supplies and were fed by local people, although their gardens had already been invaded by the Japanese, who at first paid for food but later just went and stole what they wanted. They were thoroughly disliked by the Solomon Islanders, especially because of their behaviour when the fighting turned against them. They had no help from the islanders, and they greatly resented the assistance that the local people gave to the Americans, none of whom they betrayed. The Americans, especially the black soldiers, got on well with the Melanesians.

While the Melanesian Mission staff were continuing their pastoral, medical and educational work at Fauabu Hospital and in various places in the bush on Malaita, the Japanese had been establishing themselves on the islands of the Gela group. Their ships at Tulagi had been badly smashed up in a terrible air attack, which they told the Gela people they hoped would not be repeated! Those Japanese who got ashore raided the villages for calico and food, while the local people retired to their hill gardens. The Japanese also pillaged the Mission's Headquarters at Taroaniara, taking furniture and animals and food and burning what they did not want -- books and china. Later, they dismantled the Bishop's house and another one used by bachelor missionaries, and used them elsewhere. Then they pillaged Siota.

The beautiful little Christ the King church at Tulagi, built in memory of Bishop Patteson, and the Cathedral at Siota, did not survive the war. The houses for the school at Bungana had all been destroyed. On Guadalcanal, two Roman Catholic priests and two Sisters had been murdered by Japanese soldiers when they refused to reveal American positions. On Malaita, the Bishop had his 'house' at the village of Tantalau, where the mat which had been round Bishop Patteson's body, the altar silver from the Cathedral at Siota and Bishop Selwyn's staff were all being kept. Sister Stead was there too, continuing the training for a handful of women, looking after a Maternity Ward and running a dispensary. The schoolhouse where the Bishop stayed was nicknamed 'The Burrow, Stoney Rocks'. The Bishop spent long weekends visiting villages in the Kwara'ae District which he would not normally have been able to do when touring by ship. On November 8, stores arrived at last!

During August, the Americans cleared the Japanese from Tulagi, Bungana, Gavutu and the mainland of Gela, while fighting continued on Guadalcanal.

They then established a seaplane base in the harbour near Tulagi,and Gela became a secondary base for allied operations for the duration of the war in the Solomons.There was also a watering point on Gela for the US Navy, which diverted water from an underground source. Japanese ships continued to patrol, using Thousand Ships Bay on Isabel as a harbour, just as the first (Spanish) explorers had done. When General Vandergrift expressed his wish that all expatriate women remaining in the Solomons should go south, the Bishop made arrangements for the women in the Mission to move to the New Hebrides or go on leave. Mrs Sprott, who had been hidden in the bush in Meringe by the 'mothers' when the Japanese arrived on Isabel, was sick and went south for treatment. The women all left at the end of November. The white nuns and the local Sisters (Taina) joined Mother Margaret, their Superior, at Lolowai on Ambae island in the northern New Hebrides. Harry Reynolds was asked to re-open the Headquarters at Taroaniara, and the Bishop returned there and became very popular with the Americans based nearby. They also established an anti-aircraft school at Siota, and Charles Fox spent six months with the troops there. All his valuable books, including his many books in different languages, had been destroyed or had perished during the war. The great

American naval victory of November 14-15 persuaded most people that there would be no more 'enemy occupation'.

Six months of bloody fighting on land and at sea had led to eventual victory for the Allies - the Americans, Australians, New Zealanders, Solomon Islanders, Fijians and the British who had remained. However, the losses were terrible on all sides. Probably 80,000 had died, a large number being islanders killed in the crossfire or dying for lack of food. The Japanese losses were extremely heavy. The Solomons Defence Force had increased in number to 400 and only seven of those were lost in action. There was outstanding bravery on the part of many of the islanders, some of whom were decorated by the Americans, as was Bishop Baddeley. In a letter to the “Solomon Star” newspaper of February 2, 2016, it was stated that the Coastwatchers were credited with saving 501 allied personnel and 450 civilians.

Some American soldiers and seamen had been rescued by islanders, among them Jack Kennedy, the man who would later become President of the USA. Kasolo, the island where he and his shipmates were washed ashore in the Western Solomons, was re-named Kennedy Island after the war.

On Malaita, the Japanese station with its 50 soldiers, was surrounded by the American forces at night, guided there from Fauabu Hospital by the Melanesians. Machine gun fire killed most of them while they were having their breakfast. About 500 non-Christians from the bush villages in the hills killed the wounded and any who fled by trying to swim out to sea. On the other hand, wounded Americans were always given help, and the British and other expatriates who stayed in the islands were admired. On Gela, the American Marines were called 'na vure tabu' ('holy' people) because they were fierce fighters, lived hard, did not steal, respected the women, were very generous and invited Melanesians to eat with them. Above all, they were friendly and showed no colour discrimination – perhaps because the war had shown them what Melanesian Christians were really like! However, many of the Americans were anti-colonial, and urged the people to oppose the colonial Government after the war was over. The islanders were very conscious that the Americans, not the

British, had saved them from the Japanese, who had killed not only some of them but also some of the Chinese traders who served them, and who had caused many of them to starve. A few of the Japanese revealed that they were Christians. One officer went into the Cathedral at Siota to pray as he was an Anglican, but he was killed soon afterwards by the Americans. Islanders were shocked that that often the Japanese would deliberately desecrate their churches, but that did not stop them praying wherever they could. Women and children would stay up in the hills during the night, but come down to the church for morning prayers wherever and whenever possible.

On Guadalcanal, the chapel of the Melanesian Brotherhood at Tabalia was burnt down and the altar vessels stolen, while the rest of their Headquarters was destroyed. The few Brothers remaining there fled for their lives and swam out to sea. One was killed, Brother Simon Sigai. Sergeant Major Vouza of Guadalcanal became a war hero, as he was captured and refused to divulge any information about the Americans. He was tied to a tree and bayonetted in the chest and throat and left for dead. Amazingly, he survived and managed to reach the Americans, covered in wounds, and insisted on reporting the Japanese position before receiving treatment. Twenty years after the Americans landed he sent a message to the veterans who had greatly admired him, saying: 'Tell them I love them all. Me old man now, and me no look good no more. But me never forget.' He named his village California.

The Americans were amazed that the people prayed each day, morning and evening, whenever possible, either in the village church, if still standing, or in a temporary leaf house in the hills. If a priest was available, Holy Communion would be celebrated, sometimes in spite of the presence of Japanese nearby. On the island of Savo, near which a terrible naval battle had taken place, the Melanesian priest found hundreds of bodies had been washed up. The Americans had lost that battle, but he tried to read the burial service over them and bury them. However, he would not do that for the Japanese (although some were Christians) but deposited their bodies in the sea. The American and Australian navies had lost 1,023 dead in one night, more than the Americans' First Marine Division would lose in four months of fighting. The comment of Admiral King in Washington D.C. was that 'it was the blackest day of the war'. He was Commander-in-Chief of the US fleet, and thought the future to be 'unpredictable' after that.

On Guadalcanal a great number of Melanesian Christians, mainly Anglican, constructed a memorial chapel for the Americans in the cemetery where 1600 American men of the Armed Forces were buried. It took two months to build and it was dedicated on September 12, 1943. Jason, a Melanesian leader in the Labour (Labor) Corps, dressed in a singlet and white 'calico' (long loin-cloth) presented the church to the Americans assembled outside. Then two American chaplains said dedicatory prayers and the assembly passed into the chapel, led by the Labor Corps members singing 'Onward Christian Soldiers' in harmony. The chapel was 90 feet long, 26 feet wide and seated 280. It was built in locally supplied materials, different timbers being used for the rafters, roof and altar. Woven matting in varied patterns formed the walls. The bell-tower rose above the thatched roof and was surmounted by a carved wooden cross. It was an act of thanksgiving to the Americans and their Allies 'who have fought to push the enemy out of our land,' as Jason put it. He added, however, 'This Church no longer belong to you and me. This Church belong God.' The Americans were deeply moved. After the War, many bodies were exhumed and returned to the U.S.A.

The Chapel and cemetery were near the coast and looked out over Sealark Channel to Gela. After the war, the channel became known as Ironbottom Sound, as so many ships of both sides were sunk there. The bodies of Americans which were recovered on land and at sea were buried in the cemetery. For years afterwards, until they were too old to make the journey, some of the Marines returned regularly to visit Guadalcanal. In the early 1980s the Japanese erected a large memorial on Mount Austen,east of Honiara, which was dedicated in 1984, and eventually the Americans erected one on a hill in the middle of the town. This was dedicated on August 7, 1992, marking the 50th anniversary of the landing of American Marines on Guadalcanal. A ceremony of remembrance is held there every year on August 7. The monument has inscriptions recording all the land and sea battles of the Solomon Islands campaign, which had prevented the Japanese reaching any further south. It did not list the names of the fallen Americans or their allies, but the battles which had affected not only them but the people of the Solomon Islands, for whom the Second World War had been the most traumatic experience ever undergone by the people of the Western and Central islands of the group. However, the Japanese did not leave some islands of the Bismarck group in the New Guinea Islands further north until they finally surrendered on August 15, 1945. After leaving Guadalcanal they based themselves for a while at Munda on New Georgia, where further battles took place in June and October 1943.

Father Wall survived the war and, as a New Zealander, was eventually given the OBE by a grateful British Government although, in typical Antipodean style, he said that rather than meaning 'Officer of the British Empire' it really meant 'Other B----'s Efforts' – an example of his bluff sense of humility! He had been ten years in the islands when war had come. He had hidden in the bush to escape the 'Japmen' as the Melanesians called them. He, with others, had been rescued by Marine patrols, some missionaries being very sick by then. The patrols had found the bodies of the two priests and two nuns (Religious Sisters) who had been killed by the Japanese. Before the Americans had landed, they had destroyed some of the Roman Catholic mission stations and the homes of Melanesians nearby, and their owners had to flee.

After the conflict on Guadalcanal had ceased, some Americans had attended Mass and heard Fr Wall explain with emotion that 'it was impossible for the priests and nuns to carry on their work effectively. They were as hunted animals. It was a terrible setback to them. ' A Marine Corps captain wrote: 'Our landing gave them a new start, and priests were able to return to their duties in the recaptured areas.' He had been present at the Mass, and was impressed by the words of Fr Wall, who congratulated the whites present for showing the Melanesians that the Christian religion was practised in the 'great outside world', as few of the whites in the Solomons, other than missionaries, were regular worshippers or attended Church at all.

The war deeply affected the Melanesian Brotherhood. The Gela Household at Tulagi had closed, and Brothers in Households in the rest of the Solomons, New Britain and the New Hebrides, had dispersed and resigned without being properly released from their vows. Only on Malaita, where Brother Charles

Fox had been based, had a Household survived at Gwounatolo. Charles Fox appointed James Vasethe from Isabel as Elder Brother. Bishop Baddeley returned to Gela from Malaita where, he said, he had been 'living like a rabbit'. He re-established the Diocese's headquarters at Taroaniara, and a visitor reported what he had seen there: 'His flag flies over what is probably the least pretentious Episcopal palace in the world. It is a leaf hut erected by natives on the concrete foundations of the mission warehouse which, like all the other buildings on the station, was left in ruins by the Japanese. Outside this humble but airy abode (whose cool veranda you are likely to find crowded with American servicemen appreciatively devouring generous helpings of fruit salad, in the preparation of which His Lordship proudly specialises) there hangs a wooden plaque bearing the whimsical but defiant legend 'Bishop's Court, 1942 - ?'

The same visitor noticed a cluster of leaf buildings on the hill behind, which had been the site of the theological college, and where the Principal, Fr Jim Edwards, was back in residence, awaiting the eventual arrival of his former students. His house had lost its roof and walls of permanent materials, but these had been replaced by leaf panels, and Fr Jim told the visitor he was 'very comfortable' as he had two canvas chairs and a camp bed 'borrowed from the Marines'. Five of the Mission's stations had been left by the Japanese in ruins, and the Cathedral at Siota had been despoiled. The beautiful fonts, lecterns and altar crosses in the churches, usually inlaid with shell, had been taken or destroyed, but they would in time be replaced. When Bishop Baddeley preached to an American unit, the chaplain announced that the following Sunday a box would be put out for donations to the work of the Mission. A hundred or more servicemen gave $187 to show their appreciation - a generous donation under those conditions.

In 1944 the Bishop removed the Brothers from Gwounatolo on the Mission ship 'Mavis' to stay with the Mission Carpenter at Fauabu, Mr C R Buffett, who was from a Norfolk Island family, before being taken on to Taroaniara. The profession of a new Brother took place there on October 28, the Feast of St Simon and St Jude, and Households were opened at Maravovo on Guadalcanal (as Tabalia was not yet available) and at Maka on South Malaita, where there had been a Household before. The Brotherhood had been saved, with the encouragement of the Bishop, and would soon increase again. The founder, Ini Kopuria, who had broken his life vow, joined the Labour Corps and also married, was relieved to know that the Brotherhood had not been destroyed - but was also filled with sorrow that he himself, probably believing that all was lost, had been unable to keep his vow or to lead its revival. He continued as a Deacon till his death in 1945, deeply missed by his former fellow Brothers and the Companions of the Brotherhood.

The Japanese, according to their custom, later requested that they be allowed to recover the bodies of the fallen and repatriate their remains to Japan. This was agreed and a recovery mission collected the bones and burnt them in a ceremony at the Japanese monument. The Solomon Islanders, in a spirit of reconciliation, even established a Solomon Islands - Japan Friendship Association. Later still, the Anglican church in Japan, the Nippon Sei Ko Kai, expressed its deep sorrow over the numbers of Christians killed both in Papua New Guinea - 333 in all - and also in the Solomon Islands, and expressed the penitence of its members for not speaking out against the militaristic policies of their Government, which had led to great tragedy both for themselves and for millions of others in Asia and the Pacific. In the Solomons conflict, 38,000 Japanese had lost their lives, while the US forces had suffered the loss of 7,000 of their numbers.[33] Also, among the casualties were 27 Coastwatchers and 20 Solomon Islanders, while 18 Coastwatchers and 40 Solomon Islanders had been captured, but had survived. Starting in 2013, Solomon Islands Scouts' and Coastwatchers' medallions were presented to those Solomon Islanders who had served as Scouts during World War Two, usually by the

---

[33] The author had a relative in the US Navy, Lt Frank Smith, his father's second cousin. He may have spent time at or near Tulagi, as his duty was to pay naval personnel. His grandfather had emigrated from north-east Scotland to the USA. He served in the Solomons for over a year and he survived, although he suffered, like many others, from malaria. His sister-in-law says he was stationed on Guadalcanal.

Australian High Commissioner in the Solomon Islands, and sometimes on Australia Day. In 2016 the Prime Minister of the Solomon Islands spoke of his Government's intention of establishing a 'war memorial park' centred on Bloody Ridge on Guadalcanal in time for the 75th anniversary of the Battle of Guadalcanal and the landing of Allied forces.[34]

The Second World War was a defining incident in the history of the Solomon Islands. In August 2016, on the campus of the Solomon Islands National University, opened in 2013, the Solomon Islands Pacific War Centre was opened. It will act as an information and education centre, and it has been established through the work of the Solomon Islands' Scouts and Coast-watchers Memorial Trust. It will help Solomon Islanders know and value this important period in their history.

On August 7, 2011, Solomon Islanders were able to see for the first time a monument to all their fellow islanders involved in the events of the Second World War in their country. Designed by Solomon Islander Frank Haikiu, the monument is called 'Pride of our Nation' and it is a fruit of the work of the Solomon Scouts and Coastwatchers Trust. The ceremony coincided with the annual American memorial programme, and began at the American memorial and moved to Commonwealth Street for the dedication of the memorial by the Anglican Archbishop of Melanesia after it had been unveiled by the Governor-General. It ended at Honiara Yacht Club, where there is a memorial plaque to Douglas Munro, a member of the US Coast Guard mortally wounded on Guadalcanal in September 1942. A bronze statue of the war hero Sgt Major Jacob Vouza, whose bravery had been recognised with the granting of a knighthood, had already been placed outside the central Police Headquarters in Honiara, having been made in Australia and paid for by the Americans in 1990. The history of the Solomons campaign and the contribution of Solomon Islanders to it are

---

[34] Information in this paragraph is largely drawn from a communication by Frank Short to the Editor of the 'Solomon Star' (see www.solomonislandsinfocus.com and Solomon Islands Information Network February 2, 2016.)

now included as subjects in the national education curriculum. In 2016, the Solomon Islands National University and the Solomon Scouts and Coastwatchers Memorial trust hosted the Inaugural Guadalcanal Military History Conference, planned around the 74th anniversary of the landings on August 7,1942 ,of allied forces on Guadalcanal and Tulagi/Gavutu. It also marked the opening of the Solomon Islands Pacific War Centre on the campus of the University.

When in 2013 the Australian Government provided, belatedly, 500 Solomon Islander Coastwatchers and Scouts' medallions, only three of the Solomon Islander veterans were still alive. However, the 70th anniversary of the US Marine Corps's landing on Guadalcanal was marked in 2012 by a message from President Barack Obama, in which he wrote: 'The landing of United States Marines on Guadalcanal on August 7, 1942, marked the beginning of the arduous journey to victory in the Pacific theater. Its success owed much to the critical intelligence provided by the Coastwatchers and the Solomon Scouts. When Solomon Scouts rescued LTGJ John F Kennedy after his PT boat sank, they secured a lasting place in history.'

Anna Annie Kwai, an islander from Malaita, makes significant comments about the campaign in her book 'Solomon Islanders in World War II : An Indigenous Perspective', published in 2017, saying: 'For an ethnically divided nation, the war was a common denominator and a time when Solomon Islanders worked together for a common cause. The reminder of this co-operative effort through the physical presence of the Pride of Our Nation monument is symbolically helping to restore the co-operative spirit. In order for this understanding to gain momentum, people need to be aware of islander participation in the war.'

Figure 31 : St Peter's Theological College, Siota, Gela 1963. [Credit : Mrs Jennifer Probets]

CHAPTER 14

RECOVERY AND RENEWAL

The eastern Solomons had not been the scene of fighting by land, but nobody knew how far the Japanese would reach. Some Americans were stationed at Alangaula, on the shore of Ugi island, and for much of the war Alfred Hill had continued to run Pawa School on a hill nearby. Having been a Master Mariner, he related easily to the troops, who sometimes invited him to eat and drink with them. On one occasion, they had added something to his drink, which caused him to oversleep on a Saturday night. It was the only time he was unable to celebrate Holy Communion on the Sunday morning for the staff and students there. Later the boys were astonished to see their headmaster carrying bags of small stones up the hill for adding to the surface of the pathways - this was a punishment he gave to the boys for misdemeanours. He explained to them that he had let them down, and so had given himself the same punishment! It was significant actions like this which endeared him to his pupils.

Among them was a boy who was paler in colour than the rest, called Norman Kitchener Palmer. His great-grandfather had been one of the head-hunting chiefs of the Western Solomons, who had invited a white trader to establish himself in his area, as he wanted trade goods. However, his daughter heard him saying one day that he intended to kill the trader, and then he would get all the trade goods for himself without having to pay for them. She had another idea. Bravely she said to her father: 'Don 't kill him, I'll marry him!' (That would be another way of getting permanent access to the trade goods he wanted!) The chief agreed, and the couple had a daughter, who later had a son with another white man who had arrived in safer times to work in the Western Solomons. His surname was Palmer. When the Japanese arrived, the question for his mother, who had subsequently married a dark-skinned local man, was: What could they do to save young Norman, as the Japanese might assume he was a European, and kill him? Although they were Methodists, they sent him to Pawa School, hoping he would be safe there. After the war, he trained overseas as a teacher and later became an Anglican priest – then bishop.

Boys at Pawa School were able to continue their studies without much interruption, but what about Maravovo School? All that remained of it was a cement platform, the foundation of the former sanctuary of the school chapel. The Japanese had used the place as a command post, and it had become a battleground. The Marines had rid the compound of the Japanese, and F A Rowley was then given permission to return there. On arriving with his pupils, he set about re-erecting in local materials all the buildings that they required: a chapel, two dormitories, a dining hall, a 'hospital' and houses for the Melanesian teacher and himself.

He also managed to salvage and repair water-tanks and re-erect them. The altar and school desks were made from driftwood found on the beaches, and from some other timbers. Items hidden hurriedly from the Japanese in the bush were recovered - altar vessels, some medicines and a few school books. Gardens were re-planted. During the conflict, the number of pupils had been reduced to 45, although there had been 200 before, brought by the Bishop from islands all over the central and eastern Solomons. Some of them would be selected after three years to go on to Pawa Senior School. The Reverend Donald Mayberry, a chaplain in the US Naval Reserve serving in the Solomons, was invited by Rowley, who was still a deacon, to celebrate Holy Communion just before Christmas. He travelled to Maravovo on the Mission vessel 'Patteson'. He noted down the school programme: Rise at 5.45, chapel at 6.15, then breakfast, cleaning and 'brushing' the station, cutting the grass with strips of bamboo stick. Each day, some worked on rebuilding the permanent chapel. Three hours were then spent in class, learning English, arithmetic, writing, the Bible and the Catechism. At noon the boys ate a lunch of biscuits, tea and fruit, then they would go out to their individual gardens. Sport and 'swim' (bathe) followed. Their teacher Nelson Gao led them in Evening Prayer at 5.15pm. If a Melanesian priest visited, he would celebrate Holy Communion in the morning. The boys prepared their own evening meal in groups in their gardens, using what they had grown, or fish that they had speared.

Padre Mayberry was impressed, and shared his experiences with readers of a magazine of his Episcopal (Anglican) Church in the United States, which was called 'The Living Church' in a special article.

The rebuilding at Maravovo was typical of what was happening all over the islands in places where the Japanese had been; but there were more significant changes taking place on Guadalcanal than on other islands. It now had a large airfield, which was named Henderson Field after a Marine Major, Lofton R Henderson, a dive-bomber squadron commander killed in the Battle of Midway Island south-west of Hawaii. The American general who opened it wanted to honour him. He was Major-General A Archer Vandergrift, Commander of the First Marine Division, which included not only Marines but infantry, artillery and specialists of various kinds. The American camp at Honiara, was largely made up of big 'Quonset huts' (the British equivalent was Nissen huts) constructed of corrugated iron, but it became the capital, as Tulagi had been gutted. The Anglicans and the Roman Catholics acquired two of the Quonset huts as their temporary cathedrals, the Anglicans dedicating theirs to All Saints. It replaced the 'leaf' Cathedral at Siota on Gela, which had been bombed.

In March 1943, a month after the Japanese had withdrawn from Guadalcanal, US Army's black troops began to arrive on Guadalcanal. Some of them had been building airfields in New Caledonia, as they formed two aviation engineer battalions. In the Solomons, they built the 'bomber airdromes' south of Koli Point. The islanders thus began to see people the same colour as themselves doing the same jobs under the same conditions as the white troops they had got to know. This led some to ask among themselves whether Solomon Islanders should not be ruling themselves and making their own decisions.

After the Second World War the process of decolonisation began. India, Pakistan and Ghana (formerly the Gold Coast) in West Africa gained Independence from Great Britain in 1947, and other parts of the British Empire followed in the next few years. Decolonisation also led to the Independence of Indonesia from the Dutch in 1949, although this did not include Dutch New Guinea, the western part of that island. It became part of Indonesia in 1963 by questionable means, in spite of the matter being the responsibility of the United Nations. However, Independence came to territories in the Pacific Islands much more slowly, the first being Western Samoa, gaining its Independence from New Zealand in 1962. White Americans were generally against the continuation of the British Empire -

- including Franklin D Roosevelt, President of the United States during the war. American troops had been somewhat surprised to find that Britain ruled the Solomon Islands and questioned why, and the arrival of black soldiers led to more questioning of why white people were ruling black people. The Second World War had also proved to whites how much more capable Melanesians were in many ways, if given both the encouragement and the resources. The Americans in most cases had treated the Melanesians with respect - sometimes they had had to rely on them for their lives! They also invited them to eat with them. Dr Charles Fox was very aware of the underlying racism in the way that many Government officers, traders, plantation owners and even a few missionaries treated the islanders. He wrote: 'They feel very much being treated as inferiors. The colour feeling is real. The test of colour feeling is whether a man will eat with another or not. That is the Melanesian test.'

Many whites felt it was beneath their dignity to eat with Melanesians, while Melanesians felt that their dignity had been affronted by this attitude. By the Second World War, Melanesians had already had experience of dealing with white men, not just in the Solomons and New Hebrides but also, through labouring abroad, in Australia, Fiji, New Caledonia and Samoa. Some stayed in those places, but most returned, especially with the enforcement of the white Australia policy from 1906. That policy caused deep resentment. Many of the labourers were from Malaita and some were converted to Christianity in Australia through the work of either May Robinson, an Anglican who was the wife of a sugar planter in Mackay in Queensland, who ran a school on behalf of the Melanesian Mission, or the Queensland Kanaka Mission, founded in 1886 by Florence Young, an Evangelical and sister of two of the largest planters in Queensland. There were 6,389 Melanesians in Queensland in 1906. 4,800 were from the Solomons, and of them about 2,500 were from Malaita. One of those influenced (and taught to write) by May Robinson had the name Jack Malayta, and he wrote a widely circulated letter in which he complained that 'the white people ... want to turn us out'.

In 1904, before the eventual repatriation of most of the labourers, the Queensland Kanaka Mission relocated itself to Malaita, establishing its head station at Onepusu. Some of the returned labourers were still alive during and after the Second World War, and their families were conscious of their feelings. By 1942 about 18,000 people on Malaita had accepted Christianity and had joined one of the four churches working there - the South Sea Evangelical Mission (as the Kanaka Mission had been re-named), the Melanesian Mission (Anglican), the Roman Catholic Mission, or the Seventh Day Adventists. The SSEM had about 9,000 adherents on the island. The rest of the population were still animists, called 'heathen' by the Christians.

There were, then, memories of how the Australian Government had treated Melanesians, of how Melanesians had initiated the missionary work of the South Sea Evangelical Mission in the Solomons, and of how Americans during the war had urged them to reject colonialism. Also circulating were stories of the temporary success of the 'parliament' movement promoted by Richard Fallowes. This all led to a significant movement, with its base on the island of Malaita, called Maasina Rule or 'Brotherhood' Rule, anglicised to 'Marching Rule'. Some Melanesians had been attacked and killed on plantations by white overseers in the 1920s, and they had been from Malaita. The whites, however, had been acquitted of the crime. In 1927 on Malaita, District Officer Bell and a white cadet had been killed, together with 13 of their Melanesian assistants, when Bell attempted to confiscate rifles and collect tax. Six Malaita men were hanged for that, and their district of Kwaio brutally punished. People there did not forget. About 2,000 men, the majority from Malaita, joined the Solomon Islands Labour Corps, and others the Defence Force. However, rumblings of dissent began in 1943. A group of military 'scouts' declared they were fighting not for the British, but for the Americans. On Gela, Oliver Alogobu, a dismissed Government headman (accused of adultery) organised meetings at which he declared to receptive audiences: 'We don't want the Government back at Tulagi' and 'The Americans must stay'.

Also, following the example of George Kabini (a man from the Lau area on Malaita) in 1943, Alogobu gathered donations for the American Red Cross. In December 1944, the District Officer on Gela, C S Belshaw, reported to the D.O. on Guadalcanal: 'It has come to my notice that there has been a resumption of activity by several natives with the object of collecting names for a petition to be presented to the U.S. Major Trench has discovered activity on Malaita with its origins in Nggela. I would be grateful for any information you may have as to similar activity on Guadalcanal and Savo, since there is reason to believe that Vouza and Soro have been contacted by the people involved in Nggela ... I think it would be advisable to discourage communication with Nggela for a while - say on medical grounds. No Nggela boys[35] are being permitted to leave Nggela except in exceptional circumstances...'

In 1945 a delegation from the Labour Corps and later a SSEM teacher were told categorically by the American commander that the Americans would not be taking over the administration of the Solomons. The centre of protest moved to Malaita when members of the Labour Corps were demobilised. Resistance to Government authority started in 1944 in North Malaita, and it linked up with a self-help group in Are'are district. Two strong leaders emerged, Hoasihau and Nono'ohimae, who had both attended the Fallowes meeting held in 1939. The movement demanded a 'Native Council' and until early 1946 the movement went by that name. It then adopted the title 'Maasina', based on the Are'are language word for 'brotherhood'. Elements of various schemes were incorporated into the overall planning, including an experiment in local government conducted on Gela in 1941 under the direction of the then Resident Commissioner, W S Marchant. Some whites had not believed that the Malaita people, with their different languages and customs, could come together to form a single authority for their island, but they did so by dividing the island into nine districts, each with a Head Chief, of whom five were from the SSEM. The nominal head of the movement was Nori, one of the delegation which had earlier gone to see the U.S. commander. Nori was a pagan till 1947, when he became a Roman Catholic. They started to gather people into large villages, forbidding them to 'recruit' for work elsewhere, and instructing them to plant large communal gardens. On December 26, 1946,

---

[35] The word 'boys' may have been used instead of the word 'men', an indication of a certain attitude towards Melanesians !

about 5,000 people gathered at the Government station at Auki, demanding higher wages for Melanesians, an insistent demand.

At the same time, the movement began to spread to other islands. From Are'are it went to the island of Ulawa, and from there to San Cristoval (Makira). Men from Are'are also brought it to Guadalcanal, where Jacob Vouza, now Headman of Tasiboko District, supported it, having already been involved in campaigns for higher wages for the Labour Corps and for stevedores in Honiara. In June 1947 he sent Brown Zalamana ,a man from Hograno District on Isabel who was an Anglican teacher and former follower of Fallowes, to spread the word to Gela and Isabel regarding the need for self-help and rejection of British rule. Zalamana (sometimes called Julumana) preached that the British were 'wolves clothed in sheep's clothing' and 'false prophets'. The Anglican clergy on Gela opposed him. Dr Fox went with the Gela priest Fr Stephen Hagesi and Gela schoolmaster John Manebona to every village on Gela to answer the points which Brown had made. The Government later arrested Brown.

On Isabel, Brown's reception was very different. He had a hearing there because he had worked as a chaplain's assistant on an American base during the war, and he had got to know Jacob Vouza the war hero when he was posted to a church school on Guadalcanal. He had joined in Maasina Rule meetings organised by Vouza. In Hograno, he met the senior Isabel priest, Father Ben Hageria, who expressed enthusiastic support and gave him the history of the British Parliament which he had written down in Bugotu language, based on Fallowes's teaching. This became a key text for the Isabel supporters of the movement. Zalamana had also been a member of the Melanesian Brotherhood, and had been training to be a deacon. He held his meetings in village churches, beginning with a ceremonial procession, dressed as a catechist with robes given him by the American chaplain. In his speeches, he quoted from the Bible, as well as repeating points made by Vouza and other leaders on Guadalcanal. At his trial in the High Court in 1948, he stated his understanding of the movement's religious basis:

'When I was asked to explain on Gela about Marching Rule, I thought it must be the same as what Mr Fallowes had explained before... This

Marching Rule wanted taxes to be used by the people, which Mr Fallowes wanted... Mr Fallowes had wanted to help the Solomon Islanders before and give us a parliament, but the Government had sent him back to England... Marching Rule was taken from his teachings.'

Zalamana was sentenced to four years in prison for his involvement in what was described as a 'seditious' movement - but the movement had forced change. The Protectorate Government had to respond to the demand for local government of some sort. In 1948 the Government headman on Isabel formed a 'native council' with ten leaders from around the island, and a 'committee' in each village. Elections for councillors were introduced in the 1950s. Zalamana himself was later elected to the Isabel Council and served for 12 years.

On Guadalcanal, the arrest of Zalamana and Government attempts to suppress the movement caused Vouza and his followers to reconsider their position, especially when Vouza himself was arrested in 1947, although he was not charged. In January 1948 Vouza was one of five Solomon Islanders whom the Government sent to Fiji to study local administration. However, another movement then arose on Guadalcanal which its leader, Matthew Belamatanga, called the 'Development Society for the Native Races' or 'The Freedom Movement'. In 1949 he and four of his associates were found guilty of forming an 'illegal society' and imprisoned. Popular support for Maasina Rule continued on Malaita and San Cristoval.

When the Government recruited 50 Malaita men for work in Honiara, Maasina leaders responded by threatening a strike. On June 30, 1947, 7,000 people gathered outside the Malaita District Commissioner's office, when their leaders met the D.C., Mr Sanders. The people wanted to establish their own courts, following their own rules and regulations. Ownership of Mission lands began to be questioned as well. Some of the Anglican clergy saw dangerous tendencies in the movement, and some leading Melanesians were alarmed at the adoption by some members of uniforms and dummy weapons and military drill. In anticipation of a Government backlash, the villages began to be 'fortified' by fences, tall towers and sentry boxes, from 1948.

The Government took action on August 31, 1947. Seven European officers and 50 Melanesian policemen from the Western Solomons, where there had been hardly any support for the movement, arrested 253 Maasina leaders, who were tried and imprisoned for up to six years. In July 1948 further action was taken to do away with the fences. Those resisting were arrested. By June 1949 about 2,000 were in prison. Some believed the Americans would come to help them with cargo, but the last group of them, a surveying party, left in October. Hopes of an American return gradually faded, but Government demands for the payment of tax led to further mass protests, and police reinforcements were brought in. The Resident Commissioner, H G Gregory-Smith, decided in 1950 to release the nine principal chiefs if they would urge their supporters to back the Government. They agreed. However, a movement like the 'Freedom Movement' had developed in Kwara'ae, similar to Balamatanga's in its aims - but it also issued a 'Malaita Declaration of Independence', which was formally rejected by the British Minister of State for the Colonies, John Dugdale, in a speech in Auki in 1951. The leader, Ariel Sisisi, was jailed for three years.

The movement ceased in 1952 when the Government promised to help Malaita attain higher educational, economic and health standards. King George VI School, the first full secondary school and the only one run by the Government, was established at Aligegeo near Auki in the 1950s and later moved to Honiara. A Legislative Council for the country was established in 1960. In 1975 the name 'British Solomon Islands Protectorate' was changed to 'Solomon Islands', a Governing Council having been established in 1970.

There were two movements on Malaita which offered other possibilities of development. Dr Fox, while still living there, tried to start a movement called Patana (Partner) with the aim of increasing partnership between the British and the Melanesians for the sake of the Solomons, but especially of Malaita. Some Malaita people had sought an alternative to Maasina Rule. However, the Resident Commissioner did not allow it to go ahead. Instead, on Malaita in 1953 and on all the main islands, the Government set up Native Councils with their own Presidents and officers. The local Council governed the island, collected taxes, ran the courts and established schools, all with the advice and necessary consent (for major decisions) of the District Commissioners and District Officers.

Gela had its own Council and its own Education Committee. Culturally, the people were used to making corporate decisions at the village level, and now new levels of administration and local government were being introduced - but Gela and Isabel had tried them once before! The other movement which spread from Malaita to Gela and other islands was called 'The Church Association' initiated in 1953 by a Malaita priest, Fr Willie Masura'a (later a Canon), who saw the need for 'self-help' and worked out a specifically Christian way in which some of the aims of Maasina Rule could be achieved socially rather than politically. The majority of the Malaita Anglicans believed in the need for more self-government and eventual Independence, but were realistic enough to see the need for better education first. The reaction of Gela people to Maasina Rule was to offer to pay double the tax which the Government required, as a sign of support for its authority!

The US Navy had had a station of Siota, and Dr Fox was there from 1943 to 1949. He was at Fiu on Malaita from 1949 to 1952, and returned to Tabalia (though no longer a Brother) from 1952 to 1954, so that the Brothers had again a priest among them. His last appointment was to Taroaniara on Gela, an island he loved, from 1954 to 1973.

Figure 32 : Bishop Charles Koete, first Bishop of the Diocese of Central Solomons 1997-2010, with members of his diocese. [Credit : The Anglican Church of Melanesia]

CHAPTER 15

INDEPENDENCE AND INSURRECTION

In the twentieth century, the Gela Church had sent out its own missionaries, including Tome and Ivo to Malaita and Toke and Toganiade to Guadalcanal. In 1946 there were the ordinations of two Gela men, Eli Huri and Charles Vunda. Others had served in the Melanesian Brotherhood, and Alfred Bula had died as a missionary in Fiji. Bishop Hill was a strong supporter of the Melanesian Brotherhood and on his retirement became Chaplain to the Brothers in the New Guinea Region, based in West New Britain, where he had commanded a Mission ship when he first came to Melanesia in 1936. The Brothers thought that a Household of Brothers should go to the New Guinea Highlands, and this idea was welcomed by Bishop Hill and the Bishop of New Guinea, Philip Strong. Dr Fox gave them a course of preparation at Taroaniara for a few months, and then they toured the Gela villages, preaching to the people. The congregations gave £60 to support them in their work, and the Companions of the Brotherhood raised some more. The group of eight included two Brothers from Gela. They went to work in 1956 near Goroka in the Highlands of New Guinea among recently discovered tribes there.

Whilst at Taroaniara, Dr Fox produced some key publications. In addition to the Gela dictionary which had been published in New Zealand in 1955, he produced a booklet 'Gela for Beginners', printed and published by the Mission Press at Hautabu near Maravovo in 1941, before the arrival of the Japanese. Indeed, he wondered if Gela might replace Mota in the Solomons as the common language for Anglicans there. The Press, which had begun its work in New Zealand, had then transferred to Norfolk Island and ended up on a hill called Hautabu in west Guadalcanal, near Maravovo. After the war it was re-established at Taroaniara, which was ideal for Dr Fox as some of his books were now printed there, and so could be easily checked by him on the spot. He was then in his eighties. His history of the Mission, entitled 'Lord of the Southern Isles', was however published by A R Mowbray and Co in London in 1958. Its sub-title was 'Being the Story of the Anglican Mission in Melanesia 1849-1949'. It celebrated the centenary of the work in Melanesia, which had also been marked in London by a special meeting at Mary Sumner House, the Headquarters of the Mothers' Union, in 1949. This was chaired by the Patron of the Mission, the Archbishop of Canterbury, Dr Geoffrey Fisher. Dr. Fox had written the history in 1952, prior to his settling at Taroaniara,and Bishop Hill sent him to England to try to get it published. Originally, it had been three times longer! His account followed on from 'The History of the Melanesian Mission', the story of the first 50 years written by Mrs E S Armstrong and published in London in 1900. Both books were later carefully supplemented by the book 'God's Gentlemen: A History of the Melanesian Mission 1849-1942' written by the Australian historian Dr David Hilliard, and published by the University of Queensland Press in 1978. However, Dr Fox was not just writing about the history - he had also been part of it himself since 1902, when he joined the Mission at Norfolk Island. The story of his ministry was published by Hodder and Stoughton in London in 1962 under the title 'Kakamora', a name by which he was known in San Cristoval, when he worked in Arosi District from 1911 to 1924. He had earlier prepared and published a dictionary of the Arosi language, and done a study of the people there and their customs. This was entitled 'Threshold of the Pacific ', and was published in London in 1924. He had also done a dictionary of the language of Lau while on Malaita. His study of the Arosi people had led to the award of the degree of Litt.D (Doctor of Letters) from the University of New Zealand in 1922. Thereafter he was known in Melanesia as Dr Fox, 'Fokis' or 'Kakamora' - described by Norman Palmer as a 'small naughty creature', a character in the traditional mythology of San Cristoval (Makira). Dr Fox was quite small in stature and could be quite playful and provocative in what he said !

With Dr Fox at Taroaniara for a while was Fr Daniel Sade, who came from the same area of Guadalcanal as Ini Kopuria, and had been suckled by the same woman. They were sometimes described as 'brothers' because of this. Father Dan was an old friend of Fox from their days in the Melanesian Brotherhood; they could converse in Mota or English, and probably some Gela as well, as Fr Dan's language was related to Gela. They took services in the chapel and ministered to the Marine Workshops which had been established there by the Mission after the war, so that the 'Southern Cross' did not have to go to Auckland to be serviced, as it had had to do before. There were by then other Mission vessels to be cared for as well.

A small hospital dedicated to St Clare was also established nearby, and Matron Christine Woods, who had served on Malaita during the war, took charge and made it into a valued maternity clinic for the whole of the Gela group of islands. Mr Bryan Ayres from New Zealand was in charge of the workshops at different periods, before handing over to trained Melanesians.

The presence of Dr Fox on Gela was of great significance to the people there. He would sometimes go down the Boli Passage to Siota and seek for shells on the reef nearby. His extensive collection of shells was later presented to the Solomon Islands Museum in Honiara. He was for many a living link with the past, and especially with the period when the headquarters of the Mission was on Norfolk Island. He had also grown up knowing a great deal about the Maori people in New Zealand. He was greatly revered, and people would bring their problems to him and also seek his guidance, especially in helping to find people or things when they were lost. In effect, he became a kind of spiritual advisor to the people of Gela, whose language he knew well, and in which he could communicate with all of them. He did not use Solomons Pijin. In the 1960s and 1970s he and Fr Brian Macdonald-Milne were the only white priests who conducted worship in the Gela language.

The theological college was moved from Taroaniara to Siota when the station there was rebuilt. The College Chapel was erected on the site of the former Cathedral. There were permanent houses (for the only two members of the teaching staff then) on one side of the 'square' and classrooms on the opposite side, with the chapel between them on the third side. On the fourth side was the wharf, which jutted out into the Boli Passage. Philip Baker, from New Zealand, was tutor there from 1951 to 1954 and Warden from 1958 to 1963 after being district priest on Malaita from 1954 to 1956. He was succeeded by a priest from England, Alan Dutton, whose wife Susan came from Australia and was the daughter of a bishop in South Australia. Her first-born son Stephen was born on board the ship 'Fauabu Twomey' en route from Siota to Honiara! A trained nurse, she provided medical care for the staff and students and their families, although there was sometimes a nurse among the students' wives who could assist her or take over. Fr Desmond Probets arrived from England in 1962 as Sub-Warden and married his English fiancée Jennifer in a wedding at Bungana, where a girls' school, dedicated to St Hilda, had been re-established. Years later, it became for a time a training centre for young women run by the Mothers' Union. In 1964 Fr Probets was replaced by Fr Brian Macdonald-Milne from England, when he moved on to be Headmaster of Pawa School, taking over from Fr Harry Standley, who with his wife returned to England. Fr Standley later wrote about his experiences at Pawa School in his book entitled 'My Heart's in the Islands.' Fr Dutton handed over the Secretaryship of the Gela Education Committee to Father Brian, as he was usually known – or sometimes Mama Brian, as 'Mama' is a Mota word for 'Father'. Refresher courses for deacons were held at the College, and their priestly ordinations took place there as well, when necessary. Rural Deans would also come for meetings or courses. With the constitutional changes taking place in both the Solomon Islands and New Hebrides, Fr Brian taught Pacific studies, including history and culture, to prepare students for both their ministry and the coming constitutional changes. Some of the students of that period became MPs in both countries, while one of them, Fr Walter Lini (pronounced Lingi) became the first Prime Minister of Vanuatu in 1980, and another, Fr John Bani, became President of the Republic of Vanuatu some years after independence. Tulagi was rebuilt, and became the centre of local government, shipping and general stores. Ships could be repaired there, as well as at Taroaniara, not far away.

Alfred Hill was elected Bishop in 1954 and a bishop's house, a bungalow, was erected west of the town of Honiara in an area which became known as Bishopsdale. For a while, there was no longer a bishop or a cathedral on Gela, but that would change. Bishop Hill had replaced Bishop Sidney Gething Caulton, from England, who had served as Bishop of the diocese from 1948, succeeding Bishop Baddeley, having at one time been a district priest on Gela and also the Vicar-General of the Diocese.

At the theological college, the son of Fr Stephen Hagesi, Robert, was a student from Gela, and Fr Brian, then the Sub-Warden of the College, asked him to teach his language to him. Fr Brian also encouraged the theological students to learn Gela and use it to take services in villages nearby, stressing the importance of acquiring the language of the area, wherever one was called to minister. Fr Alan Dutton and his family left for Australia, his wife's homeland, in 1967. Two of their children were born in the Solomons and spent their early years at Siota. Their son Stephen continued to consider himself to be a 'Gela man'. His mother Susan had done much for the medical work based at the College, and had hosted meetings of the Mothers' Union. Women came from villages near the College, especially Belaga, for Mothers' Union events, often smoking their pipes, which they extinguished on arrival and pushed between the branches of the dwarf palms in front of the Chapel. Their skirts were usually worn below their stomachs in front, and higher up at the back. Before entering the chapel for their service they put on their blouses which only covered the upper part of their bodies. This gave them a very distinctive look. Their singing, like that of the Isabel women, was different from that of the other islands, being very high-pitched and audible from some distance.

Dr Fox wrote in his chapter on Gela in his book 'Kakamora': 'The women have great influence. A man's wife decides when the next crop is to be planted, and how large the garden is to be. She is 'Lord of the garden'. She is also called 'Lord of the Reef' and she knows far more about it than the men do. Being a conchologist, I used to go to the women to get the Gela names of the shells. On one beach about 100 yards long I found 46 species of 'Conus'.' The land on Gela passes through the female line, as on Guadalcanal, and this also gives them a special position in their society.

For many years there was a triumvirate of experienced men living in the Solomons who had served the Diocese for very many years -- Bishop Alfred Hill, Archdeacon Harry Reynolds and Dr Fox. When Bishop Hill left for Papua New Guinea in 1967, Harry Reynolds became Administrator of the Diocese until the arrival of the next Bishop. The 'Sacred Synod' of the clergy, who exercised their right of nomination for the last time, could not come up with one name to recommend to the New Zealand bishops, so the bishops chose the Assistant Bishop of New Guinea, John Wallace Chisholm, an Australian, to be the tenth and last Bishop of the Diocese of Melanesia. On the departure of Fr Dutton from Siota, Fr Brian Macdonald-Milne became Acting Warden for a year. He had become convinced that the theological college should move to Guadalcanal for various reasons. Fr Andrew Scott, an Australian, had taught for a while at Siota before becoming the Principal of St Andrew's Catechist College, Kohimarama, which was situated on ground next to the Brothers' Headquarters at Tabalia. He agreed that it would be good to combine both institutions, so that future clergy and others chosen for lay ministry, including a few male and female members of the Religious Orders, could study together. Fr Brian's successor, Fr Eric Jones, agreed, as did Bishop Chisholm. The whole College moved from Siota to Guadalcanal in one day in 1970 on a large amphibious vessel, and Brothers, Novices and students carried everything up to Kohimarama, much of it on their backs. Fr Brian, who was Chaplain and Tutor of the Melanesian Brotherhood from the end of 1968 to 1973, also continued as a teacher of Pacific studies and religious education at the College. This move affected Gela, and a decision had to be made as to what would happen at Siota. It returned to its original role as a school, carrying on the long tradition of education there, but now dedicated to the teaching of Gela children.

Bishop Chisholm had been contacted by Bishop Dudley Tuti of Isabel after his arrival in the Solomons. Bishop Dudley was not only in charge of the Anglican Church on Isabel, as one of the Assistant Bishops of the Diocese, but was later anointed as its Paramount Chief in 1975. He had heard Fr Brian speak about Bishop Steward's idea in the 1920s of forming a 'Pacific Province' consisting of the island dioceses of New Guinea, Melanesia and Polynesia. Fr Brian had thus encouraged discussion about the future of the Anglican Church in the Pacific, which was also the concern of Bishop Dudley. The bishop was later a participant in the discussions which led to the establishment of the three 'tikanga', parallel streams in the Anglican Church of Aotearoa, New Zealand and Polynesia for the Pakeha (whites), Maori, and Polynesians, each with their own archbishop, bishops and clergy.

Bishop Dudley from Isabel and Bishop Leonard Alufurai from Malaita had been consecrated as bishops in All Saints' Cathedral in Honiara in 1963, in a ceremony conducted by the Archbishop of New Zealand, Norman Lesser. The question for the Dioceses of Melanesia and New Guinea was what should be the next step in their development, especially when Polynesia Diocese decided to continue with the New Zealand Church. Bishop Chisholm saw his role as promoting the spiritual, educational and material development of the Church of Melanesia. Decisions were therefore made to rename the theological college the Bishop Patteson Theological Centre (later College), as 1971 was the centenary of the Bishop's death; to raise the standard of training for the Brotherhood by bringing Novices from Papua New Guinea and the New Hebrides to train with Solomon Islanders at Tabalia; to build a new Cathedral in Honiara dedicated to St Barnabas (in remembrance of Norfolk Island), and to establish a new Anglican Province, initially with four dioceses, to replace the enormous Diocese of Melanesia. The Province was established in 1975 and John Chisholm was then installed twice in the new St Barnabas's Cathedral -- as Archbishop of Melanesia and as Bishop of Central Melanesia -- with his see in Honiara. St Barnabas's became both the Provincial Cathedral (with its Canons and Honorary Canons) and the Cathedral for the Diocese of Central Melanesia. The Assistant Bishops became the Bishops of the new dioceses of Isabel and Malaita, and the Archdeaconry of the New Hebrides became a diocese for the New Hebrides and New Caledonia, with the Assistant Bishop there, Derek Rawcliffe from England, as its first Bishop. This pre-dated the Independence of the Solomon Islands in 1978 and also of the New Hebrides, which eventually became the Republic of Vanuatu in 1980.

These developments in the Anglican church much affected Gela. In 1975 Gela had found itself as part of the largest diocese, the Diocese of Central Melanesia, which also included Savo, Guadalcanal (with Honiara), San Cristoval (Makira), Ugi and Ulawa, and the Eastern Outer Islands. Casper Uka, a Tikopian, was consecrated to be the Assistant Bishop and he was based on San Cristoval, to look after the Eastern parts of the Diocese. He was the first Polynesian bishop in the Church of Melanesia. After a few months, Archbishop Chisholm died on a visit to Australia. Therefore, immediately after his funeral in St Barnabas's Cathedral and his burial in the Cathedral Garth, the Electoral College met and elected the Dean of the Cathedral, Norman Kitchener Palmer, to be the next Archbishop. He was the first Solomon Islander to fill that post. He invited Fr Brian to be his Vicar-General, so that he could deal with the administration of the large diocese. He also had to take on the role of Diocesan Secretary, as

Archbishop Chisholm had not appointed one for his Diocese of Central Melanesia. So the Archbishop, the Assistant Bishop and the Vicar-General, with no Diocesan Office, had to work out how to minister effectively as a team. The former Diocesan Office which John Chisholm had had built had now become the Provincial Office, so Fr Brian had to ask the Provincial Secretary, Basil LePine-Williams, for a room in that building to use as the Diocesan Office for Central Melanesia. Much later, a separate building was erected with the help of skilled people from Gela.

As his appointment was only for two years, Fr Brian also had to seek and train a successor. He approached one of his former students, Fr William Tarai from Gela, and he took over as Diocesan Secretary in 1978. Before the Independence of the Solomon Islands in 1978, Fr Brian was invited to become Secretary of the Solomon Islands Christian Association for a second time, in order to arrange the ecumenical celebrations of that great event. He then left for work in the New Hebrides, at the invitation of Fr Walter Lini, the leader of the Vanua'aku (Nationalist) Pati, another former student of his. Meanwhile Fr Robert Hagesi of Gela went on for further study at the Pacific Theological College and then Fuller Theological Seminary in Pasadena, California. He later became Principal of the Bishop Patteson Theological College. Fr Peter Atkins, who had taught at Siota in Fr Dutton's time as Warden, and Fr George Connor, who had taught with Fr Brian and Fr Eric Jones at Siota and Kohimarama, both returned to New Zealand, and the staff of the College over the years gradually increased in number and became completely Melanesian.

Fr Atkins eventually became the Bishop of Waiapu and then Principal of St John's College, Auckland, and Fr Connor eventually became Bishop of Dunedin. They had all helped to raise the academic standards of the Theological College, and it eventually became the first degree-granting institution in the country. One of the last white members of staff was Terry Brown who had returned to Canada, but was later elected Bishop of Malaita in 1996. He eventually returned to Canada, after four years as the Provincial Archivist based in Honiara, having handed over the diocese to a Melanesian bishop, Sam Sahu, fifth Bishop of Malaita.

The Province gradually developed new dioceses. First, the Outer Islands became the Diocese of Temotu in 1980, then San Cristoval, Ugi and Ulawa, with neighbouring islands, became the Diocese of Hanuato'o in 1991, and Gela and Savo became in 1997 the Diocese of the Central Solomons, together with much of the island of Guadalcanal, and the islands of Rennell and Bellona. Honiara the capital (having nearly a fifth of the population of the country) became the diocese of Central Melanesia; it also included part of the north coast of Guadalcanal. But Guadalcanal, except for the capital, together with Rennell and Bellona, became a separate diocese in 2014. In 1980 the Diocese of the New Hebrides changed its name to the Diocese of Vanuatu on the independence of that country, and later to the Diocese of Vanuatu and New Caledonia, and a new Diocese of Banks and Torres was separated from it in 1996. Where the Anglicans had first established themselves in the Banks Islands was now, significantly, a Diocese.

John Coleridge Kuvi of Gela became Head Brother of the Melanesian Brotherhood from 1991 to 1995 and visited England with another Brother, and toured various dioceses. He made his island and the Brotherhood better known in the United Kingdom.

The establishment of the Diocese of Guadalcanal meant that Gela, the first Christian island group in the Solomons, was now with Savo a diocese of its own, albeit a small one, like the Diocese of Banks and Torres. But the people of both dioceses had something in common -- the inhabitants were nearly all Anglican. The first Bishop of the Diocese of the Central Solomons, while it still included parts of Guadalcanal, was a Gela man from the village of Boromole, Charles Koete, who also became Gela's Paramount Chief, while his wife Edith Mary became Provincial President of the Mothers' Union.. He retired in 2010 and was succeeded in 2011 by another Gela man, Ben Seka, who had been the second Gela priest to be Principal of the Bishop Patteson Theological College. The Diocese had its beautiful cathedral at Tulagi, replacing the church destroyed by the Japanese, and the Diocesan Office was placed there as well. Taroaniara continued to serve the ships of the Province, and was staffed by Melanesians. Fr Hagesi and Fr Tarai, in retirement, undertook the revised translation of the New Testament in Gela language -- some portions of the Bible had been translated before. This was done with the assistance of the Bible Society of the South Pacific. Fr Tarai and Fr Hagesi also advised Professor Andrew Pawley, Professor of Linguistics at the Australian National University, on the revision of Dr Fox's Gela dictionary, at the suggestion of Fr Brian, as Dr Fox had asked him to try and get that done. Tulagi's role increased as it became the headquarters of the Central Provincial Government and the site of a new educational institution, the McMahon Secondary School. A new era had opened up for the people of Gela and its neighbouring islands - but then in 1998 a civil war broke out, known as the 'ethnic tension'. Before this, there had been promising economic development on Gela. Exploratory fishing by Solomon Taiyo at Tulagi began in July 1970. The mainstream fishery opened in 1971. Tulagi was the shore base for the fishing fleet, as it was clear from the beginning that there would be the possibility of onshore facilities there. All agreements were sorted out by the Financial Secretary of the Government, John Smith, before he left the Solomons in May 1973, on being appointed Governor of the Gilbert and Ellice Islands. A cannery was soon established. In those years, 'Solomon Taiyo' was considered the best canned tuna in the world. The fish was caught in environmentally sound ways by pole and line fishing. It was never deep frozen, as it reached the cannery within a couple of days of being caught. There was plenty of employment in the industry and a good revenue stream for the Government without any investment by it. The fishing was controlled to ensure protection of the stock. The joint venture between the Government and the Japanese company Taiyo was regarded as a model around the world.

The agreement had been reached with the strong support of David Kausimae, Chairman of the Natural Resources Committee of the Governing Council -- the Ministerial system of government had not yet been introduced. However, the operation was deeply affected by the strife between Malaita and Guadalcanal in the 'ethnic tension'. Gela was caught between the two. However, a branch of the company or 'joint venture' had been established by then in the Western Solomons, which was not so deeply affected by the conflict[36]. The operation continued at Noro, but the

---

[36] Personal communication from John Smith, 26th November 2015.

cannery at Tulagi was closed. Tulagi, and Gela generally, became a much quieter place as a result.

The people of Guadalcanal had seen the capital, Honiara, grow and grow, with people arriving to work, or just to settle, on what they considered their land. Much land had already been alienated by the British Protectorate Government by moving the capital from Tulagi to Honiara after the Japanese withdrawal. People, especially from Malaita, were establishing settlements on the edge of the city, and all over the northern side of the island. Some were marrying local women. This was sometimes regarded as a way of acquiring land as, according to Guadalcanal custom, land passed through the female line, whereas on Malaita it passed through the male line. The indigenous population of Guadalcanal, which was not great, felt increasingly disempowered. At the east end of the island around Marau, people had already come from Are'are and neighbouring districts on Malaita to settle, over a long period. The Guadalcanal people wondered if this would be repeated elsewhere on the island. On the neglected south coast, called the Weather Coast, there was also the Moro Custom Movement. Moro had called on the people there to go back to following their old custom, as developments on the north coast had, he thought, not helped them. The resulting conflict, which began in 1998, was mostly between Guadalcanal and Malaita militias, and led to fighting and deaths, with the Police, mostly from Malaita, opening their armoury in Honiara and issuing people from Malaita with weapons. The Anglican and Roman Catholic Religious Communities' Houses, which were in the conflict area of North Guadalcanal, acted as peace-makers and provided refuge for people fleeing the violence. A rebel leader, Harold Keke, on the Weather Coast, did not accede to the Peace Agreement signed in Townsville in 2003, and he and his men killed one Melanesian Brother, and then proceeded to torture and kill six other Brothers who had volunteered to rescue him, if still alive,or recover his body. They were sent out from Tabalia with the agreement of the Archbishop and the blessing of the Chaplain of the Brotherhood, who was then Brother Richard Carter from England. The whole country was horrified, as no members of Religious Orders had been killed during the actual fighting. It was as if history was repeating itself, Gela becoming again an island of comparative peace in the midst of violence, especially on Guadalcanal and Malaita.

Figure 33 : Archbishop Sir Ellison Pogo, Archbishop of Melanesia 1994-2008 and Lady Roslyn Pogo outside Buckingham Palace after his investiture as a Knight Bachelor, March 27, 2001. [Credit : Revd Canon John Pinder]

Figure 34 : Archbishop Norman Kitchener Palmer, Archbishop of Melanesia 1995-1987 and Mrs Elizabeth Palmer. [Credit : Revd Canon John Pinder]

Figure 35 : Some of the graves of the Seven Martyred Brothers of the Melanesian Brotherhood and the grave of Brother Charles Elliot Fox, Tabalia, Guadalcanal. [Credit : The Melanesian Mission and the Rt. Rev. Keith Joseph, Bishop of North Queensland, Australia]

AFTERWORD

When I went ashore at Honiara, capital of the British Solomon Islands Protectorate, in April 1964, the town seemed to be a sleepy, laid-back sort of place. There were stores, almost all run by Chinese originally from Hong Kong or Rabaul, there were flame trees which blossomed around Christmas time along the main coastal road (then still named Mendana Avenue), and it appeared to be a quiet place like the two towns I had visited in the New Hebrides during the voyage from Sydney. The island of Guadalcanal seemed to have recovered from the traumas of the Second World War over 20 years earlier, and the relics of it, scattered along some of the beaches and further inland, were valued mainly because they attracted tourists, then few in number, and returning veterans, mostly of the US Marine Corps. The Japanese would later return for a short period to recover the remains of their fallen soldiers and return them, as Japanese custom required, to be buried in the homeland. A Japanese-Solomons association would be formed to enable this to happen more effectively, and as an indication of a desire for some reconciliation.

I was advised soon after my arrival to call on the District Commissioner of Central District at his office not far from the wharves at Point Cruz. He seemed to be rather preoccupied and remarked: 'Beware of Malaitans with flowers in their hair'! I went to Evensong in All Saints' Cathedral wondering what he had meant. I heard a rumour that a group of Malaita men were planning to storm the Central Police Station, where one of their number was being held after being arrested for some offence, and they were determined to get him out. The then Bishop of Melanesia, Alfred Hill, wanted to meet me and have a talk at his residence at 'Bishopsdale' at the western end of the town, and he had brought his car to the Cathedral. As we drove back, he was alarmed to find that we were passing through what appeared to be smoke, and it was making us cough. 'What on earth...?' he began to say, and I replied 'It is tear gas, Bishop' - and I shared with him what I had heard from the D.C. and others. It was my introduction to violence in the capital, which in later years erupted from time to time. It was significant that it was people from the most heavily populated island of the Protectorate, Malaita, who were protesting. The people from Malaita provided much of the labour force. A large number had formerly been recruited for work on the plantations in Queensland and also for those on Guadalcanal and in the Western Solomons, but the number of plantations had been much reduced as a result of the war. Malaita people, mostly young men seeking jobs, flocked to the expanding capital and increasingly settled there in certain areas, sometimes encroaching on the land of Guadalcanal people and gradually coming to dominate the town. They obtained jobs in the stores, in the houses of expatriates and, significantly, in the Police and other key occupations.

While the population of the capital was only about 2,500 and the total population about 250,000 in 1964 - a round guess by the authorities - there seemed to the colonial Government to be no cause for alarm, and the national (and then the only) radio station optimistically called itself 'Radio Happy Isles'. However, the apparent calm would not last indefinitely. The Malaita people were often energetic, hard-working and keen to get on, contributing to the progress of the country.

During the 1970s, the country made slow but steady progress to political Independence, in contrast with the political tensions in the neighbouring Anglo-French Condominium of the New Hebrides. The Churches also moved towards autonomy, with the Church of Melanesia (the Anglican Church in the Solomon Islands, New Hebrides and New Caledonia) achieving ecclesiastical 'independence' in 1975, with an Australian, John Wallace Chisholm, the Bishop of Melanesia, becoming instead the first Archbishop of Melanesia and also the Bishop of the Diocese of Central Melanesia. Two other dioceses of Malaita and Ysabel had then been formed in the Solomons, both with Melanesian bishops, and another diocese was formed for the New Hebrides and New Caledonia, to replace the Archdeaconry of Southern Melanesia. The Archdeacon, Derek Rawcliffe, an Englishman, became its first bishop. By 2019 there were seven dioceses in the Solomons and two in Vanuatu, all with Melanesian bishops. This was all very different from when I first arrived in 1964 !

The population of the Solomons began to increase rapidly after Independence in 1978. Much of the activity was centred on the capital or the Guadalcanal Plains. the largest agricultural area of the country. The people of Guadalcanal began to realise that they were beginning to lose control of their island, as people from around the country and businessmen from other countries moved into the island. The churches were working together in the Solomon Islands Christian Association (SICA), of which I had been the first Executive Secretary in 1966, and I took up that role again just before Independence in 1978 to deal with the religious celebrations associated with that event. The first Archbishop of Melanesia had died from cancer in Australia soon after the inauguration of the Anglican Province, and he had quickly been replaced by a Solomon Islander, Norman Kitchener Palmer, who had been Dean of the recently built Provincial Cathedral of St Barnabas, and he remained Archbishop until 1988. I was his administrative assistant as Vicar General and Diocesan Secretary, based in Honiara. The first Prime Minister, Peter Kenilorea, was from Malaita and a leading member of the South Sea Evangelical Church, and the first Governor-General, Baddeley Devesi, was an Anglican layman from Guadalcanal. The Solomon Islands had decided to become a monarchy, with H.M. Queen Elizabeth II as Head of State. There was a great deal of optimism that, with the Governor-General and the Prime Minister working together, some of the growing problems of Guadalcanal could be dealt with, and peaceful developments would ensue. Soon after that, I left the country at the invitation of the leading nationalist politician in the New Hebrides, Fr Walter Lini, a former student of mine, to give whatever help I could as a new staff member of the Pacific Conference of Churches -- seconded by the Anglican Church of Melanesia --as that country moved with greater difficulty towards Independence in 1980.

Meanwhile, there had been rumblings of violence from Bougainville island across the border which had divided the Solomon Islands archipelago ever since an agreement had been made between the former colonial powers, the British and the Germans. When Papua New Guinea became independent in 1975 some of the people of the North Solomons (as the former German Solomon Islands were known) objected to being forcibly included in the new country, not least because much of the revenue from the vast Panguna copper mine run by the Conzinc Riotinto Company would be going to the National Government, and not to help the people of the island of Bougainville, where the mine was situated. A Bougainville Revolutionary Army was formed and a civil war between it and the PNG

Defence Force ensued, and so the copper mine, which I had once visited, was closed. Arms began to slip across the border into western parts of the Solomon Islands and eventually to Guadalcanal. Then weapons left over from the Second World War began to suddenly appear or be dug up. A Guadalcanal Revolutionary Army, or Isatabu Freedom Movement, was formed with the aim of expelling people of other islands from Guadalcanal (especially Malaitans) and, if possible, to gain control of the capital.

Before I left the Solomons, I was invited to a farewell feast by the people from the isolated atoll of Sikaiana, who had established a settlement at Red Beach, so named because it had been the scene of bloody conflict during the Second World War between the Americans (and their allies) and the Japanese on Guadalcanal. I had been best man to a priest from Sikaiana, so I had connections with the community, but I wondered why they in particular wanted to farewell me. During the feast a spokesman stood up and challenged me, saying 'Why are you going? We need you here.' Later I realised that they had a conviction that after Independence their residence on Guadalcanal might be challenged. The 'ethnic tension' which began in 1998 and lasted till 2003 proved them right, as much of the fighting took place on the Guadalcanal Plains where they lived, between the Isatabu Freedom Movement and the Malaita Eagle Force. They seemed to think that somebody like myself, who would not have taken sides, would have been able to help somehow. In the event, it was mainly the Solomon Islands Christian Association and the Anglican Religious Orders – the Melanesian Brotherhood, the Society of St Francis, the Community of the Sisters of Melanesia, and the Community of the Sisters of the Church - who fulfilled that role. The main houses of the four Orders acted as places of sanctuary and were not attacked by either side. The Melanesian Brothers guarded people and properties, including the Governor-General, and they actually camped between the opposing sides on various occasions, but were never attacked themselves. However, over 100 people were killed and over 20,000 people became internal migrants. The Archbishop of Melanesia, Ellison Pogo, formerly Bishop of Ysabel, who had succeeded Archbishop Amos Waiaru in 1998, attempted to mediate, and was later a participant in the negotiations which led up to the Peace Agreement signed in Townsville, Queensland, between the warring parties in October 2003. He was, however, still deeply concerned about the divisions the 'ethnic tension' was causing among Christians and others, and their effect on members of the Religious Orders, all of whom had been in grave danger and had endured the experience of much violence in the areas around their main households. The Archbishop's efforts were later recognized by the award of a knighthood.

Despite the Peace Agreement, Guadalcanal was still far from peaceful.

Guns were still being held by those involved in the tension, from Guadalcanal or Malaita, or indeed in Police hands, and this continued to create a climate of violence and insecurity and deep division. Trauma arising from the violence was far from healed. With no confidence in the Police, the Melanesian Brotherhood was again called upon to organize collection of weapons from both sides, including those issued by the Malaita-dominated Police to the anti-Guadalcanal fighters. This de-commissioning of weapons was highly successful, and the guns handed over to the Brotherhood were taken out to sea and dumped in deep water.

However, there was just one rebel leader, Harold Keke, on the rather isolated Weather Coast of Guadalcanal, who rejected the agreement and refused to disarm. He and his followers continued to carry our acts of violence and murder. A Melanesian Brother, Nathaniel Sado, felt he knew Keke well enough to go and plead with him and his followers to lay down their arms. They killed him. At the Motherhouse of the Brotherhood there was deep concern when rumours arrived there about their Brother's fate. Six Brothers, including the Assistant Head Brother, Robin Lindsay Umbude (who was from Papua New Guinea) volunteered to go and negotiate with Keke in order to either bring him back or recover his body, if he had indeed been killed. The other Brothers were Francis Tofi, Tony Sirihi, Alfred Hill, Patteson Gatu, and Ini Paratabatu. As they arrived on the beach, they were attacked, and three were killed. The other three were tortured and killed the following day. However the Brothers and Novices back at the Motherhouse were informed that these Brothers had been taken hostage. The Chaplain, the Reverend Brother Richard Carter from England, organised a vigil of prayer throughout the night for them for three months, but still no news of their whereabouts came from Keke. The experience deeply affected Brother Richard, who later wrote a book about the tension and its aftermath which vividly recalls the courage of the Brotherhood and all that its members had endured. His e-mail letters to the wider Anglican Communion led to the Brotherhood becoming a focus of prayer in Churches of the Communion around the world. This terrible event was one of the catalysts too, along with the threat of continuing violence and instability, which led Australia and a number of Pacific nations to form the Regional Assistance Mission to the Solomon Islands (RAMSI), in order to bring peace and stable government back to the country. RAMSI arrived in 2003 at the invitation of the Solomon Islands Government, and its operations continued until June 2017. After its arrival, Keke confessed to the murder of the Brothers, and was imprisoned in Honiara in the Central Prison.

The Brotherhood had lost some of its finest Brothers, its future leaders, and yet the death of these brave young men from different islands became a sign of solidarity and courage to the whole nation. The Brotherhood had been constantly working for peace, guarding others from all sides of the conflict, and enduring months of speculation about what had happened to their seven Brothers on the Weather Coast – only to learn eventually that they had all been brutally murdered. All seven Brothers were buried at the Motherhouse at Tabalia which became a place of pilgrimage and an inspiration for many. In 2004 the then Archbishop of Canterbury, Dr Rowan Williams, visited the Motherhouse and blessed the graves of the martyred Brothers. They became known throughout the Anglican Communion as the Seven Martyrs of the Melanesian Brotherhood, and April 24 is kept as the day when their deaths are specially remembered by Anglicans worldwide. Their graves are all carefully tended by the Brothers and Novices at the Motherhouse, and are next to the grave of Charles Elliot Fox, who died in 1977 as a Brother.

There was also pain and trauma that needed to be addressed because of the ethnic tension, and Brother Richard Carter in his role as Chaplain organized retreats and trauma counselling with the help of Anglicord in Australia – for many in the Brotherhood had witnessed horrific acts of violence. The wider nation also needed to come to terms with what had taken place. The Brothers held missions around the islands, in which the story of death and resurrection was enacted in a modern Passion play. The courage of the modern martyrs brought hope beyond the Solomon Islands when missions were also held in Australia, the Philippines, Papua New Guinea and Britain. In 2008 Richard Carter – by then a priest in England – and members of the Brotherhood were invited by Archbishop Rowan Williams to join the chaplaincy team for the Lambeth Conference of Anglican Bishops from around the world, being held that year in England, and the Seven Martyred Melanesian Brothers were remembered by the members of the Conference in a memorable service in Canterbury Cathedral. Later, they were commemorated in the Basilica of St Bartholomew in Rome, which is dedicated to the remembrance of modern martyrs of different Christian denominations. Their legacy lives on. "Blessed are the peacemakers, for they shall be called the sons and daughters of God", as Jesus declared to his first disciples.

In 2005, because of his deep pastoral concern for the Melanesian Brotherhood, Archbishop Ellison Pogo invited me to pay visits to different parts of the Brotherhood to see what could or should be done to help it regain its former strength and purpose. With the agreement of the Brotherhood Committee, and especially of the then Head Brother, Caulton Weris, I became its Advisor until 2013, paying regular visits from the UK. The Brotherhood gradually renewed its spiritual life and discipline and gained the leadership it needed. The Brothers' deaths shocked the whole of the Solomon Islands and many throughout the Anglican Communion, but especially the thousands of Companions of the Brotherhood, who pray for the Brotherhood and support its work – of whom I am one. So it was with a willing but initially heavy heart that I undertook this role.

For a while, it looked as if conflict had returned to wreck the Solomon Islands, but the witness of the Churches working together, the action of the women's organisations who demanded a return to peace, the example of the Anglican and Roman Catholic Religious Orders who refused to take sides (and provided refuge for those fleeing the violence), as well as the work of RAMSI, eventually led to a restoration of peace –but grievances remained.

A Truth and Reconciliation Commission was established by the Solomon Islands Government, and it opened on April 29,2009, with a speech by Archbishop Emeritus Desmond Tutu. He had been Anglican Archbishop of

Cape Town, and later the Chairman of the Truth and Reconciliation Commission in South Africa. Time will tell whether its recommendations will be fully implemented and lead to a lasting peace or not.

There are still many in the islands who are seeking peace in the Pacific, especially in the Solomon Islands. In 2019 the people of Bougainville declared by an overwhelming majority in a referendum that they wanted Independence from Papua New Guinea. The people on both sides of the border in the Solomons archipelago are still working out their future. Whatever happens, it will be of significance for the people and nations of the Pacific, and especially those of the islands of Melanesia. The country of Fiji had earlier been through a series of coup d'etats and had returned to democracy. The country of Solomon Islands has a larger land area than Fiji, and its population has increased rapidly to over 600,000, of whom nearly a fifth are in the capital, Honiara. The country will have an increasingly important part to play in the Pacific region in the future, if it can maintain peace and unity across its many islands, based above all on what is valued now in its Melanesian and Polynesian cultures and on the widely practised Christian faith of the majority of its scattered and diverse peoples.

SELECT BIBLIOGRAPHY

GENERAL

Harcombe, David. *Solomon Islands: A Travel Survival Kit.* Lonely Planet.

Pacific Theological College. 2009. *The Pacific Islands at the Beginning of the 21st Century – Religion, Culture, Society.* PTC Institute for Culture and Social Analysis, Suva, Fiji, and Evangelisches Missionswerk in Deutschland, Germany

Wheeler, Tony. *Papua New Guinea: A Travel Survival Kit.* Lonely Planet.

MIGRATION

Barrau, Jacques (ed.) 1963. *Plants and the Migrations of Pacific Peoples: a Symposium.* Tenth Pacific Science Congress, Honolulu, Hawai'i, 1961. Bishop Museum Press, Honolulu, Hawai'i.

Kirch, Patrick Vinton. 1997. *The Lapita Peoples: Ancestors of the Pacific World.* Blackwell. Oxford, England, and Cambridge, Massachusetts.

LINGUISTICS

Codrington, Robert Henry. 1885. *The Melanesian Languages.* Oxford.

Pawley, Andrew. 2010. *'Prehistoric migration and colonization processes in Oceania: a view from historical linguistics and archaeology' in Migration History in World History, Multidisciplinary Approaches.* Edited by Jan Lucassen, Leo Lucassen and Patrick Manning . Brill Publishers . Leiden, Netherlands.

SOLOMON ISLANDS HISTORY AND CULTURE

Armstrong, E.S. 1900. *The History of the Melanesian Mission.* London: Isbister and Company Ltd.

Burt, Ben. 2015. *Malaita : A Pictorial History from Solomon Islands.* British Museum.

Codrington, Robert Henry. 1891. *The Melanesians: Studies in their Anthropology and Folklore.* Oxford. Reprinted 1969.

Hilliard, David. 1978. *God's Gentlemen : A History of the Melanesian Mission 1849-1942.* University of Queensland Press.

Hopkins, Arthur Innes. 1928. *In the Isles of King Solomon : An Account of Twenty-Five Years spent among the Primitive Solomon Islanders.* London: Seeley, Service and Company.

Ivens, Walter G. 1920. *The Island Builders of the Pacific : How and Why the People of Mala Construct their Artificial Islands.* London: Seeley, Service and Company.

Jack-Hinton, Colin. 1969. *The Search for the Islands of Solomon 1567-1838.* Clarendon Press, Oxford.

Jastrzemski, Frank. 2019. *Admiral Albert Hastings Markham: A Victorian Tale of Triumph, Tragedy and Exploration.* Pen and Sword-Maritime, Barnsley, Yorkshire, England, and Hovertown, Pennsylvania, USA (Includes a chapter on 'The Martyrs of Nukapu')

Laracy, Hugh (ed.)1989. *Ples Blong Yumi: Solomon Islands, The Past Four Thousand Years.* Institute of Pacific Studies, University of the South Pacific. Suva, Fiji. (Articles by Solomon Islanders.)

Lawrence, David Russell. 2014. *The Naturalist and His Beautiful Islands.* ANU Press, Australian National University, Canberra. (Biography of Charles Morris Woodford.)

Markham, Albert Hastings (Commander, Royal Navy). 1873. *The Cruise of the 'Rosario' amongst the New Hebrides and Santa Cruz Islands exposing the Atrocities connected with the Kidnapping of Natives in the South Seas.* London: Sampson Low, Marston, Low and Searle

Montgomery, Bishop H.H. 1896. *The Light of Melanesia.* SPCK, London.

Moore, Clive. 2019. *Tulagi, Pacific Outpost of British Empire.* Acton ACT: Australian National University Press

Penny, Alfred. 1887. *Ten Years in Melanesia.* London : Wells Gardner Darton and Co.

Smith, John. 2011. *An Island in the Afternoon.* Librario.

Standley, R.H. 1981. *My Heart's in the Islands.* Becket Publications, Oxford.

Veronica of the Cross, Sister. 1949. *The School Island.* SPCK for The Melanesian Mission. (About Bungana)

Walter, Richard and Shepherd, Peter. 2017. *Archaeology of the Solomon Islands.* University of Hawai'i Press.

Wench, Ida. 1961. *Mission to Melanesia.* Elek Books, London and the Ryerson Press, Toronto, Canada.

Whiteman, Darrell. 1983. *Melanesians and Missionaries: An Ethno-historical Study of Social and Religious Change in the Southwest Pacific.* William Carey Library, Pasadena, California.

Yonge, Charlotte Mary. 1874. *Life of John Coleridge Patteson, Missionary Bishop of the Melanesian Islands.* Macmillan and Co. London. 2 volumes.

SANTA ISABEL

Wilson, Ellen.1935. *Dr Welchman of Bugotu.* London: Society for Promoting Christian Knowledge.

White, Geoffrey M. 1991. *Identity through History : Living Stories in a Solomon Islands Society.* Cambridge University Press.

Whiteman, Darrell. 1983 (see above)

VANUATU (NEW HEBRIDES)

Kolshus, Thorgeir Storesund. 2007. *We, the Anglicans. An Ethnography of empowering conversations in a Melanesian island society.* Oslo University Press, Norway. unipub.forlag. (Report about research on Mota island.)

RELIGIOUS ORDERS

Anglican Religious Life : A Yearbook of Religious Orders and Communities in the Anglican Communion. Canterbury Press, Norwich, England.

Carter, Richard Anthony. 2006. *In Search of the Lost: The Death and Life of Seven Peacemakers of the Melanesian Brotherhood.* Canterbury Press, Norwich, England.

Macdonald-Milne, Brian James. 2003. *The True Way of Service : The Pacific Story of the Melanesian Brotherhood 1925-2000.* Christians Aware, Leicester, England and the Melanesian Brotherhood, Tabalia, Guadalcanal, Solomon Islands

ROMAN CATHOLIC CHURCH

Laracy, Hugh. 1976. *Marists and Melanesians : A History of Catholic Missions in the Solomon Islands.* Australian National University Press, Canberra.

Willgren, Ralph M. 1979. *The Founding of the Catholic Church in Oceania 1825 to 1850.* Australian National University Press. Canberra and London and Norwalk, Connecticut, USA.

COLONIALISM

Laracy, Hugh (ed.) 1983. *Pacific Protest : The Maasina Rule Movement, Solomon Islands 1944-1952*. Institute of Pacific Studies, University of the South Pacific. Suva, Fiji.

McIntyre, W. David. 2014. *Winding up the British Empire in the Pacific. (The Oxford History of the British Empire).* Oxford University Press.

FICTION

Brooke, Charles. 1881. *Percy Pomo : or, the Autobiography of a South Sea Islander.* London. (A novel about Gela.)

Penny, Alfred. 1903. *The Headhunters of Christabel: A Tale of Adventure in the South Seas.* SPCK, London. (A children's novel.)

WAR IN THE PACIFIC

Among those Present : The Official Story of the Pacific Islands at War. Prepared for the Colonial Office by the Central Office of Information. 1946. London : Her Majesty's Stationery Office. Printed with permission by the Government Printing Office, Honiara, Solomon Islands, 1967.

Baddeley, Walter Hubert. *The Bishop's Report for 1942 (Passed by censor).* Sydney, The Australian Board of Missions.

Clemens, Martin. 1998. *Alone on Guadalcanal : A Coastwatcher's Story.* Naval Institute Press, Annapolis, Maryland, USA. Revised edition 2004. Bluejacket Books.

Dixon, Chris. 2018. *African Americans and the Pacific War 1941-45: Race, Nationality and the Fight for Freedom.* Cambridge University Press.

Feldt, Eric. 1946. *The Coast Watchers.* Angus and Robertson. Sydney, London, Melbourne.

Henrich, Ruth. 1944. *South Sea Epic: War and the Church in New Guinea. A record of events in the Anglican Diocese of New Guinea between the years 1939 and 1943.* London: Society for the Propagation of the Gospel.

Holland, John. 2019. *The Destiny and Passion of Philip Nigel Warrington Strong.* Lake Publishing, Holy Trinity Parish, Kawana Waters, Meridian, Australia. (The subject of the biography was the Bishop of New Guinea from 1936 to 1963, and also ministered in England and Australia.)

Horton, D.C. 1970. *Fire Over the Islands : The Coast Watchers of the Solomons.* A.H. and A. W. Reed. Sydney, Melbourne, Wellington, Auckland.

Horton, D.C. 1971. *New Georgia : Pattern for Victory.* Pan/Valentine Illustrated History of World War II.

Jersey, Stanley J. 1968. *Postal History of United States Forces in British Solomon Islands Protectorate during World War II.* The American Philatelic Society, Inc.

Kent, Graeme. 1971. *Guadalcanal : Island Ordeal.* New York : Ballantine Books

Kwai, Anna Annie. 2017. *Solomon Islanders in World War II : An Indigenous Perspective.* Australian National University Press.

Lord, Walter. 1977. *Lonely Vigil : Coastwatchers of the Solomons.* The Viking Press, USA. Republished 1978. London : Allen Lane, Penguin Books Ltd.

Merillat, Herbert C. 1990. *Guadalcanal Remembered.* New York: Avon Books.

van Dusen, Henry P. 1945. *They Found the Church There.* New York: Charles Scribner's Sons.

WORKS BY THE REVEREND DR. CHARLES ELLIOT FOX

The Threshold of the Pacific : An Account of the Social Organization, Magic and Religion of the People of San Cristoval in the Solomon Islands. 1924. London: Kegan Paul, Trench, Trubner and Co. Ltd. and New York : Alfred A. Knopf.

Lord of the Southern Isles : Being the Story of the Anglican Mission in Melanesia. 1958 . London: A. R. Mowbray and Co. Ltd.

Kakamora. 1962. London: Hodder and Stoughton. (Autobiography)

A Book of Common Prayer in Simple English. 1965. Diocese of Melanesia Press, Taroaniara, Solomon Islands. (Subsequent editions used the term Modern English.)

The Story of the Solomons. 1967. Diocese of Melanesia Publications, Taroaniara, Solomon Islands. Republished 1975 in a revised edition by Pacific Publications (Aust.) Pty. Ltd., Sydney.

My Solomon Islands. 1985. Provincial Press, Church of Melanesia, Honiara, Solomon Islands.

JOURNALS

Island Voyage. Melanesian Mission.

Southern Cross Log. (NZ and UK editions). Melanesian Mission.

The Gazette. Solomon Islands Planters and Settlers Association. 1920 – 1923 only.

INTERNET

www.anglicanhistory.org (Project Canterbury – Oceania)

Kolshus, Thorgeir Storesund. *New keys to a Cold Case : Reassessing the Death of Bishop John Coleridge Patteson.*
Available at :
www.tandfonline.com/doi/abs/10.1080/00223344.2010.530813

Akin, David and White, Geoffrey. 2016. *Artefacts of War: Art, Exchange and Politics in World War II Solomon Islands* (Published in French in 1914), Available in English at :
www.anthropology.hawaii.edu/people/emeritus/white/artifacts-of-war-akin-white.pdf

APPENDIX

PUBLICATIONS IN THE ANGLICAN CHURCH OF MELANESIA

The central Solomon Islands were the scene of significant writing, printing and publishing in the Anglican Church, much of it the work of the Reverend Dr Charles Elliot Fox. He went on writing well into his nineties. He wrote an autobiography which included an account of the years before he came to Melanesia from New Zealand, and this was published in 1985 by the Anglican Church of Melanesia, as it had become known, and printed in Honiara at the Provincial Press, as the Mission Press was re-named after it moved from Taroaniara. The book was published in his memory, as he had left Taroaniara for health reasons in 1973 and returned to New Zealand. The Melanesian Brotherhood had then asked Fr Brian Macdonald-Milne to write to him and invite him to re-join and renew his vows as a Brother, and this gave him great joy, as it maintained his strong link with Melanesia. The New Zealand Government nominated him for the award of a CBE in recognition of his services as a New Zealand citizen to the people of Melanesia. He had earlier been awarded an MBE while in the Solomons. He had wanted to be a Solomon Islands citizen, and had written to the Chief Minister before Independence about this, but his move to New Zealand prevented it happening -- although the Chief Minister had responded and indicated to him that it would be most appropriate. Dr Fox had pointed out in his letter that the country had achieved internal self-government on his birthday !

Dr Fox was invited to produce two books which were of great use for people in the islands. One was "The Story of the Solomons" published in 1967 at Taroaniara by D.O.M.Publications (i.e. Diocese of Melanesia),and intended for use in schools. It was produced at the request of Bishop Hill, former Headmaster of Pawa School, and,although Dr Fox tried in it to cover the history of the whole country, he realized that he knew little about the Western Solomons. He sought comments and suggestions from Fr.Brian, then teaching history at St Peter's College, Siota, the theological college for the Diocese of Melanesia, but he only accepted and acted on some of them, as he was not keen on making corrections !

Dr Fox's last great contribution to the life of the Anglican Church was his liturgical work. In 1965 he produced the first edition of "A Book of Common Prayer in Simple English", which included most of the services used in Anglican schools or in villages where no Prayer Book (or parts of it) were then available in indigenous languages. This was meant to replace the "Brothers' Book" which had simple forms of Morning and Evening Prayer and some other material in English. Significantly the new Prayer Book in English included the Book of Psalms, which in many places had scarcely been used after the switch from Mota to English as the common language used in the Anglican Church, with the Prayer Book in Mota subsequently being no longer used except in the Banks Islands. Only in the New Hebrides were steps taken to translate services into the local Pidgin, known as Bislama. However, the first edition of the Prayer Book did not include the service of Holy Communion, which was then being revised in the Anglican Church of New Zealand, of which the Missionary Diocese of Melanesia was still a part. A second and revised edition of the Prayer Book was published in 1967, with the Communion service included - but with a note saying that 'By direction of the Bishop the Communion service has not been changed.' Significantly, however, the second edition did not include a note which had appeared in the first edition, which said : "Though the English of this book cannot compare with that of the English Prayer Book, yet it may be better understood by Melanesian schoolboys and others whose knowledge of English is not yet very good'. In fact, the English Dr Fox used had been simple and fine, and the book quickly became widely accepted and used, and not just by Melanesian schoolboys ! The translation of the psalms was praised by those to whom he referred his translation, both in Melanesia and abroad. The book was probably the first version of the Prayer Book not to use the traditional language of the original Book of Common Prayer, and included a new version of the Lord's Prayer which boldly used the words 'holy' instead of 'hallowed', ‘rule' instead of 'kingdom' and – instead of referring to 'trespasses' – changed the wording of the phrase concerned to: 'Bring us not into trouble to try us'. This was queried by Bishop Alufurai who said that 'trouble' usually only meant one thing in Melanesia - namely questionable sexual conduct. Nevertheless, the book became very popular and a third edition appeared in 1971 with a printing of 7,500, and its title changed to "A Book of Common Prayer in Modern English". It included the new Melanesian rite called 'The Liturgy (Holy Communion)'.

This Melanesian liturgy had elements taken both from the English Prayer Book and also from the 1966 New Zealand rite, which had not been very acceptable in Melanesia as it was so different from what people were used to in the islands. The Melanesian rite had been drawn up by a Liturgical Committee appointed by Bishop Chisholm for that purpose. One reason for the popularity of the book was the clear modern English and the use of words particularly meaningful to Melanesians, but also because it could be used for translations into local languages, whether of all or just parts of the book. Once the new Communion Service was published, there was an effort to translate it into more of the local languages, as only a limited number of languages had been used for this purpose before. In the New Hebrides, there was an effort to translate the liturgy into as many of the languages used by Anglicans as possible, including Bislama, and some of the translations were done or checked by Archdeacon (later Bishop) Derek Rawcliffe himself.

The fourth edition of 500 copies in 1973 boldly adopted the title 'Melanesian Prayer Book' and on the cover appeared a map of the Solomon Islands and the New Hebrides with a cross and the words "Translation by C.E.Fox". A suitable acknowledgement of his labours ! The liturgical work continued,although Dr Fox had finished his own work.

He died in New Zealand in 1977, after a lifetime devoted to Melanesia.

The 'Brothers' Book' had had a very small number of hymns. Fr Brian, who was then teaching at Tabalia and Kohimarama, was asked to produce a 'Modern English Hymn Book' of about 100 hymns to supplement the Prayer Book. The result was a book of 107 traditional and modern hymns, including some specially written by him for Melanesia, all of which were in modern English. Fortunately, Fr. Eric Jones, the Principal of the Bishop Patteson Theological College, Kohimarama, was able to provide the Tonic Solfa for the agreed tune for each hymn. The work was done very swiftly, and subsequent editions of the Prayer book included these hymns and their tunes in Tonic Solfa. In 1984, there was a further development when the St Nicholas Christian Communications Centre, which had been established by the Church of Melanesia in Honiara, produced an Anglican book of hymns and choruses entitled "Let All the Islands Sing". The title of the book was based on the first line of a popular Pacific hymn written by Lawrence Brittain (formerly of the Diocese of Polynesia) and Fr Brian, which begins with the words "Let all the islands rise and sing". The hymn was later adopted by the Pacific Theological College in Fiji as the College hymn, with a distinctive chorus, and from there it spread around the Pacific and was later published by the World Council of Churches in a book providing suggestions for worship from around the world. The provision of services in many languages was later supplemented by the translation of the whole Bible into Bislama for the Republic of Vanuatu and into Solomons Pijin for the thirtieth anniversary of Solomon Islands' Independence.

What Dr Fox had started while at Taroaniara had therefore led to the development of two books for worship in a form of English acceptable to many Melanesians, as increasingly boys and girl have all had the opportunity to go to primary school and acquire some English there. A proportion are able to go on to secondary school, although relatives have to pay if they do so. In secondary schools, as in the Novitiates of the Religious Orders and in urban churches, the common languages known are English and Pidgin, and their worship is now usually in an English they can generally understand, thanks in large part to Charles Elliot Fox.

When Dr Fox was advised to return to New Zealand, where he could receive more care, he entrusted Fr. Brian Macdonald-Milne with his draft of an English-Gela section for his Nggela dictionary. The original, published in New Zealand in 1995 by the Polynesian Society through the Auckland Museum and lnstitute, only had Gela-English. This was helpful to the Gela people but not so helpful to others. At a conference in Cambridge University, Fr. Brian met Andrew Pawley, who was then Professor of Linguistics at the Australian National University, Canberra. He shared with the Professor the desire of Dr Fox, who had already died, to have his dictionary revised, and Prof. Pawley expressed much interest. He said he had been at the same school as Dr Fox at Napier in New Zealand, and he was one of his heroes. With the material handed over to him by Fr. Brian, including a copy of Dr Fox's 'Gela for Beginners', Prof. Pawley proceeded to do a further revision with the assistance of Pascale Jacq and Diane Kovacs, and a thesaurus was added. Extra help and advice was then provided by William Tarai and Robert Hagesi, retired Anglican priests on Gela, and a list of 360 Gela fish names with scientific identifications was also provided by Dr Simon Foale. Although printed but not so far published, this work is available for linguists and Gela people to consult through the ANU. Prof. Pawley commented in the Preface to this 2005 Extended Dictionary of Gela : 'The 1995 Dictionary is one of the largest and best of a Solomon Islands language… and has been much used by Austronesian scholars.' It is a further tribute to all the work of Dr Fox, for which many of the people of Solomon Islands give thanks to God.